Dickens refigured

DICKENS REFIGURED

Bodies, desires and other histories

EDITED BY JOHN SCHAD

❧

Manchester University Press

Manchester and New York

distributed exclusively in the USA and Canada by St. Martin's Press

Published by Manchester University Press
Oxford Road, Manchester M13 9NR, UK
and Room 400, 175 Fifth Avenue, New York, NY 10010, USA

Distributed exclusively in the USA and Canada
by St. Martin's Press, Inc., 175 Fifth Avenue, New York, NY 10010, USA

British Library Cataloguing-in-Publication Data
A catalogue record is available from the British Library

Library of Congress Cataloging-in-Publication Data
Dickens refigured: bodies, desires, and other histories / edited by John Schad.
   p. cm.
Includes index.
ISBN 0-7190-4246-1. – ISBN 0-7190-4247-X
  1. Dickens, Charles, 1812–1870 – Criticism and interpretation.   I. Schad, John, 1960– .
PR4588.D527   1996
823'.8–dc20
                                        95-25043

ISBN 0 7190 4246 1 *hardback*
ISBN 0 7190 4247 X *paperback*

First published in 1996
00 99 98 97 96   10 9 8 7 6 5 4 3 2 1

Printed in Great Britain
by Bell & Bain Ltd, Glasgow

To Martin York, our mutual friend

Contents

VII

Contents

Others

VIII

Plates

Contributors

Timothy Clark is Lecturer in English at the University of Durham. He is the author of *Embodying Revolution: The Figure of the Poet in Shelley* (Oxford University Press) and *Derrida, Heidegger, Blanchot* (Cambridge University Press), a co-editor of *The Oxford Literary Review*, and is currently writing a study of the concept of inspiration.

Steven Connor is Professor of Modern Literature and Theory at Birkbeck College London. Among his books are *Charles Dickens* (Blackwell), *Theory and Cultural Value* (Blackwell) and *The English Novel in History 1950–1995* (Routledge).

Richard Dellamora is Professor of English and Cultural Studies at Trent University, Ontario. He is the author of *Masculine Desire: The Sexual Politics of Victorian Aestheticism* (University of North Carolina Press, 1990) and *Apocalyptic Overtures: Sexual Politics and the Sense of an Ending* (Rutgers University Press).

Diane Elam is Professor of Critical Theory at University of Wales College of Cardiff. She is the author of *Romancing the Postmodern* (Routledge) and *Ms. en Abîme: Deconstruction and Feminism* (Routledge).

Patricia Ingham is Fellow in English at St Anne's College, Oxford and Times Lecturer in English Language. She is the author of *Thomas Hardy: A Feminist Reading* (Harvester), *Dickens, Women and Language* (1992), and *The Language of Gender and Class in the Victorian Novel* (Routledge).

John Lucas is Professor of English at the University of Loughborough. Among his books are *Literature and Politics in the Nineteenth Century* (Methuen), *Romantic to Modern Literature* (Harvester) and *England and Englishness* (Hogarth).

Helena Michie is Associate Professor in English at Rice University. She is the author of *The Flesh Made Word: Female Figures and Women's Bodies* (Oxford University Press) and *Sororophobia* (Oxford University Press).

J. Hillis Miller is Distinguished Professor of English and Comparative Literature at the University of California at Irvine. He has also taught at the Johns Hopkins University and at Yale. He is the author of *Charles Dickens: The World of His Novels* (1958) and of numerous other essays on Dickens. His most recent books include *The Ethics of Reading* (Columbia University Press), *Ariadne's Thread* (Yale University Press) and *Topographies* (Stanford University Press).

Nicholas Royle is Lecturer in English at the University of Stirling. He is the author of *Telepathy and Literature* (Blackwell) and *After Derrida* (Manchester University Press) and the co-author (with Andrew Bennett) of *Elizabeth Bowen and the Dissolution of the Novel* (Macmillan) and *An Introduction to Literature, Criticism and Theory*.

John Schad is Lecturer in English at the University of Loughborough. He is the author of *The Reader in the Dickensian Mirrors* (Macmillan), the editor of Thomas Hardy, *A Laodicean* (Penguin) and currently completing a book called *Victorians in Theory*.

Linda M. Shires is Associate Professor of English at Syracuse University. She is the author of *British Poetry of the Second World War* (Macmillan), co-author of *Telling Stories: A Theoretical Analysis of Narrative Fiction* (Routledge), and editor of *Rewriting the Victorians* (Routledge).

David Trotter is Quain Professor of English Language and Literature at University College London. His books include *The Making of the Reader* (Macmillan), *Circulation: Defoe, Dickens and the Economics of the Novel* (Macmillan) and *The English Novel in History 1895–1920* (Routledge).

Abbreviations and editions used

All references to Dickens's works are, unless otherwise stated, to the Penguin Classics editions (Harmondsworth, 1965–76) and abbreviated as follows:

AN	*American Notes* and *Pictures from Italy* (Oxford: Oxford University Press, 1957)
BH	*Bleak House*
DC	*David Copperfield*
Dexter	*The Letters of Charles Dickens*, ed. W. Dexter (London: Nonesuch Press, 1938), 3 vols
DS	*Dombey and Son*
ED	*The Mystery of Edwin Drood*
GE	*Great Expectations*
HT	*Hard Times*
LD	*Little Dorrit*
Letters	*The Letters of Charles Dickens*, ed. H. House *et al.* (Oxford: Clarendon Press, 1965–93), 7 vols
MC	*Martin Chuzzlewit*
NN	*Nicholas Nickleby*
OCS	*The Old Curiosity Shop*
OMF	*Our Mutual Friend*
OT	*Oliver Twist*
PP	*Pickwick Papers*
SB	*Sketches by Boz* (Oxford: Oxford University Press, 1957)
SSF	*Selected Shorter Fiction*
TTC	*A Tale of Two Cities*
UT	*The Uncommercial Traveller* and *Reprinted Pieces* (Oxford: Oxford University Press, 1958)

Introduction

JOHN SCHAD

A certain foreign body is here working over our household words.

Jacques Derrida[1]

The foreign body of literary theory has, of course, been working over Dickens's 'household words'[2] for some time now. What, though, might distinguish these new essays is that, undoing any simple theory/text opposition, they seek to locate the foreign bodies that are always already inscribed in Dickens's fiction and prose. Each chapter attempts, in very various ways, to refigure this most central of Victorian authors through attention to all that makes his work so eccentric.

Following the excellent lead of such as Jonathan Arac and D. A. Miller,[3] much recent criticism has tended to locate in Dickens perspectives that distance and indeed police the eccentric, or marginal. Far from welcoming 'the other' this Dickens, like the catechised Pip, tends to '"walk in the same"' (*GE*, 73) or indeed, as the author himself remarks, to 'regard my walk as my beat, and myself as a higher sort of police-constable doing duty on the same' (*UT*, 345). It is, perhaps, time to think again and explore the gaps that Dickens's writing lays bare within the dominant discourses and structures of Victorian culture; in short, to locate a Dickens who, like Barrett Browning's *Aurora Leigh*, 'walk[s] at all risks'[4] – in particular, at the risk of the other.

To help focus the discussion I have tentatively gathered the essays into four loosely defined sections. Whilst the last, 'Others', is on the whole self-explanatory the other three, I should explain, are concerned with particular fields of meaning – namely, the body, desire and history – in which Victorian orthodoxies are conspicuously interrupted, sometimes from within, by the very voices that those orthodoxies at once both exclude and

1

yet maintain. To be more specific, the four sections may be summarised as follows.

Bodies

As my Derrida epigraph suggests, the body is, in a sense, always foreign, always the other of the spirit, or mind privileged by nineteenth-century idealism. Writing against this hierarchy, the essays by John Schad, Timothy Clark and Nicholas Royle draw attention to the very various bodies, or materialities that inform, and indeed deform, the novels of Dickens. For Schad, the body in question is that subterranean and unreadable body of Christ which he terms Dickens's 'cryptic Church'; reading the novels through *Pictures from Italy* Schad argues that the churches in Dickens often play the part of the ritually inverted body of carnival. Clark, by contrast, is concerned with the bodies of the dead; drawing on Maurice Blanchot's claim that the 'cadaver is its own image' Clark locates in *The Uncommercial Traveller* and elsewhere an aesthetic of the corpse which, by refusing to yield some higher principle or meaning, constitutes an irreducible materiality. Though the corpse is also important for Royle, he argues that in *Our Mutual Friend* the body is most conspicuously foreign, or other in so far as it has to do with anality, excrement and – at the same time – the excesses of writing.

Desires

In so far as the body is the site of desires then this second section may be seen to develop out of the first; particularly since the circuits of desire under discussion are rarely self-identical, being often, as it were, elsewhere or other. Hence it is that, for Richard Dellamora, desire in *Oliver Twist* so exceeds the bounds of bourgeois heterosexuality as to suggest not only a homoerotic scene but also the procreative energies of working-class men – Oliver's spoon, argues Dellamora, answers to Thomas Malthus's fantasisation of the lower-class penis as a phallus that consumes as well as spends. Helena Michie explores a similarly decentred account of desire in *Nicholas Nickleby* which gestures, she argues, beyond Freud's nuclear family romance and towards what she terms 'an extended family theatre, or melodrama' which features, in particular, the figure of the uncle. Developing this familial theme Patricia Ingham, in her discussion of *Little Dorrit*, reads the titular heroine as a contradictory child–woman persona whose relationship with her father as, at once, daughter, mother and lover is acutely disruptive of the family as a model of social harmony.

Histories

Much like desire, history in Dickens is often being defamiliarised, often eluding the realm or horizon of the same. This is, in part, Linda Shires's point in a discussion of *David Copperfield* which concerns the historiography of literary careers; complicating the tendency of Victorian/modern biography to centre on a defining secret or originary trauma, Shires reads the novel in terms of the complex intersections of Dickens's career with both personal and cultural history. By contrast, in an essay that takes in *A Child's History of England*, John Lucas is very particularly interested in national history and the way that *Bleak House*, feeding off the radical republicanism of the times, succeeds in wresting the history of England from the grasp of Tory and, indeed, Whig historiography. Finally, drawing on both Marx and Heidegger, Diane Elam considers the very different history of the everday; dwelling on questions of being and debt Elam argues that in *Little Dorrit* this most familiar history, or temporality turns out to be the least familiar to theory, or what she terms our 'epistemological accounting'.

Others

This final section loosely aligns three essays which, directly or indirectly, address and complicate the now familiar notion of the other in Dickens – an interest which works out in discussions of, very variously, improbable spaces, marginal spectators and other people. In an essay on *Martin Chuzzlewit* Steven Connor explores the vulnerability of architecture *to itself* as he argues that this novel about architecture entails an urgent anti-architectural impulse which opens up what Connor calls 'spasmodic or incoherent space', a space that the novel develops into nothing less than an organising aesthetic of unbuilding. David Trotter rehearses this concern with a seemingly marginal Dickensian impulse as he traces the role of idleness right across the novels; locating a whole series of 'lazy gentlemen' who stare rather than interpret, Trotter identifies a figure who, unlike the *flâneur*, is radically resistant to the hermeneutic intensity of institutional surveillance of the Victorian city. If otherness is only an implicit feature of Trotter's discussion, in Hillis Miller's essay on *Our Mutual Friend* it becomes explicit. Reading jealousy as a curiosity about the other's other, Miller talks about an encounter with not only the wholly other but also the anarchic depths of otherness within the self; this otherness, he concludes, is mapped by the novel in terms of the depths of the Thames.

3

John Schad

Notes

1 Jacques Derrida, 'Foreword' to N. Abraham and M. Torok, tr. N. Rand, *The Wolf Man's Magic Word; A Cryptonymy* (Minneapolis: University of Minnesota Press, 1986), p. xxv.
2 Dickens, of course, edited a weekly magazine called *Household Words*.
3 I refer, in particular, to Arac's *Commissioned Spirits: The Shaping of Social Motion in Dickens and Melville* (New Brunswick: Rutgers University Press, 1979) and Miller's *The Novel and the Police* (Berkeley: University of California Press, 1988).
4 Elizabeth Barrett Browning, *Aurora Leigh*, ed. Margaret Reynolds (Athens: Ohio University Press, 1992), vol. 2, p. 106.

1

Dickens's cryptic Church: drawing on *Pictures from Italy*

JOHN SCHAD

> What is a crypt? . . . All is cryptic.
> Jacques Derrida, *Fors*[1]

Undermining the city

In *Pictures from Italy* (1846) Dickens records his visit to the Cathedral in Parma, which is followed by a descent to what he calls a 'subterranean church'. The 'roof', we read, was

> supported by marble pillars, behind each of which there seemed to be at least one beggar in ambush. . . . From every one of these lurking-places, such crowds of phantom-looking men and women, leading other men and women with twisted limbs, or chattering jaws, or paralytic gestures, or idiotic heads, or some other sad infirmity, came hobbling out to beg, that if the ruined frescoes in the cathedral above, had been suddenly animated, and had retired to this lower church, they could hardly have made a greater confusion, or exhibited a more confounding display of arms and legs.[2]

Beneath one church lies another, a lower or subterranean church which – to echo Derrida – is not only a crypt but cryptic, a quite confounding 'confusion . . . of arms and legs'. To 'decrypt' the crypt we might, in the first place, read this confusion (this very foreign body of Christ) as a displaced version of that mid-century Church of England which Dickens himself termed a 'quarrelling body' (Dexter, 3.402). It was, of course, a Church divided and disrupted from within, both by her Catholic and Dissenting others – 'here more Popery, there more Methodism', to cite

Dickens again. For all their obvious differences, Victorian Catholicism and Dissent were, like the 'cathedral above' and the 'lower church' in Parma, mirror-images of each other in the sense that, standing beyond 'the sacred pale of [the] established church',[3] both were the object of fear and suspicion.

Not limited, though, to refiguring the domestic Church, Parma's crypt may also be read as, say, asylum, clinic, prison, slum, hell, or night; indeed, the crypt's very overdetermination thoroughly inscribes it within what Dickens himself goes on to call 'my dream of churches' (387), an oneiric 'vision of great churches which comes rolling past me like a sea' (385). Dream-like and unfixed, the Italian churches differ radically from Dennis Walder's account of Dickens's 'churches [as usually] stable . . . features of the landscape'.[4] But it is not simply that in *Pictures* Dickens is anatomising the cryptic body of Catholicism; for the church that Dickens writes is always, in some sense, cryptic – always, as it were, written from below. In *Great Expectations*, for instance, when Pip is turned upside down by Magwitch 'the church . . . [is] made to go head over heels' (36); likewise, in *Our Mutual Friend* the Church of St John 'with [its] four towers at the four corners . . . resembl[es] some . . . monster . . . on its back' (271); and equally upturned is Coketown's 'New Church', the steeple of which terminates 'in four short pinnacles like florid wooden legs' (*HT*, 66). Whilst the early Church was renowned for 'turn[ing] the world upside down' (Acts 17.6),[5] Dickens's churches – as if subject to the inversion of carnival – are often themselves the wrong way up. Of course, in *Great Expectations*, once Pip is upon his feet again he confidently recalls that 'the church [finally] came to itself' (36); however, given that Joe quite happily holds the 'Prayer-Book upside down' (75), Pip's confidence is perhaps misplaced. Though Mr Wopsle still looks forward to the time when 'the Church [is] . . . "thrown open"' (55, 57) that time, it seems, has already come in the sense that the Church no longer occupies a fixed, or privileged cultural space. Indeed when, at the conclusion of Magwitch's trial, 'the audience', we read, 'got up (putting their dresses right, as they might at church or elsewhere)' (468), church shades into courtroom, theatre and, indeed, 'elsewhere'.

The name for that elsewhere, according to Thomas Carlyle, is writing: 'Pamphlets, Poems, Books', he declares in 1840, 'these *are* the real working effective Church of a modern country'; for Carlyle, the Church – as traditionally conceived – belongs to the now superannuated world of the voice: 'While there was no Writing . . . or Printing, the preaching of the voice was the natural sole method [of guiding souls].'[6] There is, then, an especial significance in Dickens's remark in *Pictures* that '[although] many churches have crypts and subterranean chapels . . . I do not *speak* of them' (385: my italics); if, as Derrida argues, 'to crypt is to cipher'[7] (to write in code) then these crypted churches are always already a kind of writing. But then so too is that early, underground Church of the catacombs which so interests Dickens in his visit to Rome (386) and which exists for us, in the New Testament, primarily as a collection of letters – or rather, purloined letters since we read what is not addressed to us. To be still more precise, or Derridean they are 'post cards' in the sense of being at once both private and public.[8] Indeed, *Pictures* effectively returns us to these New Testament post cards for here too the Church is written in letters that are not, in the first instance, addressed to us: 'the greater part of the descriptions', remarks Dickens, 'were . . . sent home, from time to time, in private letters' (260).

To speak, though, of Dickens's 'Post Cards from Italy' – the original name for the travelogue was 'Travelling Letters'[9] – is to distinguish Dickens very sharply from Carlyle. For the latter, the writing into which the Church is displaced is still invested with all the ontology and indeed Englishness of the Book – 'He that can write a true BOOK . . . is he not the Archbishop of . . . All England?';[10] by contrast, in Dickens's 'Post Cards from Italy' the Church issues in a writing that is, quite literally, homeless and open-ended. To draw again on Derrida,[11] the 'grand and dreamy structure[s]' (332) of Italy's churches cannot supress their own structurality; St Peter's Church in Rome, we learn, 'is an immense edifice, with no one point for the mind to rest upon' (367) – its archi*texture* affords no centre.

Ecclesia again shades into *écriture*, or at least a parable of its adestination in *A Tale of Two Cities* where, although the 'destination' (186) for Roger Cly's funeral procession was the 'old church of St Pancras', the body never arrives since, unknown to the procession, Cly is still alive. With Cly as a kind of dead letter, the church here takes part in a parable which anticipates Derrida's dictum that '"a letter *can* always *not* arrive"'.[12] The dead and the dead letter become, in fact, indistinguishable in the case of the 'solitary coffin' which, in *Pictures*, Dickens encounters at the great 'Pits' outside Rome; the coffin enacts a failure to arrive both in the sense that its final destination is not 'the church' but this 'blank, open, dreary space' and in the sense that Dickens recalls how, seeing 'two initial letters scrawled upon the top . . . [I] turned away' (380). Such parables of adestination were soon, of course, to become a fact of Victorian death as, in response to exhausted church graveyards, the Cemetery Acts of 1852 and 1853 decreed that the dead would not be interred in churchyards but, instead, taken to suburban burial grounds.[13]

To assume, though, that Dickens's cryptic Church should be read solely in terms of writing and its detours would be to follow Carlyle mistakenly; for, unlike his mentor, Dickens sees the Church as part of an enduring oral/aural economy. Substituting the 'labyrinth' (386) of the crypt for that of the ear, Dickens's churches (like Manette's Soho corner) are very often an 'Ear of a place' (*TTC*, 129) – a place, that is, for sound; whether it be the 'grand tones' of the organ (*MC*, 126), the resounding of the 'clergy-man's voice' (*DS*, 887), or simply 'echoes of the roof' (*AN*, 387). Indeed, in *The Old Curiosity Shop* once Little Nell is outside the church she stops 'to fancy how the noise [of the children] would sound inside' (496). For Nell, the church here represents a place not just to hear but, more particularly, to hear herself – she is, inevitably, a part of the noise outside. The highly invested notion of hearing oneself is, of course, for Derrida (who talks of *s'entendre parler*)[14] one of the characteristic features of phonocentrism; and, to listen to the 'knell' in 'Nell', we might well remark that one sure measure of the Church's implication in phonocentrism is, in Dickens, the sheer ubiquity of the church bell – for, in vibrating, it not only rings but acts like an eardrum. In short, it epitomises the seeming unmediated self-presence of *s'entendre parler*. Thus, in *Little Dorrit* the bells of Ludgate Hill, after initially ringing out 'Come to church', proceed to hammer out, 'They *won't* come' (68) and in so doing appear as if to hear themselves speaking.

Although its implication in the oral economy of Dickens's Church may align the bell with the conservatism of a nostalgia for presence, that same economy also places the bell within an oral subculture that in relation to the period's newly dominant literate culture is a subversive, or subterranean force. Anticipating 'the madness of bells'[15] in Derrida's *Glas*, the church bells in Coketown are 'barbarous' (*HT*, 66), whilst those in Genoa and London are indeed 'maddening' (297/*LD*, 67). In fact, when we hear of 'discordant bells' (*LD*, 40), 'conflicting bells' (*UT*, 87), 'bells of all degrees of dissonance' (*LD*, 67), or of 'a confusion of bells' (*DS*, 888) the church bell becomes, via a cryptic slippage, a kind of Ba*bel(l)* – as in *Hard Times* where 'bell' and 'babel', respectively, begin and end one sentence (118).

Of course, what gives this Babel of bells a subversive resonance is its sheer independence of the conventions of signification – an independence most obviously pictured in *Little Dorrit* where, at the close of the Sparklers' wedding celebrations, 'the thousand churches [of Rome] rang their bells *without any reference to it*' (668: my italics). If, though, the church bells of Rome affect a Babelian anarchy, those of pre-Revolutionary France threaten nothing less than full-blooded insurrection – in *A Tale of Two Cities* we read that 'the church bells [now] . . . ringing pleasantly in many an airy steeple over France, should [soon] be melted into thundering cannon' (216).

Clearly, in so far as maddening and barbarous bells are always already a kind of thundering cannon, or rebellious noise, the churches in Dickens align themselves with that oral or rhetorical energy which so often troubles the silences of the Dickensian page. This becomes clear in *Little Dorrit* when Mr Meagles explains how, when the fifth commandment is read out on Sundays, he is always inclined, for the sake of the orphan Tattycoram, ' "to call out, Church [meaning 'shame!']" ' (241) though he never actually does so. Here then the liturgical, or literate church is contested by 'Church' as an oppositional cry – this latter Church, the 'Church' that Meagles would but does not call out, being both enigmatic and supressed, is doubly cryptic. Indeed, since the Church's Greek name is *ecclesia*, meaning 'called out', this vocal Church is also cryptic in the sense that it punningly uncovers an ancient and deep-buried sense of Church, one that here remains under the erasure if not censorship of the literate institution.

This literate Church is never more conspicuous than in *Bleak House* where the illiterate Jo is mystified to 'see the good company going to the churches on Sundays, with their books in their hands' (274). Here, though, the literate Church is an extension of the literate city – 'the town awakes [and] . . . all that unaccountable reading and writing . . . recommences' (275); in so far, then, as the novel opens up, through Jo, a space outside, or below the literate Church – literally, in the sense that he sweeps the churchyard-step (272) – it is also involved in a deconstruction of the city itself. Thus it is that Jo, as ' "dweller in the tents of Tom-all-Alone's and a mover-on upon the surface of the earth" ' (414) recalls the New Testament declaration that 'here we have no continuing city' (Heb. 13.14). That Dickens's urban churches – no longer, of course, the burial ground, or dead centre of the Victorian metropolis – might undo any sense of the city as place is mirrored in *Pictures*. For not only does the Cathedral of Modena house 'people . . . kneeling in all directions' (320) and 'St Peter's . . . tires itself with wandering round and round' (367) but Dickens talks of Rome as 'a vast wilderness of consecrated buildings' (387). As we know, a wilderness is where one gets lost; if 'the crypt', as Derrida remarks, 'leads astray'[16] then Rome's crypted churches lead *the city* astray. In short, the conventional understanding that the nineteenth-century city subverts the Church[17] is, to some extent, turned on its head. As Dickens observes 'it is an awful thing to think of the enormous caverns that are entered from some Roman churches, and *undermine the city*' (385: my italics).

9

What, perhaps, makes these caverns so unthinkable is not just that they house 'graves, graves, graves' but that as 'ghastly passages . . . with cold damp stealing down the walls, drip-drop, drip-drop' they return Dickens to those damp passages that were increasingly and literally undermining Victorian cities – namely, the sewers. It is no accident that Victor Hugo, writing eighteen years later, talks of sewers as 'excremental crypts'; indeed, echoing the intensely moral tone of Victorian sanitary reform, Ruskin goes even further toward churching the sewer: 'a good sewer', he writes, '[is a] far holier thing . . . than the most admired Madonna ever printed'.[18] The sewer–Church analogy undergoes, though, a tacit but radical reversal with Nietzsche who writes, in 1889, that 'the Christian movement has been from the very first a . . . movement of outcast and refuse elements of every kind'.[19] For all his seeming revulsion Nietzsche only rehearses, of course, a conceit already inscribed in the garbage dump that was Golgotha and which Terry Eagleton, in his Catholic phase, positively celebrated: 'the Church', he wrote, 'is [not just] a city on a hill [but] . . . the dung of the earth'.[20] Whether Dickens is closer to Nietzsche or Eagleton is impossible to determine, but the conceit they share is certainly anticipated in both the 'pestiferous and obscene' (*BH*, 202) churchyard in which Mr Krook is buried and the churchyards surrounding Todgers's which are 'overgrown with such straggling vegetation as springs up . . . from damps . . . and rubbish' (*MC*, 186). Indeed, given the widespread Victorian construction of the poor as 'moral sewerage',[21] Parma's dark crypt of beggars, idiots, and the infirm *is* a sewer–church.

Of course, if Italy's crypts operate as a displacement of that which undermines the Victorian city then the 'chattering jaws . . . paralytic gestures [and] . . . idiotic heads' (319) of Parma's subterranean church may be read as an inflection of all the disease and infirmity which characterised and, indeed, caricatured Britain's urban underworld. The Church's very literal connection with such disease are those overflowing and miasmic churchyards of the Victorian city which so concerned Dickens.[22] There is, though, in his fiction an apprehension that the Church is itself a kind of disease, that it somehow stands outside a conception of health which, as Foucault has argued, was increasingly an instrument of social control.[23] This is never clearer than in *Little Dorrit* where the description of London on a Sunday in which nothing stirs save church bells culminates in the remark that 'up almost every alley . . . some doleful bell was . . . tolling, as if the Plague were in the city' (67). Here again Dickens has not the decency to wait for Nietzsche, who was to write that '*making* sick is the true hidden objective of the Church';[24] Dickens writes better than he knows when declaring, in a letter written in 1864, that 'as to the Church, I am sick of it' (Dexter, 3.402).

Amongst the churches of Italy Dickens, it seems, is sick in the sense that they disrupt his very ability to think; not only does St Peter's allow 'no one point for the mind to rest upon' but he dreams of a Cathedral that is 'unreal, fantastic . . . inconceivable throughout' (332) and remarks that 'sitting in any of the churches [in Genoa] towards evening, is like a mild dose of opium' (298). This capacity to disorder the mind may well be more obviously a feature of Italy's Catholic Church but it also characterises Dickens's Protestant churches – and not just the 'lunatic' revivalists. Mrs Snagsby's 'becoming cataleptic' whilst listening to Chadband getting his evangelical 'steam up' (*BH*, 416, 414) is perilously close to David Copperfield on his wedding-day when 'the church,' he observes, 'might be a steam-power loom in full action, for any sedative effect it has on me' (*DC*, 697). Again, Mrs Snagsby being carried upstairs 'like a grand piano' endures a reification shared by Mrs Miff the Anglican pew-opener who is herself 'such a pew of a woman' (*DS*, 901). If Mrs Snagsby loses not only consciousness but identity (becoming, in effect, a grand piano) then both David and Mrs Miff also come close to doing so; all three, that is, are like that 'score of people' in *Dombey and Son* who 'lost themselves every Sunday . . . among the high-backed pews' (887–8). Pip's 'vague sensation' that 'it was Sunday, and somebody was dead' (*GE*, 143) is, perhaps, not so vague. Indeed, of Parma's cryptic church we might echo 'it was Sunday and somebody was in-bits-and-pieces'; for like Lacan's pre-Oedipal infant this church constitutes a *corps morcelé* [25] – 'if the ruined frescoes in the cathedral above [with its "heaps of foreshortened limbs"] . . . had retired to this lower church, they could hardly have made a greater confusion . . . of arms and legs' (319). In their very various ways, Dickens's churches make light, it seems, of not just being human but being. This is hardly surprising in the sense that Dickens is, on the whole, writing from within a Church of England that is, of course, a 'quarrelling body' and, according to Cardinal Newman, 'the veriest of nonentities';[26] moreover, in *Pictures* Dickens is writing about a Church whose doctrine of transubstantiation puts into question the ontological status of both bread and wine. In this sense an emblematic figure within Dickens's cryptic Church is the malevolent Quilp seated in Bethel chapel and 'chuckling inwardly over *the joke of his being there*' (*OCS*, 452: my italics).

Of course, if to be is to be seen then being also endures a kind of lightness amongst the dark churches of Marseilles since, in *Little Dorrit*, they are not only 'the freest' from the 'universal stare' (40, 39) – the Church Invisible, as it were – but they are 'dreamily peopled with ugly old shadows' (40). For Foucault, as we know, the universal stare is primarily medical in that, after the French Revolution, 'Western man constitutes himself in his own eyes as an object of [medical] science';[27] however, for Dickens the cryptic Church is equally free of this clinical gaze. Of the 'heaps of foreshortened limbs' painted upon the cupola of Parma's Cathedral we read that 'no operative surgeon, gone mad, could imagine [them] in his wildest delirium' (319); in so far as the Cathedral is subjected to a clinical gaze, that gaze is blinded by the very madness against which it defines itself. According to Foucault, following the seventeenth century's marginalisation of 'Christian unreason . . . men would have to wait two centuries – until Dostoyevsky and Nietzsche' to recover that 'madness . . . which belonged so intimately to the Christian experience of the Renaissance'[28] – Dickens's account of Parma's insane Renaissance frescoes surely comes close to bringing that wait to an end.

'Not my father's house'

This same account, indeed, envisages a church that threatens not only reason but property – 'behind each of [the] marble pillars there seems to be', Dickens writes, 'at least one beggar in ambush' (617). When, in *A Tale of Two Cities*, we read of 'churches that are not my father's house but dens of thieves' (399) we might well return to Parma's subterranean church. We might also return to the old crypt into which Little Nell is taken where 'in the time of the monks . . . amid . . . gold and silver . . . and precious stuffs and jewels . . . hooded figures . . . told their rosaries of beads' (*OCS*, 498). If here the church again shades into an underworld of an almost criminal kind, the reverse is the case in *Oliver Twist* where a reference to the Quakers is encrypted in the ironic chapter-heading that reads 'How Oliver passed his Time in the improving Society of his reputable Friends' (177) – for Fagin's den of thieves read the Society of Friends. Victorian fears of both Catholicism and Nonconformity obviously play a part at such moments but in so far as the Church that Dickens writes is shrouded in criminality it is closer to the Nietzschean intuition that 'here public openness is . . . lacking; the hole-and-corner, the dark chamber is Christian'.[29] The Church, of course, was born in the hole-and-corner in the sense that it was initially an outlawed and cryptic body – as the reader of *Pictures* is reminded not only by Dickens's visit to both the Roman catacombs (386) and St Peter's dungeon (384) but also by *Great Expectations*'s intriguing presentation of the jailbird Magwitch as a kind of St Paul. Compare Magwitch's '"I've been put out of this town and put out of that town . . . stuck in the stocks, and whipped and worried and drove"' (360) with St Paul's 'five times received I forty stripes save one. Thrice was I beaten with rods, [and] once was I stoned' (2 Cor. 11.24–5).[30]

A den of thieves by another name might just, of course, turn out to be a prison, and so it often proves with Dickens's churches. Anticipating Foucault's observation that 'for the Church . . . confinement represents . . . a police whose order will be entirely transparent to . . . religion',[31] Dickens not only describes London's sabbatarian churches as a 'stringent policeman' (*LD*, 68) but in *Pictures* he writes of priests who carry 'candles . . . like truncheons' (369); little surprise, then, that the 'innumerable churches [of Florence] . . . *arrest* our lingering steps' (431). Elsewhere in Dickens's crowded cities, church and prison at times appear almost contiguous: Marshalsea Prison stood only 'a few doors short of the church of Saint George' (*LD*, 97); 'the great black dome of Saint Paul's bulg[es] . . . at [Pip] . . . from behind . . . Newgate Prison' (*GE*, 189); whilst in Rome the dungeon of St Peter so presses on the oratory above that the 'gloom of the . . . old prison . . . [is] on it' (385).

To read, then, 'prison' for 'den of thieves' – thus 'the churches are not my father's house but a prison' – clearly makes some sense; indeed, this reformulation also makes illuminating non-sense in that for Dickens the church is a prison precisely in so far as it *is* 'my father's house'. Crucial to this intuition is the time when Dickens's own father was in Marshalsea for debt, a time of which the author himself remarks that 'Sundays . . . I passed in . . . prison'.[32] For the young Dickens church-going shades into prison-going; prison, like church, is 'my father's house'.[33] There is then considerable autobiographical resonance in the adult Dickens's observation of the way that, following one particular ceremony involving figures representing Mary, Joseph and the Infant Saviour, the presiding monk 'locked up the whole concern (Holy Family and all)' (381). This picture of the Church incarcerating the model family not only tells an autobiographical story but also and at the same time enacts the sense in which for Dickens the Church, in so far as it is joined to the prison under the sign of 'my father's house', serves to discipline or police the family – to underwrite, that is, the patriarchal Victorian family. In this light the priest's candle is not just a 'truncheon' but a phallus, whilst the sacrament of marriage is an elaborate policing of desire – thus it is that Wemmick and Miss Skiff are 'ranged in order at those fatal rails' (*GE*, 463), whilst David Copperfield, recalling his wedding, describes 'the pew-opener arranging us, like a drill-sergeant, before the altar' (*DC*, 697). To marry is to enter, it seems, not just a church but the quasi-military regime characteristic of the nineteenth-century prison.[34]

Indeed, merely to begin to desire outside marriage incurs the penal system's ultimate sanction; or at least that is the lesson of Stephen Blackpool's nightmare in which he who is already married finds his marriage to 'some one in whom his heart had long been set' turning into a burial service at his own execution – 'in an instant what he stood on fell below him, and he was gone' (*HT*, 122–3).

Though Stephen begins his nightmare alongside his bride, he ends it alone 'before a crowd so vast, that . . . all the people in the world . . . could not have looked . . . more numerous' (123); in becoming, then, a place of execution the church subjects Stephen to an appalling isolation and thereby mimics something of the solitary prison system so vigorously attacked by Dickens in the 1840s.[35] A system in which solitude was expected to cause 'the prisoner . . . to turn inward . . . and repent'[36] drew heavily, of course, on various institutional practices of the Church, in particular meditative prayer and the confessional. And that Dickens knew this well is clear from the way in which the inspectors of Mr Creakle's solitary system prison, upon encountering the dazzling piety of Uriah Heep, 'shad[e] . . . their eyes . . . as if they had just come into a church' (*DC*, 927). Indeed, in so far as the churches in Dickens do constitute a species of prison it is one run on the solitary system; 'in my father's house', after all, 'are many mansions [or rooms]' (John 14.2). This is all but literally the case when, in his 1860 essay, 'City of London Churches', Dickens recalls how he 'open[ed] the door of a family pew, and shut myself in' (*UT*, 85). If Foucault is right that the Catholic 'confession [is] . . . inscribed at the heart of [Western] . . . procedures of individualization'[37] then for the Protestant Dickens the family pew is a displacement of not just the solitary cell but the confessional box; shutting himself in is an act of individuation as well as incarceration.

What, though, distinguishes Dickens's pew from Foucault's confessional is that the former entails visibility – 'the clerk', records Dickens, 'glances at me knowingly'. Thus, like the pew rather than the confessional, Dickens's churches – though cryptic – are never, I suggest, a site of absolute invisibility; indeed, what invisibility there is tends to serve the interests of visibility, the visibility of others. The principle is that of Bentham's panopticon prison 'in the central tower [of which] one sees everything without ever being seen'.[38] It is not for nothing that when Oliver Twist spends hours at Fagin's garret window looking out without ever being seen it is 'as if he . . . lived inside the ball of St Paul's Cathedral' (*OT*, 179). The same panoptic principle is at work in that 'mouldy old church' in *Dombey and Son* where the very hiddenness of the worshippers increases their powers of surveillance – 'Miss Nipper', we read, '[felt] that the eyes of [the congregation] which lost itself weekly among the high-backed pews, were upon her' (887–8). Might it be, then, that the churches of Marseilles are 'the freest' from 'the universal stare' simply because, on the panoptic principle, the unseen is the one who sees?

After all, for both Dickens and his contemporaries the Church, in the form of St Paul's Cathedral, frequently functions, literally as well as symbolically, as a surveillance tower. Not only does Lucy Snowe, in *Villette* (1853), 'mount to the dome' to look out over London but Henry Mayhew records that to gain 'a bird's-eye view of the port, I went up to the Golden Gallery', whilst another mid-century social investigator begins his study of London by imagining precisely the same.[39] Indeed, social investigation shades into social policy as, according to the *Examiner* in 1849, '"crow's nests"' were erected 'above the cross of St Paul's for the purposes of [a] sanitary survey'.[40] It may not surprise us, then, that, as well as the 'great black dome . . . bulging at' Pip (*GE*, 189), in *Martin Chuzzlewit* 'the cross . . . of St Paul's . . . tak[es] . . . note of what[ever the murderer Jonas] . . . did' (662); whilst in *Little Dorrit* the talk following the death of the murderous Merdle 'swell[s] . . . into such a roar . . . that a solitary watcher', we learn, '[on the gallery] above the Dome . . . would have perceived the air to be laden with [the rogue's] . . . name' (776).

For all its implication in panopticism the dome of St Paul's does not, in Dickens, so much reproduce Bentham's 'hierarchical organisation . . . of power'[41] as lay bare the ambiguities of surveillance. If the watcher above the dome is 'solitary' then her fate resembles not just the guardian in the central tower but also the prisoner in the cell; likewise, since *Oliver Twist* is not free to leave Fagin's house, 'living inside the ball of St Paul' describes not just his view but his incarceration. Refigured in terms of St Paul's dome, Bentham's observation tower no longer represents a position of pure power. To put it another way, as part of Dickens's intuitive reworking of the politics of surveillance, St Paul's dome serves to feminise, or *dome*sticate, the gaze; not only in the sense of turning the phallic tower into a mammary dome (Peggotty's work-box displays a 'pink-dome[d]' St Paul's (*DC*, 65)) but also by complicating the gaze of surveillance with the gaze of the mother. For 'dome', that is, read 'dame' as in *A Tale of Two Cities* where the whole of Paris is overlooked by 'the watching towers of Notre Dame' (136). Church, mother and gaze again coincide in *Bleak House* when, in the chapel at Chesney Wold, immediately after the vicar declares '"O Lord . . . in thy sight"' Esther suddenly, and for the first time, encounters her mother's 'handsome proud eyes': 'shall I ever forget the . . . beating at my heart, occasioned by [that] . . . look' (304). Rivalling as it does 'thy sight', the maternal gaze here operates at the expense of the Father's; if Notre Dame is the 'Cathedral of Our Lady' (204) then this is the church of 'my Lady', Lady Dedlock.[42]

That the gaze of Dickens's Church should play between dome and dame may not surprise (a Victorian woman's place being in the dome, or *domus*), but what does surprise is that 'my Lady' does not leave the house of God as she finds it. For her look is set in opposition not only to a heavenly Father but also to an earthly one in that this meeting of eyes between mother and daughter reflects that mirror-stage in a child's development which precedes the entry of the father:[43] 'her face [was] . . . like a broken glass to me . . . I . . . seemed to arise before my own eyes' (*BH*, 304–5). In excluding the father, however, 'my Lady' is no less subversive than 'Our Lady' of the Virgin Birth.[44]

Violating, as they do, the endogamous code of the Victorian bourgeoisie, Our Lady and my Lady together suggest not only that 'the churches are not my *father's* house' but also that the house of God is not a home. For all its disciplining of the family, the Church that Dickens writes is never, it seems, a purely domestic space, it is only ever home *from* home. The beggars and idiots in Parma's crypt are not so much a home as a community or crowd; the dark and hooded monks who once lived in the crypt that Little Nell is shown are, of course, a disturbingly homosocial group; and in *Little Dorrit* the tourists who 'prowled about the churches . . . in the old . . . prison-yard manner' were there, we read, like prisoners through a 'general unfitness for getting on at home' (565). There is, indeed, a sense in which the church is always to some extent unhomely in precisely the sense of *unheimlich*, that term of Freud's which translates as 'uncanny'. The dark, unnerving and even Gothic aspects of Dickens's churches have often been observed[45] and none, of course, is more Gothic than the churches of Marseilles which are not only peopled with shadows but dotted with 'winking lamps' (40), lamps that seem as if to be communicating some secret; if, as Freud argues, 'the uncanny [is] . . . something which ought to have remained hidden but has come to light',[46] then these Marseilles churches are profoundly uncanny. Indeed, when later in the novel Little Dorrit seeks temporary refuge in St George's Church only to be greeted by the registrar, a specifically sexual secret threatens to come to light; at first he recommends she just wait by his fire, however 'his surveying her with an admiring gaze suggested', we read, 'something else to him', namely:

'Stay a bit. I'll get some cushions . . . and you and your friend shall lie down before the fire. Don't be afraid of not going in [to the prison] to join your father when the gate opens. *I'll* call you.' (*LD*, 219–20)

In so far as the registrar's homely way suggests an unhomely motivation, so his 'gaze' becomes an uncanny wink, a wink in our direction. This church that is not my father's house ('"don't be afraid of not . . . join[ing] your father"') corresponds, then, to what Freud calls the '*unheimlich* house', the unhomely home that translates, according to Freud, as the 'haunted house'[47] – in this case it is the house of God, and what haunts is sexuality.

As Foucault has argued,[48] for the Victorians sexuality functions, paradoxically, as an open secret and indeed, as here, it is in bringing sexuality to light that Dickens's Church is most uncanny. For Freud, a crucial instance of that which the uncanny discloses are the '*heimlich* parts of the human body, the pudenda'[49] and, of course, it is precisely 'those members of the body [of Christ] which we think to be less honourable' (1 Cor. 12.23) that are, as it were, exposed to view when Dickens, rehearsing the 'ritual inversion of the body in carnival',[50] quite literally turns his churches 'head over heels'. Equally uncanny is the disclosure of sexuality implicit in Parma's subterranean church; Italian crypts had, that is, a notorious reputation – writing in 1820, for instance, one British travel writer remarks of the 'subterranean chapel' beneath St Peter's in Rome that it was no longer open to both sexes since 'the sanctity of the place had not saved it from being converted into the scene of those licentious intrigues which its obscurity seemed calculated to favour'.[51] When Dickens describes a crypt occupied by both men and women as an animated version of the 'arms and legs . . . entangled . . . involved and jumbled together' in the Cathedral frescoes above we cannot but infer some dark and licentious secret.

Of course, the very notion of a secret, of something obscured and therefore deferred, undermines traditional realist accounts of truth as unmediated presence and in this sense the uncanniness of Dickens's churches is indicative of the way that in general, because so secretive or cryptic, those churches beg the question of truth. The one moment in which this becomes explicit is in *A Tale of Two Cities* where, within a page of reading that 'Notre Dame [is] almost equidistant' from the two extremes of poverty and wealth in pre-Revolutionary Paris, we learn that 'Man had got out of the Centre of Truth' (136–7) – in so far as equidistance implies a kind of centrality then the eccentric exception to this rule of eccentricity is Notre Dame, though of course she is only almost an exception since she is only 'almost equidistant'. The connection is itself eccentric; Notre Dame, we might say, renders the relationship between Church and truth as a riddle. As such Notre Dame takes us a long way from that dominant position of mid-Victorian Britain in which truth, as

made in the image of contemporary Anglicanism, was national, established and male. Indeed, we are closer to that more cryptic account of
truth articulated by the Catholic Newman in 1843 – 'in certain cases a lie
is the nearest approach to truth'; still closer, perhaps, is Nietzsche's later
and deconstructive invitation to 'suppos[e] . . . truth a woman'[52] – in
Dickens's case, Notre Dame. What is for sure, though, is that we are a long
way from the early Ruskin's phallocentric declaration that one of 'the
moral habits to which [Protestant] England in this age owes . . . [its] greatness [is] . . . a sincere upright searching into religious truth [which is] . . .
only traceable in the [church] tower, sent like an "unperplexed question
up to Heaven"'.[53] It is no accident that with regard to the question of
truth Dickens should, by contrast, focus on Notre Dame – a church that
is neither male, Protestant nor English. Indeed, just as Dickens's churches
are always in some sense cryptic so his English churches are often,
somehow and to some extent, foreign: in *Little Dorrit* a 'Congregationless
Church . . . [in Cheapside] seem[s] . . . to be waiting for some adventur-
ous Belzoni [the Egyptian explorer] to dig it out and discover its history'
(70); in 'City of London Churches' Dickens explores structures 'unknown
to far greater numbers . . . than the ancient edifices of the Eternal City'
(*UT*, 92); and in *Dombey and Son* the London congregation that lost themselves among high-backed pews constitute an 'integral portion of Europe'
(889).

In so far as the foreignness, or elsewhereness, of Dickens's churches
entails an account of truth, or knowledge, it is most obviously inscribed
in that description of St Peter's in Rome as 'an edifice, with no one point
for the mind to rest upon . . . and [that] tires itself with wandering round
and round'. Though for Dickens the cathedral's perpetual refusal of intellectual stasis is 'not religiously impressive', for Ruskin, writing just seven
years later, exactly the same experience is celebrated as the very spirit of
the Gothic church: 'The vital principle', he writes, 'is not the love of
Knowledge, but the love of *Change* . . . that restlessness of the dreaming
mind, that wanders hither and thither among the niches . . . pinnacles . . .
wall and roof'.[54] Though both men write a Church which entails a mind
that changes rather than knows, where Ruskin sees a vital principle, a
principle of life, Dickens sees the repetition and exhaustion ('a wandering round and round') of the death instinct; however undecidable or
unfollowable it may be, the Church that Dickens depicts never erases the
crypt in cryptic. In other words, the perpetual displacement implicit in
Dickens's cryptic Church is not so much a case of always already elsewhere – as in Ruskin's Gothic church – but of always already below.

Thus, just as Dickens leaves Parma's Cathedral only to enter a subterranean church so, at the very end of *Little Dorrit*, having 'walked out of the church', the newly-wed couple 'went down. Went down . . . Went down . . . Went down . . . went quietly down into the roaring streets, insep-arable and blessed' – in so far as we misread the *streets* as 'blessed' it is as if here too Dickens chances upon a 'lower church'. Moreover, in much the same way as Parma's beggars-in-ambush momentarily threaten an inversion of the economic order so here the sheer noise of the blessed streets effects a coded inversion of the 'down, down, down, down, down' of the couple's descent with the 'up' of the 'uproar' that is the novel's final word. In each case, in writing the Church from below, from socially below, Dickens uncovers a shadowy, cryptic community which threatens a love of change that is not only intellectual but economic and political. To quote from the very end of Barrett Browning's *Aurora Leigh*, published in the same year as *Little Dorrit*: 'new churches, new oeconomies'.[55]

Notes

1   Jacques Derrida, '*Fors*', Foreword to N. Abraham and M. Torok, *The Wolf Man's Magic Word: A Cryptonymy*, tr. N. Rand (Minneapolis: University of Minnesota Press, 1986), pp. xi, xxxix.

2   *AN*, 319; all subsequent references to *Pictures from Italy* are to this edition and appear parenthetically in the text.

3   Mrs Trollope, *The Vicar of Wrexhill* – as quoted in Valentine Cunningham, *Everywhere Spoken Against: Dissent in the Victorian Novel* (Oxford: Clarendon Press, 1975), p. 22.

4   Dennis Walder, *Dickens and Religion* (London: Allen & Unwin, 1981), p. 25.

5   All references to the Bible, unless otherwise indicated, are to the Authorised Version and appear parenthetically in the text.

6   Thomas Carlyle, *On Heroes, Hero-Worship and The Heroic in History* (Cambridge: Cambridge University Press, 1914), p. 166.

7   Derrida, '*Fors*', p. xxxvi.

8   'What I like about post cards', writes Derrida, 'is that . . . they are made to circu-late like an open but illegible letter' – *The Post Card: From Socrates to Freud and Beyond*, tr. Alan Bass (Chicago: University of Chicago Press, 1987), p. 12.

9   See Fred Kaplan, *Dickens: A Biography* (London: Hodder & Stoughton, 1988), p. 198.

10 Carlyle, *On Heroes*, 166.

11 See Jacques Derrida, *Writing and Difference*, tr. Alan Bass (London: Routledge, 1978), p. 278.

12 *The Post Card*, p. 123.

13 See Owen Chadwick, *The Victorian Church* (London: Adam & Charles Black, 1966), p. 327.

14 'The system of "hearing (understanding)-oneself-speak" [*s'entendre parler*] through the phonic substance – which *presents itself* as the nonexterior . . . noncontingent sig-nifier – has necessarily dominated the history of the world during an entire epoch' – Jacques Derrida, *Of Grammatology*, tr. Gayatri Chakravorty Spivak (London: Johns Hopkins University Press, 1974), pp. 7–8.

15 John P. Leavey, *Glassary* (Lincoln: University of Nebraska Press, 1986), p. 104c – Leavey is here attempting to describe the place and significance of bells in *Glas* (which means, of course, 'passing-bell'). As Leavey remarks, 'the movement of the bell . . . clapper swinging one way, barrel the other, is the motion of Derrida's [own] text' and indeed 'an emblem for the . . . movement of . . . his theory of writing as difference' (pp. 93a, 89c).

16 Derrida, '*Fors*', p. xxxvi.

17 J. Hillis Miller, for example, writes that 'life in the city is the way in which many men have experienced most directly what it means to live without God in the world' – *The Disappearance of God* (Cambridge, Mass.: Harvard University Press, 1963), p. 5.

18 Victor Hugo, *Les Misérables*, tr. N. Denny (Harmondsworth: Penguin, 1980), vol. 2, p. 368; quoted in A. S. Wohl, *Endangered Lives: Public Health in Victorian Britain* (London: Methuen, 1983), p. 101.

19 Friedrich Nietzsche, *Twilight of the Idols / The Anti-Christ*, tr. R. J. Hollingdale (Harmondsworth: Penguin, 1990), p. 178.

20 Terry Eagleton, *The Body as Language: Outline of a 'New Left' Theology* (London: Sheed & Ward, 1970), p. 70.

21 This phrase appears in an essay published in 1853 and is quoted by David Trotter in *Circulation: Defoe, Dickens, and the Economics of the Novel* (London: Macmillan, 1988), p. 73.

22 See Trotter, p. 105.

23 Michel Foucault, *Power/Knowledge: Selected Interviews and Other Writings 1972–1977*, ed. Colin Gordon (Brighton: Harvester Press, 1980), pp. 166–82.

24 Nietzsche, *Twilight*, p. 177.

25 See Jacques Lacan, *Écrits: A Selection*, tr. Alan Sheridan (London: Routledge, 1977), p. 4.

26 John Henry Newman, *Apologia Pro Vita Sua* (London: Fontana, 1959), p. 326.

27 Quoted in Simon During, *Foucault and Literature* (London: Routledge, 1992), p. 50.

28 Michel Foucault, *Madness and Civilisation*, tr. Richard Howard (London: Routledge, 1989), pp. 78–9.

29 Nietzsche, *Twilight*, p. 141.

30 This Pauline allusion was first observed by Joseph A. Hynes – see 'Image and Symbol in *Great Expectations*', *ELH*, 30 (1963), 260–1.

31 Foucault, *Madness*, p. 63.

32 Quoted in John Forster, *The Life of Charles Dickens*, ed. A. J. Hoppé (London: Dent, 1966), vol. 1, p. 24.

33 As Forster observes, at this time in Dickens's life, when he was living in lodgings, 'at home' meant Marshalsea (*Life*, vol. 1, p. 26).

34 See Michel Foucault, *Discipline and Punish*, tr. Alan Sheridan (Harmondsworth: Penguin, 1991), pp. 6–7.

35 See Natalie McKnight, *Idiots, Madmen, and Other Prisoners in Dickens* (New York: St Martin's Press, 1993), pp. 18–21.

36 McKnight, pp. 22–3.

37 Michel Foucault, *The History of Sexuality*, tr. Robert Hurley (Harmondsworth: Penguin, 1990), pp. 58–9.

38 Foucault, *Discipline*, p. 202.

39 Charlotte Brontë, *Villette* (Harmondsworth: Penguin, 1979), p. 109; E. P. Thompson and Eileen Yeo, *The Unknown Mayhew: Selections from the 'Morning Chronicle' 1849–50*

(London: Merlin Press, 1971), pp. 97–8; see James Grant, *The Great Metropolis* (New York, 1837), vol. 1, p. 19.

40 See the *Examiner*, 14 July 1849, cited in Robert Partlow (ed.), *Dickens the Craftsman* (Carbondale: Southern Illinois University Press, 1970), p. 119.

41 Foucault, *Discipline*, p. 205.

42 Throughout *Bleak House* Lady Dedlock is, of course, referred to as 'my Lady' by the anonymous narrator.

43 The 'assumption of his specular image', writes Lacan, takes place whilst the child is 'still sunk in his . . . nursling dependence' – *Écrits*, p. 2.

44 For a fuller discussion of the subversive significance of the Virgin Mary, in a Victorian context, see John Schad, '"No one dreams": Hopkins and Lacan', *Victorian Poetry*, 32 (1994), 141–56.

45 See Harry Stone, *The Night Side of Dickens: Cannibalism, Passion, Necessity* (Columbus: Ohio State University Press, 1994), pp. 240–5.

46 *The Complete Psychological Works of Sigmund Freud*, tr. Alix Strachey, vol. xvii (London: Hogarth Press, 1955), p. 241.

47 *Ibid.*, p. 241.

48 Foucault argues that since the nineteenth century our society, with respect to sex, 'speaks verbosely of its own silence' – *History*, p. 8.

49 Freud, p. 225.

50 Peter Stallybrass and Allon White, *The Politics and Poetics of Transgression* (London: Methuen, 1986), p. 185.

51 Charlotte A. Eaton, *Rome, in the Nineteenth Century* (London: Henry G. Bohn, 1852), vol. 1, p. 408.

52 John Henry Newman, *The Oxford University Sermons* (1892), p. 341.; Friedrich Nietzsche, *Beyond Good and Evil*, tr. R. J. Hollingdale (Harmondsworth: Penguin, 1990), p. 31.

53 John Ruskin, *Unto This Last and Other Writings*, ed. Clive Wilmer (Harmondsworth: Penguin, 1985), pp. 107–8.

54 *Ibid.*, p. 99.

55 Elizabeth Barrett Browning, *Aurora Leigh*, ed. Margaret Reynolds (Athens: Ohio University Press, 1992), Book 9, l. 947.

2

Dickens through Blanchot: the nightmare fascination of a world without interiority

TIMOTHY CLARK

La poésie vint d'une insomnie perpetuelle.

René Char

Dickens's work has often seemed to call for its own peculiar aesthetic. Robert Garis, for instance, coined the famous phrase the 'Dickens theatre' in response to the way in which 'there is something about Dickens's way of looking at people that is unacceptable by the ordinary standards of serious fiction'.[1] If the last phrase dates Garis's account, written in the mid-1960s, his notion of the Dickens theatre still usefully describes Dickens's texts as the work of a self-conscious verbal showman who tends to deal with characterisation, narration and use of figures in ways that foreground the skill of the performance itself. If one removes Garis's stress on the author's subjectivity, it is a view that may come close to anti-humanist readings of Dickens's work as 'nothing but figure' (Henry James). In this chapter I try to sketch such a Dickensian aesthetic, drawing largely from the thinking of Maurice Blanchot and Emmanuel Levinas, suggesting a new reading of some well-known Dickensian traits for which the notion of the Dickens theatre is inappropriate. Blanchot's work enables us to trace in the darker aspects of Dickens a latent if pervasive anti-humanist aesthetic at odds with that writer's expressed romanticism.

The philosophical complexity of Maurice Blanchot's work may seem a long way from Dickens's often less conceptualised complexities. Yet, while he has devoted no essay to Dickens, Blanchot's thinking on what he terms the 'image' intersects productively with Dickens's work in three areas: first, the elaboration of what might be termed an aesthetic of the cadaver; second, an attention to the distinctive mode of being of the urban everyday and, lastly, a concept of insomnia as a peculiar mode of inspiration.[2] Finally I turn to a particular late essay, 'Night Walks', as an intense exemplar of all these features.

In 'Reality and its Shadow' (1948),[3] a seminal text for Blanchot on the image, Levinas makes explicit reference to Dickens:

> We think that an exterior vision – that of a total exteriority . . . where the subject itself is exterior to itself – is the true vision of the novelist. Atmosphere is the very obscurity of images. The poetry of Dickens, who was surely a rudimentary psychologist, the atmosphere of those dusty boarding schools, the pale light of London offices with their clerks, the antique and second-hand clothing shops, the very characters of Nickleby and Scrooge, only appear in an exterior vision set up as a method.[4]

Some of Levinas's generalisations may seem hard to accept. Is exteriorisation the only method of Lawrence, Joyce or George Eliot? Is Dickens really so rudimentary a psychologist, or in fact a subtle analyst of modes of psychic repression? Yet Levinas has described one of the most striking and pervasive features of Dickens's work. The novels manifest the combined horror and fascination of a world without interiority.

Blanchot and Levinas

Blanchot is now, belatedly, being recognised as one of the twentieth century's most original thinkers on literature.[5] Emerging from and against the phenomenological and existentialist thinking of the 1940s and 1950s, especially the work of Sartre and Heidegger, Blanchot is the decisive figure in the emergence at this time of notions of *écriture*, transgression and irrecoupable negativity now more usually associated with Jacques Derrida. Literature, for Blanchot, is understood as a mode of language whose ambiguity is essential to it. Against Heidegger's valorisation of poetic language (*Dichtung*) as giving access to some realm of truth fundamental to human consciousness, literature is testimony to being as dissimulation: it is an impersonal realm in language that can neither be totally conceptualised nor interpreted as the representation of some prior reality or consciousness. Writing escapes or exceeds the grasp of subjective consciousness, resisting criticism and philosophy's obsession with meaning, and 'the desire to master death and find fulfilment for human finitude'.[6] It is language in the guise of an unworking, an experience of powerlessness, pointing 'towards an exteriority that would scatter meaning . . . in the space of dying itself'.[7]

Towards the end of *The Space of Literature* (1955)[8] appears an essay entitled 'Two Versions of the Imaginary'. The first version of the imaginary is a familiar one, since Blanchot's definition might cover any known use of the term in literary criticism. To make an image is an intentional creative act, one whereby the mind, in its effort to grasp something, renders it manageable in the form of a concrete representation. It is 'the ideal operation by which man, capable of negating nature, raises it to a higher meaning, either in order to know it or to enjoy it admiringly' (206). The image is a function of human mastery and expressiveness – in Dickens Blanchot's first notion would cover not only much of his fanciful animism but also those complex structures of symbolism and analogy that structure the later 'dark' novels.

The second notion of the imaginary stems from what looks initially like an exercise in a phenomenological discipline of attention to the things themselves, purged of all presupposition. Yet this exercise comes to overturn the very notion of intentional consciousness at the basis of such a phenomenological reduction:

> when we are face to face with the things themselves – if we fix upon a face, the corner of a wall – does it not also sometimes happen that we abandon ourselves to what we see? Bereft of power before this presence suddenly strangely mute and passive, are we not at its mercy? Indeed, this can happen, but it happens because the thing we stare at has foundered, sunk into its image, and the image has returned into that deep fund of impotence to which everything reverts. (255)

Particularly striking to the reader of Dickens is the close connection made between an aesthetics of the image and a kind of phenomenology of the corpse. The connection is introduced through an analogy:

> we might . . . recall that a tool, when damaged, becomes its *image* (and sometimes an esthetic object like those outmoded objects, fragmented, unusable, almost incomprehensible, perverse, which André Breton loved). In this case the tool, no longer disappearing into its use, *appears*. This appearance of the object is that of resemblance and reflection: the object's double, if you will. The category of art is linked to this possibility for objects to 'appear,' to surrender, that is, to the pure and simple resemblance behind which there is nothing – but being. (258–9)

Blanchot's implicit target here is the argument of Martin Heidegger, first in *Being and Time* (1927) and later in 'The Origin of the Work of Art' (1950)[9] that an object which is broken, or detached from its context in some way, may acquire a peculiarly disclosive nature. Instead of disappearing into its use, the object, precisely by no longer accommodating itself to the network of possible uses, purposes, etc. that had hitherto defined its being, renders unusually apparent to us that 'world' or network of possible assignments. A whole way of life may seem latent, newly exposed, in say 'the useless fragment of a wooden bowl' (Wordsworth). There is a homology between the broken and the aesthetic.

Blanchot's work on the corpse as image is an argument with this phenomenological view. What could be more disclosive of a world of human aims and desires than the corpse of a dear friend? This violent disjunction, though, is not only the uncovering of a world: it is also the manifestation of an irreducible materiality, one that is nul, without world. The corpse is an image in the sense of an appearance – but of what?

> he is, I see this, perfectly like himself: he resembles *himself*. The cadaver is its own image. It no longer entertains any relation with this world, where it still appears, except that of an image, an obscure possibility, a shadow ever present behind the living form from which now, far from separating itself from this form, transforms it entirely into shadow . . . And if the cadaver is so similar, it is because it is, at a certain moment, similarity par excellence: altogether similarity, and also nothing more. (258)

Similarly Levinas's 'Reality and its Shadow' argues for a related concept of the aesthetic as a mode of being that is not to be understood as an imitation of nature or reality, or as the expression of a subjectivity or representation, referrable to some higher principle, such as meaning or the idea. Rather it is *sui generis*. A corpse-like realm of imagery and resemblance is inherent to the very apparentness of phenomena:

> A being is that which is, that which reveals itself in its truth, and, at the same time, it resembles itself, is its own image. The original gives itself as though at a distance from itself, as though it were withdrawing itself, or through something in a being delayed behind being.[10]

Any entity, as it appears, bears in its sensuous aspect an allegory or resemblance of itself. Even the most perfect likeness is also an 'insurmountable caricature'.[11]

A pertinent point about this notion of the image is that it is not referrable to psychology. The image is not a subjective expression or instrument of understanding. It is a realm of irreducible materiality whose relation to consciousness is one of what Blanchot terms 'fascination' or 'passion for the image' (32). The image fascinates subjectivity as something which possesses an immediacy to which one is subject. A point that immediately strikes the reader of Dickens is that fascination, for Blanchot, is an especial feature of childhood: 'If our childhood fascinates us, this happens because childhood is the moment of fascination, is itself fascinated' (33).

This experience relates to Blanchot's anti-phenomenological model of subjectivity, which is not that of an enclosed interiority, or of a consciousness whose experience is an intentional object in the phenomenological sense. It is a model of subjectivity as a heteronomy, close to the thinking of Georges Bataille as well as that of Levinas. Subjectivity is not an agency whose relation to things can be ultimately one of intentionality. Rather, 'the susceptibility to the exterior which defines subjectivity is precisely the impossibility of such a transcendence on the part of consciousness'.[12] With deceptive simplicity, Blanchot's *The Infinite Conversation* (1969) schematises these issues into an opposition between a notion of intentionality as an active or passive synthesis, and experience in the Bataillean sense of the undergoing of an affect too immediate or 'close' to be securely conceptualised or represented.[13] Subjectivity is fundamentally a heteronomy, an opening to exteriority, at depth not an *ego cogito* but a *cogitatur*. It is this model of subjectivity that is corroborated, Blanchot argues, by the second experience of the image.

Dickens: the image and characterisation

If we return now to the quotation from Levinas at the beginning of the chapter – on the novelist's exterior vision – we see that 'exteriorisation' here would mean a method that renders appearances and speech from the viewpoint of fascination. Scenes, characters and their speech pass into the mode of being of images, i.e. phenomena detached from notions of interior animation or intention and so become image-like as aesthetic phenomena that are compulsive in their irreducible materiality.

The aspect of Dickens's technique that first comes to mind here is his art of characterisation and caricature. A Dickens character is often notoriously 'flat', i.e. one or two salient characteristics, gestures or items of speech are repeated in different situations without reference to the possibility of some sort of psychological change or development. The current tendency in criticism is to relate this method of characterisation to a reading of Dickens as a defender of a romantic psychology. Dickens is said to be advocating an ideal of psychic wholeness, of an integrated relation between all aspects of the psyche and between the psyche and its environment.[14] He is thus seen as giving satirical portraits of a world of atrophied or perverted development in which people have been reified into mere fetishised fragments of some putative fuller personality, those 'extraordinary specimens of human fungus', for example, 'that spring up spontaneously in the western streets of London' (*BH*, 426). David Simpson writes of 'characters who evidence an abdication or enforced loss of the essential or inward self in favor of outward attributes'[15] – Turveydrop, for instance, the model of deportment in *Bleak House*, an atrophied embodiment of fashions from the Regency period: 'a fat old gentleman with a false complexion, false teeth, false whiskers, and a wig' (242).

This view of Dickens as a romantic novelist surely gives us the correct historical context for work on this writer. Yet figures like Turveydrop, Grandfather Smallweed, Heep, Mrs Skewton and others also possess a compulsion and interest that is other than that of satire or comedy. They transmit the fascination of the image in Blanchot's sense. Of Silas Wegg we read, in *Our Mutual Friend*:

> Wegg was a knotty man, and a close-grained, with a face carved out of very hard material, that had just as much play of expression as a watchman's rattle. When he laughed, certain jerks occurred in it, and the rattle sprung. Sooth to say, he was so wooden a man that he seemed to have taken his wooden leg naturally, and rather suggested to the fanciful observer, that he might be expected – if his development received no untimely check – to be completely set up with a pair of wooden legs in about six months. (89)

I do not find this passage easy to assimilate to any straightforward sense of Dickens's moral vision or a conception of the world as one of fragmented pieces that call for reintegration. Wegg is, in his way, complete. The uneasy comedy of the text, tilting as it does towards horror, may be as much part of a metaphysical as a social viewpoint – that of a world without interiority. James R. Kincaid argues that Dickens's work makes us question notions of selfhood as some isolable, inner series of stable qualities: 'If we ask: "Who is the true Dick Swiveller, Wilkins Micawber, Abel Magwitch, Noddy Boffin?," we find ourselves so helplessly bobbing about in deep waters that we begin to see that we have cast off in the wrong boat, formulated the question in a way that will frustrate a good answer.'[16] The difference between roles and role-playing is often non-formulable in Dickens. His is a technique of characterisation as mimicry which realises a possibility which is fleeting in the appearances of actual people: 'In the rare instances when a living person shows similitude with himself, he only seems to us more remote, close to a dangerous and neutral region, *astray* in *himself* and like his own ghost already: he seems to return to no longer having any but an echo life' (258).

The crowd who gather round the corpse at the Paris morgue in 'Some Recollections of Mortality' in *The Uncommercial Traveller* (1860) are characterised by 'general, purposeless, vacant staring . . . like looking at a waxwork without a catalogue, and not knowing what to make of it. But these experiences concurred in possessing the one underlying expression of *looking at something that could not return a look*' (192). This stare seems to enact more than a morbid curiosity. It is possessed by the combined horror and fascination of a state of total exposure in an existential sense, and not merely in the sense of nakedness. Intentionality is taken over by the cadaver as a place of transgression between people and things, between the inner life and thinghood. Two little girls are among the spectators of the bodies, 'one showing them to a doll' (191). The scene recalls Dickens's own dread of being looked at while asleep. The custodian in Paris refers to the morgue as a 'museum', reminding us again of the close relation of the phenomenology of the corpse to the phenomenology of the aesthetic. This connects the morgue to the numerous stores and piles of bric-à-brac and *nature morte* to be found in Dickens, from the old curiosity shop itself, to Krook's shop in *Bleak House*, Sol Gills's naval store in *Dombey and Son*, or Mr Venus's collection of human and animal fragments in *Our Mutual Friend*.

The Dickensian villain is invariably a body in animation. Uriah Heep, for instance, possesses 'a cadaverous face' with 'hardly any eye-brows, and no eyelashes, and eyes of red-brown, so unsheltered and unshaded, that I remember wondering how he went to sleep' (*DC*, 275). Heep can easily be read as a double for aspects of David Copperfield that he cannot openly avow – the shared characteristics of social aspiration, shame connected with poverty (Heep comes to know through Micawber of Copperfield's having been 'in the streets' (817)), and latent rivalry for Agnes Wickfield. Yet aspects of Heep also relate to the pervasive nightmare of a world without interiority. One night Heep has to be accommodated at Copperfield's lodgings:

There I saw him, lying on his back, with his legs extending to I don't know where, gurglings taking place in his throat, stoppages in his nose, and his mouth open like a post-office. He was so much worse in reality than in my distempered fancy, that afterwards I was *attracted to him in very repulsion*, and could not help wandering in and out every half-hour or so, and taking another look at him. (443–4: my italics)

This passage recalls the phrase 'the profound fascination of repulsion' associated by Forster with Dickens's relation to London.[17] It also anticipates Dickens's account in 1860 of the power that attracts to an urban churchyard in 'City of the Absent'.[18]

Blanchot's argument on the image helps us conceptualise one of Dickens's idiosyncrasies, his delight in bad acting, not just for its giving a sense of the ridiculous but also for its eliciting the almost hypnotic consciousness of a realm of physical movement and expression which enacts no cogent inner or psychological dynamic. At the Britannia Theatre at Hoxton, for instance, 'We all knew what was coming when the Spirit of Liberty addressed the king with a big face, and His Majesty backed to the side-scenes and began untying himself behind, with his big face all on one side'.[19] Here bodies take on the mode of being of objects in the environment, mask-like and clumsily automatised.

The urban everyday

Blanchot's notion of the image is also applicable to Dickens's modes of characterisation because his characters and urban scenes are often presented in the guise of the habitual or customary. That is, a place or person is often presented not precisely as appearing on a particular occasion but in terms of qualities that reliably recur on all or most occasions, habitually or recurrently. The mode of being at issue is that of an habitual performance of a series of attributes or epithets. These often spill over to apply to the environment around a character or all things associated with it. The effect of this habitual mode of presentation is to detach the entity from the here and now except in so far as the present appearance takes on the mode of being of the image. This is characterisation as the making of a mask. In his 'Masking: Toward a Phenomenology of Exteriorization', Robert L. Grimes writes of masking as a kind of rigidifying process, like dying itself: 'To die is not to become powerless but to become powerful in a fixed mode.'[20] Such masking is a reduction to one dimension, that of 'empowered exteriority'. Grimes writes:

A character-type is to drama what a death-mask is to ritual, namely, a concretizing of *dunamis* in a fixed form. What is at once terrifying and comical, i.e. grotesque, about masked figures is the paradox of form and dynamic. At any moment the mask can come off revealing that it is a mere lifeless thing and the man underneath a mere mortal. But the lifeless thing also threatens to attain a life of its own.

For Garis, the sense of puppetry and the grotesque is part of the performative dimension of Dickens's work. Behind the mask Garis and many others would have us find the writer himself, demonstrating his showmanship. Such a notion of the grotesque humanises or rehumanises it, making inner and safely psychological once more the vision of exteriority inherent in the mask-like quality of Dickens's characters. Yet a character also appears to us, not as the outward manifestation of an inner personality but as a performance in the mode of similarity and resemblance.

This habitual, image-making mode of presentation is a strong part of Dickens's art of the urban everyday. It is the mode of being of that peculiarly anonymous and ceaseless theatre which is the street. In an essay in *The Infinite Conversation* Blanchot, unknowingly repeating contemporary responses to Dickens's *Sketches by Boz*, assimilates the everyday to the mode of being of the image: 'the everyday is what we never see for a first time but can only see again, having always already seen it by an illusion that is constitutive of the everyday'.[21] The streets of a large city make up a space that touches those that walk them with the anonymity of a public thing, the 'visible-invisible' character of the passer-by: 'When we meet someone on the street it comes always by surprise and as though by mistake, for we do not recognize ourselves there; in order to go forth to meet another one must first tear oneself away from an existence without identity' (*SB*, 243). The streets in Dickens not only embody the threat of a lost identity – especially for children such as Oliver Twist, Florence Dombey and Charlie Necker who seem to vanish into them – they also acquire an image-like quality through Dickens's mode of presentation in terms of the habitual. The Seven Dials, for instance, are

> streets of dirty, straggling houses, with *now and then* an unexpected court composed of buildings as ill-proportioned and deformed as the half-naked children that wallow in the kennels. *Here and there*, a little dirty dark chandler's shop, with a cracked bell hung up behind the door. (*SB*, 71: my italics)

The sharp particularity of Dickens's writing plays here against the fact that these items are presented as several, lending each detail the image-like status of being its own simulacrum or resemblance. They are themselves yet also 'here and there' and 'now and then'. The same haunting self-insistence pervades many of the 'people' in Dickens. Characters in a small room in Dickens often retain the fascinating yet disconcerting mode-of-being associated with the street.

Insomnia

Blanchot repudiates romantic idealisations of creativity in favour of fascination as a mode of reversed intentionality in which the initiative passes, to a qualified degree, to modes of automatism inherent in language itself. Levinas's essay illustrates such a notion by the transformation undergone in certain dreams, or in 'The particular automatic character of a walk or a dance to music . . . a mode of being where nothing is unconscious, but where consciousness, paralyzed in its freedom, plays, totally absorbed in this playing'.[22] Levinas's description could equally well apply to the mesmerism that interested Dickens all his life and of which he was a skilful practitioner.[23] It is a matter of an exteriority of the inward that may be read as confirming an anti-Kantian view of subjectivity as a heteronomy, an opening to exteriority. Here the impersonal overrides the personal at the very heart of personality, breaking down distinctions between interiority and exteriority.[24]

One mode in which the transformation of subjectivity which Blanchot names fascination manifests itself is the experience of insomnia (e.g. *The Space of Literature*, pp. 264–8). In calling the writer 'the insomniac of the day'[25] Blanchot is implicitly rebuffing Freud's account of the artist as the dreamer of the day whose sexual fantasies are sublimated in the form of cultural products. Blanchot's is an anti-romantic notion of 'creativity' or 'inspiration' not as enhanced subjective power but as the *ecstasis* of fascination as an opening to exteriority. Kafka remarked that if he did not undergo nights of sleeplessness he would be unable to write.[26] Dickens's work too recurrently muses on insomnia as inspiration. His attention to the vicissitudes of sleep is so exact as to have made his work the subject of an article in the scientific journal *Sleep*.[27] At the opening of *The Old Curiosity Shop* we read:

> That constant pacing to and fro, that never-ending restlessness, that incessant tread of feet wearing the rough stones smooth and glossy – is it not a wonder how the dwellers in narrow ways can bear to hear it! Think of a sick man in such a place as Saint Martin's Court, listening to the footsteps, and in the midst of pain and weariness obliged, despite himself (as though

it were a task he must perform) to detect the child's step from the man's, the slipshod beggar from the booted exquisite, the lounging from the busy, the dull heel of the sauntering outcast from the quick tread of an expectant pleasure-seeker – think of the hum and noise being always present to his senses, and of the stream of life that will not stop, pouring on, on, on, through all his restless dreams, as if he were condemned to lie dead but conscious, in a noisy churchyard, and had no hope of rest for centuries to come. (43)

In this nightmare of compulsive wakefulness, the mind is possessed by the images that impinge upon it from the sounds of the street; it has no choice but to participate.[28] In insomnia, 'The bare fact of presence is oppressive; one is held by being, held to be' (Levinas).[29] In *The Uncommercial Traveller* the narrator recounts how, falling half-asleep during long walks, he finds himself making 'immense quantities of verse' and speaking 'a certain language once pretty familiar to me, but which I have nearly forgotten from disuse, with fluency' (94). The passage from the opening of *The Old Curiosity Shop* is also reminiscent of Dickens's personal need for streets and the continuous anonymous activity of their people in order to be able to write. He found the composition of *Dombey and Son* especially difficult because of the lack of the 'magic lantern' of London (*Letters*, IV.612). Later he confides that 'The absence of any accessible streets continues to worry me . . . It is quite a little mental phenomenon . . . I don't seem to be able to get rid of my spectres unless I can lose them in crowds'. The tensions of writing often resolved themselves for Dickens through long night walks through the city (*Letters*, IV.622).[30] The streets in Dickens often possess an 'eternal' or 'incessant' quality that passes over into the mode of being of the image, physically immediate yet conceptually remote – the 'close, eternal streets' (*OCS*, 415).

'Lying Awake', an essay from *Household Words*, 30 October 1852 (*SSF*, 159–66), concerns wholly this peculiar automatism of language betweeen sleeping and waking. It is a virtuoso dramatisation, soon modulating into the present tense, of the images that present themselves willy-nilly to the insomniac mind. Ostensibly a notable piece of Dickens theatre in Garis's sense, it also yet differs from a show of verbal virtuosity in its suggestion of a process of writing fascinated by its power to go on and on, with a precise hallucinatory articulacy, with little pressure of a conscious or directive intention behind it. For instance, attempts to 'think of something on the voluntary principle' (162) on the 'balloon ascents of this last season' (162), and then 'the late brutal assaults' (165), interrupt themselves with insomniacal digressions that unfold according to their own inherent logic – quasi-public speeches, pointed and slightly over-punctuated, on the needs of ordinary people for escapist exhibitions that court danger, followed by a peroration on the case against the revival of whipping as a punishment for brutal assault. The effect, difficult to illustrate without over-lengthy quotation, is that language approaches the status of an impersonal garrulousness – it is as if, in insomnia, one reached a common space out of which emerge those various species of logorrhoea that may become speakers such as Mrs Nickleby, Mrs Skewton or Mr Micawber. The language of the novels is often performative in a comparable way, a heightened image of received discourses or of idiolects become self-caricaturing in their very repetition. This technique recalls Blanchot's description of literature as language ruled by fascination, not 'a language containing images or one that casts reality in figures, but one which is its own image, an image of language (and not a figurative language) . . . not signs, but images, images of words, and words where things turn into images' (34). *Mimesis* in Dickens is often less imitation or representation than the making of the phonological equivalent of a mask.

The connection between the image and insomnia as an experience of an exteriority of the inward can also be related to Dickens's well-known obsession with corpses and corpse-like phenomena such as effigies, waxworks, old clothes or seemingly animated furniture. The corpse etc. in Dickens is often associated, paradoxically, with a frightening kind of perpetual wakefulness or fascination. The effigy which Quilp beats as a substitute for Kit Nubbles is 'goggle-eyed and with that excessively wide-awake aspect . . . by which figure-heads are usually characterized' (*OCS*, 564). Uriah Heep's lack of eyebrows and eyelids assimilates him to the nightmare of perpetual wakefulness associated with the effigy, a fascination and power that is no less at work in Heep's appearance when he actually is asleep. The corpse which the 'uncommercial traveller' encounters in the Paris morgue in 'Travelling Abroad' is described as 'a large dark man whose disfigurement by water was in a frightful manner comic, and whose expression was that of a prize-fighter who had closed his eye-lids under a heavy blow, but was going immediately to open them' (*UT*, 65). Portraits of the Dedlock ancestors in *Bleak House* make up 'a large collection, *glassy-eyed*, set up in the most approved manner on their various twigs and perches, very correct, perfectly free from animation, and always in glass cases' (588, my italics). Jarley's waxworks are 'all . . . looking intensely nowhere, and staring with extraordinary earnestness at nothing' (*OCS*, 283). Invariably in Dickens a painting or likeness has a mask-like or corpse-like mode of being, less an aesthetic object than a frozen attitude, a perpetual vigil.

'Night Walks'

I turn finally to Dickens's most concentrated and sustained expression of the nightmare of a world without interiority, the essay 'Night Walks' in *The Uncommercial Traveller*. 'Night Walks' probably commemorates Dickens's bout of night-walking after the death of his father.[31] Its narrator refers to 'a temporary inability to sleep, referable to a distressing impression' that caused him 'to walk about the streets all night, for a series of several nights'. Given Dickens's habits of composition, the essay may be read as an allegory of Dickensian inspiration. The subject of this dramatised meditation is named simply 'houselessness' or 'the houseless mind'. The essay shifts back and forth between the first person and the third, creating a sense of blurred agency throughout, as if houselessness were a state of subjectivity other than the normal person of the narrator. The essay's climax is a sudden confrontation with a symbol of total exposure, a young man, a 'creature like a beetle-browed hair-lipped [*sic*] youth of twenty' with 'a loose bundle of rags'. These are lost as the creature flees from the narrator's outstretched hand (*UT*, 133).

The essay instantiates the relation between the image and the mode of being of the habitual or recurrent. It concerns not one walk, as a cursory reading might suggest, but several walks blurred into a composite, and presented in the peculiarly divided and yet suspended temporality of the habitual:

> Walking the streets under the pattering rain, Houselessness *would* walk and walk and walk, seeing nothing but the interminable tangle of streets, save at a corner, *here and there*, two policemen in conversation, or the sergeant or inspector looking after his men. *Now and then* in the night – but rarely – Houselessness *would* become aware of a furtive head peering out of a doorway a few yards before him . . . evidently intent upon no particular service to society. Under a kind of fascination . . . Houselessness and this gentleman *would* eye one another from head to foot. (128: my italics)

This is one sleepless walk presented in the guise of its own resemblance or image over several occasions. Resemblance, in the sense of an exterior vision of material forms detached from the instrumental or daytime purposes that normally define them, also dominates the presentation of space in 'Night Walks'. The whole city takes on the corpse-like externality, the remoteness and fascination of the image. Houselessness recurrently seeks some interior, humanising space as a respite from the compulsive pacing of the streets. Entering one of the theatres on the

South Bank, however, the narrator finds no inner shelter but merely goes from one exterior space into another:

> In one of my night-walks . . . I passed the outer boundary of one of these great deserts, and entered it. With a dim lantern in my hand, I groped my well-known way to the stage and looked over the orchestra – which was like a great grave dug for a time of pestilence – into the void beyond. A dismal cavern of immense aspect, with the chandelier gone dead like everything else, and nothing visble through mist and fog and space, but tiers of winding sheets. (129)

Houselessness wanders between some of the most famous buildings in London, from Waterloo Bridge and 'the two great theatres' to Newgate prison, then on to the Bank, thence Billingsgate and then over London Bridge to the old King's Bench prison. Then a meditation on 'Dry Rot' in men, and the horror of a human form becoming infiltrated, losing all interiority and crumbling to dust, leads to Bethlehem hospital. These digressions are carefully paced so as to suggest the temporality of the walk itself and its distractedness. For instance, a trite enough meditation on dreaming as a sort of universal madness takes the walker to Westminster:

> By this time I had left the hospital behind me, and was again setting towards the river, and in a short breathing space I was on Westminster-bridge, regaling my houseless eyes with the external walls of the British Parliament. (132)

In the quiet and dimness of the night each of these places is detached from the daytime use that defines it, becoming walls disjunct from their familiar being and yet oddly and newly visible at the same time. There is the effect, nowhere stated explicitly but pervading the piece, that all these major buildings are somehow closer together than by day, and newly available in a city that seems half necropolis and half a full-sized model of itself.

'Night Walks' may be compared to that minor genre of romantic writing that dramatises the meditations of a walk, such as Hazlitt's 'On Going a Journey', various essays by De Quincey, or Leigh Hunt's 'Walking Home by Night'.[32] Yet this night walk, which Peter Ackroyd describes as 'a strange essay, in some ways the strangest Dickens ever wrote',[33] also works against the romanticism of the genre in a way comparable to what has already been said about characterisation. The walk, in the poetry of Wordsworth and Coleridge and the essays already mentioned, engages the writer in the dramatisation of a dialectical interaction between mind and world. It is a space of encounter and reflection: it enacts a drama of consciousness, both in the release gained through dwelling upon the play of forms and topics suggested by the walk in progress and the empowerment of the mind in imaginative self-definition or discovery. In Dickens's text, on the other hand, the romantic dialectic of mind and world becomes an insomniacal fascination with an irreducible exteriority, alien to interiorisation and conceptualisation. Whereas romantic examples of the walk tend to gesture towards some sort of homecoming at the end, symbolic or otherwise, the Dickens ends only with a tempered image of escape into sleep: 'the day came, and I was tired and could sleep' (*UT*, 135).

In conclusion, Blanchot's work enables us to articulate a pervasive anti-idealist aesthetic in Dickens's work, at odds with his expressed romanticism and with individualist and humanist models of subjectivity. The pervasiveness in Dickens of the image in Blanchot's sense may also suggest limits to the critical desire to totalise and interpret, for the image is the fascination of a non-signifying materiality. It is, by definition, removed from that instrumentalising attitude that would have it mean something other than its own insistent being.

Notes

1 R. Garis, *The Dickens Theatre: A Reassessment of the Novels* (Oxford: Oxford University Press, 1965), p. 44.

2 To my knowledge, the only other essay to draw Dickens and Blanchot together, in a manner very different from my interests here, is Garrett Stewart's 'Leaving History: Dickens, Gance, Blanchot', *Yale Journal of Criticism*, 2:2 (1989), 145–90.

3 E. Levinas, 'Reality and its Shadow', in *Collected Philosophical Papers*, tr. Alphonso Lingis (Dordrecht: Martinus Nijhoff, 1987), pp. 1–13.

4 *Ibid.*, p. 10.

5 See J. Gregg, *Maurice Blanchot and the Literature of Transgression* (Princeton: Princeton University Press, 1994); Joseph Libertson, *Proximity: Levinas, Blanchot, Bataille and Communication* (The Hague: Martinus Nijhoff, 1982).

6 S. Critchley, '*Il ya* – A Dying Stronger than Death (Blanchot with Levinas)', *Oxford Literary Review*, 15 (1993), 81–132.

7 Critchley, '*Il ya*', p. 84.

8 M. Blanchot, *The Space of Literature*, tr. A. Smock (Lincoln and London: University of Nebraska Press, 1982). All further references to Blanchot are to this text unless otherwise stated and included, parenthetically, in the text.

9 M. Heidegger, *Being and Time*, tr. John Macquarrie and Edward Robinson (New York: Harper & Row, 1962); 'The Origin of the Work of Art', in *Poetry Language Thought*, tr. Albert Hofstadter (New York: Harper & Row, 1971), pp. 17–81.

10 Levinas, 'Reality', pp. 6–7.

11 Levinas, 'Reality', p. 8.

12 Libertson, *Proximity*, p. 20.

13 Blanchot, *The Infinite Conversation*, tr. Susan Hanson (Minneapolis and London: University of Minnesota Press, 1993), p. 207.

14 See D. den Hartog, *Dickens and Romantic Psychology: The Self and Time in Nineteeenth Century Literature* (London: Macmillan, 1987); L. Frank, *Charles Dickens and the Romantic Self* (Lincoln and London: University of Nebraska Press, 1984); D. Simpson, *Fetishism and Imagination: Dickens, Melville, Conrad* (Baltimore and London: Johns Hopkins University Press, 1982).

15 Simpson, *Fetishism*, p. 48.

16 J. R. Kincaid, 'Performance, Roles, and the Nature of the Self in Dickens', in *Dramatic Dickens*, ed. Carol Hanberry Mackay (London: Macmillan, 1989), pp. 11–26 (p. 12).

17 J. Forster, *The Life of Charles Dickens*, ed. J. W. T. Ley (New York: Doubleday, 1928), p. 11.

18 'The City of the Absent', in *UT*, 246–54.

19 'Two Views of a Cheap Theatre', in *UT*, 28–32.

20 R. L. Grimes, 'Masking: Toward a Phenomenology of Exteriorization', *Journal of the American Academy of Religion*, 43:3 (1975), 508–16 (p. 511).

21 'Everyday Speech', in *The Infinite Conversation*, pp. 238–45, 240.

22 Levinas, 'Reality', p. 4.

23 See F. Kaplan, *Dickens and Mesmerism: The Hidden Springs of Fiction* (Princeton: Princeton University Press, 1975).

24 Blanchot writes of Proust's experience of the 'essence of literature' in terms of such a reversal. It is: 'the metamorphosis of time into an imaginary space (the space peculiar to images) . . . that remoteness and distance which are the space and origin of metamorphosis; the place where psychology is redundant because here there is no psyche, when that which is inner becomes outer, becomes image. Yes, in such a time everything becomes image and the essence of the image is to be wholly exterior without privacy, yet more inaccessible and more mysterious than the most private thought' (*The Sirens' Song*, ed. Gabriel Josipovici (Brighton: Harvester, 1982), pp. 68–9).

25 Blanchot, *The Writing of the Disaster*, tr. Ann Smock (Lincoln and London:University of Nebraska Press, 1986), p. 121 (translation modified).

26 Blanchot, *L'Amitié* (Paris: Gallimard, 1971), p. 170.

27 J. E. Cosnett, 'Charles Dickens: Observer of Sleep and its Disorders', *Sleep* 15:2 (1992), 264–7.

28 In *Bleak House*, Esther Summerson, ill with smallpox, undergoes a sense of bad infinity, not of streets but of 'never-ending stairs . . . more and more – piled up into the sky', followed by a 'worse time' – 'strung together somewhere in great black space, there was a flaming necklace, or ring, or starry circle of some kind, of which *I* was one of the beads! . . . my only prayer was to be taken off from the rest . . . it was such inexplicable agony . . . to be part of the dreadful thing' (544). In moments of great trauma in Dickens's work, one sees a slippage into a mode of consciousness without personal subjectivity, an impersonal 'it is happening' as in the famous scene in which Fagin is on trial in *Oliver Twist* (466–7), Darnay's meditation on imminent death in *A Tale of Two Cities*, 'more like the wondering of some other spirt within his, than his own' (378), or Esther once more, recuperating from her illness, 'with so strange a calmness, watching what was done for me, as if it were done for some one else whom I was quietly sorry for' (545).

29 Levinas, *Existence and Existents*, tr. Alphonso Lingis (The Hague: Martinus Nijhoff, 1982).
30 R. Lettis, '"How I Write": Dickens in the Writer's Chair', *The Dickensian*, 89:1 (1993), 5–24.
31 Peter Ackroyd, *Dickens* (London: Minerva Press, 1991), p. 656.
32 See J. C. Robinson, *The Walk: Notes on a Romantic Image* (Norman and London: University of Oklahoma Press, 1989).
33 Peter Ackroyd, Introduction to *The Uncommercial Traveller* (London: Mandarin, 1991), p. xii.

3

Our Mutual Friend

NICHOLAS ROYLE

Do not read this

The narrator of *Our Mutual Friend* observes: 'No one who can read, ever looks at a book, even unopened on a shelf, like one who cannot' (61). This aphorism can be likened to another: 'Do not read this aphorism.'

Dickens's novel is awash, clogged, stumped with figures of reading, illiteracy, illegibility, the unread and unreadable. Charley Hexam is proud of his fireside sister Lizzie who can't read 'real books' but whose 'library of books is the hollow down by the flare' (73). Riah is said to have looked at Fascination Fledgeby and 'read his master's face, and learnt the book' (637). Mrs Lammle 'scarcely finds it necessary to look at Twemlow while he speaks, so easily does she read him' (685). In all these cases a figurative sense of 'reading' seems unambiguous. But Dickens's text disperses any such complacency or nostalgia. Threading through the comedy of Silas Wegg reading *The Decline and Fall off the Rooshan Empire*, the *Animal Register* and biographies of misers to Noddy Boffin, and stitching up the warious diwisions of characters into those to whom 'all print is shut' (93) and those to whom it is a way of life (teaching, law), *Our Mutual Friend* at once articulates and disarticulates, figures and disfigures the putative differences between 'reading' in a literal and 'reading' in a non-literal sense. *Our Mutual Friend* dumps before us the ghostliness of reading and the implacable, unending demands it makes. As Noddy Boffin affirms, there is 'no end' (546) to reading. It is this unstable, illimitable sense of 'reading' that charms the great chum of Mortimer Lightwood, solicitor Eugene Wrayburn:

'You charm me, Mortimer, with your reading of my weaknesses. (By-the-by, that very word, Reading, in its critical use, always charms me. An actress's Reading of a chambermaid, a dancer's Reading of a hornpipe, a singer's Reading of a song, a marine painter's Reading of the sea, the kettle-drum's Reading of an instrumental passage, are phrases ever youthful and delightful.)' (605)

Reading, we could say, after Iago, is nothing if not critical.

Our Mutual Friend invites us into the dark, into other scenes of reading, leading us along strange waterways, into the desiccation of headstones and crypts, the silence of the tome. To enter the world of *Our Mutual Friend* is to enter the world of the dead, living on. But once we realise we are inside, for instance in the sense of engaging with a reading of a book, even its spine, 'unopened on a shelf', we can no longer be certain what the 'outside' might have meant, or indeed whether it ever existed.

Meaning translation

Start with the title-page of volume I of the first two-volume edition (1865): 'OUR MUTUAL FRIEND. BY CHARLES DICKENS'. And at the bottom of the page, italicised in square brackets, beneath the date: '*The right of Translation is reserved*' (37). '*Our Mutual Friend*': these three words are unreadable. This illegibility is inscribed in the italicised declaration beneath it. Restrictions are imposed, rights are reserved. But where does 'Translation' begin? Doesn't the work of translation begin with, and even precede, every act of reading (in the putatively literal sense of that term)? For example, isn't there something being translated, being carried across (Latin *translatum*, from *transferre*: *trans*, 'across', *ferre*, 'to carry'), in the very process of 'look[ing] at a book, even unopened on a shelf'? Wherever there is sense-making there is translation. To read the phrase, to register the linking or articulation of the phrase 'our mutual friend', is to acknowledge the prior demand for translation, for making sense of the phrase, for carrying it across into one's own experience, oneself. But the right of translation is reserved: this title-phrase will never be translated, by right. It demands but resists translation. Not least on account of its enigmatic status as at once a title-phrase and the entirety of the text to which it refers, 'our mutual friend' says: you cannot translate me, you cannot *not* translate me. It is this cryptic mutual assurance *and* non-assurance of the title, its resistance to being translated or read, which links it to waste, and in particular to the sort that can last a long time: nuclear waste, writing or, as we will suggest a bit later on, the coprolith.

Cut adrift

If paraphrase is, as Bill Readings puts it, 'a philosophical joke',[1] how do we get beyond the title of this novel? Perhaps we don't. Seeking a definition of the phrase 'our mutual friend', we may go to a dictionary, such as *Chambers*. *Chambers* defines 'mutual friend' as 'common friend' and refers us back to Dickens. The *Chambers* joke avoids mentioning the abyss of 'our' and, by switching 'mutual' for 'common', effaces the connotations of exchange, giving and receiving, that are marked in the word's etymology (French *mutuel*, from Latin *mutuus*, from *mutare*, to change). 'Mutual' is protean in itself: it gestures at once towards what is double and other. 'Mutual', says *Chambers*, is an adjective meaning 'interchanged; reciprocal; given and received; common, joint, shared by two or more'. Of course the title-phrase seems to refer primarily to John Rokesmith. It turns up more than once 'in' the text. For instance:

> 'By-the-bye, ma'am,' said Mr Boffin, turning back as he was going, 'you have a lodger?'
> 'A gentleman,' Mrs Wilfer answered, qualifying the low expression, 'undoubtedly occupies our first floor.'
> 'I may call him Our Mutual Friend,' said Mr Boffin. 'What sort of a fellow *is* Our Mutual Friend, now? Do you like him?'
> 'Mr Rokesmith is very punctual, very quiet, a very eligible inmate.'
> (157)

Our mutant friend. The shifts from 'lodger' to 'gentleman' to 'inmate' signal the changeableness and uncertainty, while the 'very quiet' points up the play on 'mute' that is another kind of lodger, a phonemic parasite or foreign body within the title-phrase. What, though, is a title? What is going on when a title is quoted within the text to which it refers? Boffin's capitalisation of the phrase exacerbates the strangeness, as if he were a reader of Charles Dickens's novel as well as a character in it. In a so-called everyday context, 'our mutual friend' suggests shared or common feelings in relation to a third person. Dickens's novel ironises this, disfiguring or disarticulating any assurance of what might be 'mutual', not only through the shifting, mute alterations of identity that John Harmon, Julius Handford and John Rokesmith undergo, but also through a decomposition of 'our'.

How must, and why can't, we read the word 'our', as it appears in the title of the novel? What are we to make of the implied linkage generated by the first words of the opening chapter: 'In these times of ours, though concerning the exact year there is no need to be precise, a boat of dirty and disreputable appearance, with two figures in it, floated on the Thames' (43)? Who is the addressee of *Our Mutual Friend*? The opening words specify an imprecise present ('these times'), anonymously 'ours'. These opening words are at once topical and atopical, unchanging yet changed with every reading, every new addressee. If this 'our' of the title and this 'ours' in the opening sentence mean *us*, as in some sense they must, this novel is addressed to the dead. We may read the novel as though it were addressed to us, as though we must be the addressees, the living 'we' of the 'our' evoked in the title and engaged by the Dickensian narrator from the first words onwards. But we are also called upon to acknowledge a work of survival: every reader who first read this novel, as it appeared in its nineteen instalments from May 1864 to November 1865, is dead, and any addressee can in turn only ever identify herself or himself within the ghostliness of their own disappearance, engaging with a text that invokes a 'we', an 'our' for which our own presence, our own capacity to be a reader or legatee is entirely dispensable. Our deaths are written into the script. It is not that the 'first' readers of this novel were themselves exempt from effects of spectralisation, rather the reverse. The staggered, staggering appearance of Dickens's novel – suspending itself and its readers in nineteen parts – re-enacts or doubles the forms of suspended life, the suspended lives 'in' the novel itself. And if, as Richard Gaughan remarks, 'The novel must have, like Harmon, a suspended identity',[2] so must its readers. To be the reader of *Our Mutual Friend* is to submit oneself to an uncanny experiment in suspended animation – uncanny to the extent that it is impossible to know if or in what sense one is the *subject* of this experiment.

Our mutual blancmange

For Garrett Stewart, *Our Mutual Friend* is a forerunner of the work of James Joyce, in particular in so far as Dickens's novel is characterised by a pulverisation and dissemination of words and bits of words. Stewart's fine exploration of some of the linguistic densities and cavities in Dickens's text centres on the unpacking of the Joycean portmanteau word, 'Harmony'. He cites Wegg's jogged articulation of a query to the man who is taking him in a donkey-drawn truck to the late John Harmon's residence, Harmony Jail, for the first time: ' "And-why-did-they-callitharm-Ony?" ' (98). Stewart argues that this is the 'quintessential moment of disarticulation' in the novel, observing:

> 'Harm' and 'money', imbricated within a single phonemic span, encode the paired sins that at one and the same time cannot speak their names, cannot be simultaneously verbalized. They are there in the text not as a written but as a silently overheard interdependence, a reciprocal satiric indictment plumbed beneath or between inscriptions, in both senses *sounded* without being said.[3]

In focusing attention on the extraordinary disintegrations of language and on the cryptic effects of what is not said, Stewart is no doubt right to suggest that there is 'a more radical reading practice entailed by Dickensian fiction than criticism ordinarily supposes'.[4]

Who's a Freud of little Rogue Riderhood? *Our Mutual Friend* is, to adopt Wegg's term, 'terrimenjious' (725). It is radically different from other contemporaneous English novels – such as Wilkie Collins's *The Moonstone* (1868) or George Eliot's *Middlemarch* (1871–72) – and much closer to being a vast phantasmagoric sort of verbal 'Glue Monge' (to half-inch Young Blight's mispronunciation). Or alternatively, we might say, it is a text shaking all over, falling apart, like a dying drug addict. Eugene Wrayburn asks Blight where Mr Dolls is: ' "He's in a cab, sir, at the door. I thought it best not to show him, you see, if it could be helped; for he's a-shaking all over, like –" ' Blight's simile is perhaps inspired by the surrounding dishes of sweets – "like Glue Monge" ' (693). The whiteness of the 'blanc' is there, on every page of the novel, swarming with activity. It is a novel to be consumed (*mangé*) but only to get stuck, like glue. It is in a state of constant and, in principle, illimitable disintegration and disarticulation. The Joycean universe is set spinning here, with the possibilities for falling into one or other trap of language (*une glu*), for grafting or gluing bits of world (*monde*) and bits of word, for experiencing language as both the edible and the blank *and* neither. If all print is shut to Noddy Boffin, the print of Dickens's novel is as open as a grave. It may be, as Boffin puts it, 'too late' for him 'to begin shovelling and sifting at alphabeds and grammer-books' (94), but *Our Mutual Friend* institutes precisely such horticultural studies. To adopt another of the text's own verbal deformations, we could say that *Our Mutual Friend* produces a change of 'atomspear' (721) – at once the evacuation and dissemination of the world of Victorian fiction.

Invisible insects

But if *Our Mutual Friend* is, as Stewart puts it, 'more like Joyce than like Trollope',[5] it is also uncannily like Beckett. Wrayburn, by the burning rays of the fire at the Jolly Fellowship Porters, tells his chum Lightwood they can expect to have to stay there till around midnight:

> Thereupon he stirred the fire, and sat down on one side of it. It struck eleven, and he made believe to compose himself patiently. But gradually he took the fidgets in one leg, and then in the other leg, and then in one arm, and then in the other arm, and then in his chin, and then in his back, and then in his forehead, and then in his hair, and then in his nose; and then he stretched himself recumbent on two chairs, and groaned; and then he started up.
> 'Invisible insects of diabolical activity swarm in this place. I am tickled and twitched all over. Mentally, I have now committed a burglary under the meanest circumstances, and the myrmidons of justice are at my heels.'
> (212)

Alongside a Joycean explosion of the atomspear of writing, there is a Beckettian operatics of verbal and gestural repetition. Perhaps the first real example of absurdist fiction in English, *Our Mutual Friend* combines a sense that 'Everything is ridiculous' (213) with a darker logic of the foreign body: invisible insects, internal myrmidons, the incessant twitches of thought, the contamination and overrunning of any sense of fixed identity. After this novel of 1865, we could say (echoing your words, Gaffer, on page 121), there is a pest in the House of Fiction. Who speaks in a novel? Who's doing what 'in different voices' (246)? Is it a Dickensian or is it a Beckettian voice, for example, which says: 'But it was not I. There was no such thing as I, within my knowledge' (426)?

Hailstorm

What makes the title of Dickens's novel at once unreadable and unendingly readable has to do both with the ironies inhabiting the designation of the 'mutual friend' as Harmon/Handford/Rokesmith/the unnameable/the foreign body, and with the labyrinthine elaborations of the meaning of friendship in the text (whether, for instance, there can ever be a mutual friend, a friendship between three which would therefore disturb the reciprocity of two *or* a friendship between two which would not always already be riven by a foreign body). But it is also a matter of the ceaseless instability, the energies or allergies of disenfranchisement, dislocation, metamorphosis, affecting the 'our'. The 'our' is both exclusive (it does not mean you and me) and inclusive. No doubt in some sense it is not only the royal 'we', the royal 'our' of the omniscient narrator, but also the author. Indeed this would be one way of phrasing the cryptic character of this novel – to suppose that the 'our' of the title is specifically what is shared, divided, kept secret between the author and the narrator. A kind of phantasmagoric 'our' which encrypts the 'friend', buried alive, irretrievably. But then, what would the terms 'author' and 'narrator' mean here?

In an admirable essay which offers a fascinating account of Dickens's interest in ventriloquy and the emergence in the earlier nineteenth century of the phenomenon of the ventriloquist, 'biloquialist' or 'dramatic polyphonist', Patrick O'Donnell argues that 'Dickens "throws" or scripts the tumultuous voices of his many characters with an increasing sense that, the more successful or spectacular the act of ventriloquy, the more self-questioned is the singular identity who is the source of these voices'.[6] O'Donnell's argument (which might be described as being, in some ways, ultimately a Kristevan one about the suppression of the 'female' or 'maternal' in Dickens) perhaps requires a slight further inflection, however, away from the still-implicit unity and authority of 'Dickens' as author and towards a greater attentiveness to the specific nature and effects of the figure of the *narrator* as such. There is no author, no (even hypothetical) 'mutual friend' of that designation, without the *hood* or chaperon, the ghosting and disseminatory effects of the figure of the narrator.

The singularity of voice and identity in *Our Mutual Friend*, in other words, is perhaps more fundamentally dislocated than O'Donnell's account might suggest. For the narrator of *Our Mutual Friend* is not *one*. Rather the narrator is a sort of multiple personality: a polymorphous, ventriloquistic, foreign-bodied, male and female dream-being. Not only is the narrator omniscient – or at least telepathic – in the sense of being able to give a third-person presentation of the thoughts and feelings of various characters, but s/he also takes on the voice and speech of different characters, abandoning quotation marks and in the process abandoning every explicit sign of differentiation between identities. Thus the remarkable, doubly telepathic moment when the narrator takes over Lizzie, on the night of her father's death: 'Father, was that you calling me? Father! I thought I heard you call me twice before! Words never to be answered, those, upon the earth-side of the grave' (221). The narrator is at once Lizzie and not Lizzie (and furthermore, one might infer, at once alive and posthumous, both on and beyond 'the earth-side of the grave').

Elsewhere the undecidably gendered, polysexual or hermaphroditic narrator becomes 'our mutant friend' himself and moreover a John Harmon/ Rokesmith in the very moment of regressive mutation into *another* John, the little Johnny who dies: 'O boofer lady, fascinating boofer lady! If I were but legally executor of Johnny's will' (594). Or again, the narrator becomes Lady Tippins: 'And dear Mrs Lammle and dear Mr Lammle, how do you do . . . ? And Mortimer, whose name is for ever blotted out from my list of lovers, by reason first of fickleness and then of base desertion, how do *you* do, wretch?' (467).

The polyphonic, foreign-body identity of the narratorial royal 'we' in this novel, then, comports with the kind of hypnogogic dream-state assigned to Mortimer Lightwood at the Six Jolly Fellowships:

> As Mortimer Lightwood sat before the blazing fire, conscious of drinking brandy and water then and there in his sleep, and yet at one and the same time drinking burnt sherry at the Six Jolly Fellowships, and lying under the boat on the river shore, and sitting in the boat that Riderhood rowed, and listening to the lecture recently concluded, and having to dine in the Temple with an unknown man, who described himself as M.R.F. Eugene Gaffer Harmon, and said he lived at Hailstorm, – as he passed through these curious vicissitudes of fatigue and slumber, arranged upon the scale of a dozen hours to the second, he became aware of answering aloud a communication of pressing importance that had never been made to him, and then turned it into a cough on beholding Mr Inspector. (224)

Rather than see this passage as a remarkable adumbration of the psychoanalytic theory of the unconscious (in which, Freud asserts, contradictions cease to exist or at least exist side by side in uncontentious fashion, and a dozen hours can seem a second), it may be more productive to think all of this from the other side, in other words to see Freud's work as in many ways deeply Dickensian and yet at the same time to speculate on the idea that this Dickensianism is in turn insufficient.[7] In short, we might suggest that *Our Mutual Friend* presents a rendering of the unconscious and of dreamstates that is in some ways stranger but more precise than Freud's. No nodal point, no longer the dialectical model of a composite of two (of self and other), for example, but rather an overrunning multiplicity. (No) more Freud, (no) more Dickens. To be the reader of *Our Mutual Friend* is to live at Hailstorm – to consign oneself to the astonishing 'atomspear' of calls showering from a distance, multiple summons to stop or come, to live oneself *as* 'hail-storm'. To be conscious and asleep, sitting or lying or walking ('pass[ing] through') in an irreducibly multiple number of locations *at the same time*: as a hypnography or telepathy contaminating and exceeding the putative science of psychoanalysis, this figures the very narratorial form of the novel, the very structure of its telling. From Freud to Dickens and beyond: our mutant finest our.

Asocial chorus

Critics and readers of Dickens's work have always read his novels as illuminations of 'society', the social or *socius* (Latin for 'companion' or, if you will, 'friend'). But *Our Mutual Friend* suspends, dislocates and transforms the very notion of society, the very possibility of the social. We may wish to suppose that *Our Mutual Friend* offers a fictional rendering of midnineteenth-century English society. And let's be clear about this, it is 'English', not 'British': Dickens's 'British' is formidably, if insidiously, Anglocentric. As if Podsnappishly repressed until almost the last page of the text, this becomes explicit when Podsnap 'talks Britain' with Lightwood:

> Podsnap always talks Britain, and talks as if he were a sort of Private Watchman employed, in the British interests, against the rest of the world. 'We know what Russia means, sir,' says Podsnap; 'we know what France wants; we see what America is up to; but we know what England is. That's enough for us.' (887)

We are presented, then, with a rendering or translation of English society in the 1860s – a society the inequalities, injustices and barbarism of which the novel wants passionately to expose. This translation keeps its rights in reserve. The text's singularity, its unparaphrasability and untranslatability, demand to be respected. Of course, like any engaging work of fiction, *Our Mutual Friend* could be said to provoke an experience of disavowal in its reader. As Roland Barthes puts it, in *The Pleasure of the Text* (1973): the reader *disavows*, in other words he or she keeps thinking, '*I know these are only words, but all the same*'.[8] But in all its strange Joycean paronomasia, its verbal disfigurations and dispersions, and in all its Beckettian ur-absurdity, *Our Mutual Friend* constantly interrupts any logic of readerly disavowal. In this way it ceaselessly affirms itself as 'merely' writing, presenting us with identities such as 'Harmon', 'Wegg', 'Boffin', 'Riderhood' or 'Headstone', only to let them decompose before our eyes. We are thus offered, for example, the paronomastications of harm and money, harm and man, a wooden leg and German Weg, Spoffin, Doffin, Moffin, Poffin (see 365, 367), 'little Rogue Riderhood' (471), or the fitful madness of a fictional character trying to get in touch with the inhuman essence of his identity, the very form of his name: 'The wild energy of [Headstone], now quite let loose, was absolutely terrible. He stopped and laid his hand upon a piece of the burial-ground enclosure, as if he would have dislodged the stone' (454).

The pulse, the heart, the head and name, *scattered like sand.*

Our Mutual Friend stages the dispersal of fictional realism. Quite apart from the errant characterological absurdity of Harmon/Handford/Rokesmith, for example, the novel explores and perhaps breaches that extreme of characterisation which leaves the reader expected – but unable – to credit or accept the revelation of Mr Boffin's 'real' character and intentions. In this respect Mr Boffin never lives up to living, but rather is bequeathed to the reader, as a peculiar instance of character as stopped in amber or, rather, placed in a wooden 'boffin'. In this way the novel's treatment of Boffin can be set alongside the 'face in a tablespoon' (53) world of the Veneerings. The Veneerings are presented to us in a discourse that is neither realism nor caricature but something dislocating the two, that is to say what we might call veneerealist discourse or social veneerealism. J. Hillis Miller's fine evocation of Veneering, 'gradually manifest[ing] himself like an ectoplasmic vision at a seance', suggestively evokes what is ghostly or veneereal in the novel in this respect.[9]

The novel ironises the very possibility of presenting a society. This culminates in the final chapter of the novel, 'The Voice of Society' (886–92), with its abyssally ironic refutation of the sense and coherence of its own title. Whether in the sense of 'upper class' or more broadly, 'society', in *Our Mutual Friend*, is a society of ghosts and doubles, imitation and ventriloquy without decidable source or end. Every social chorus is infected by the asocial, by Glue Monge, by what interrupts the very possibility of identity, individual or communal. Thus Lavinia Wilfer's voice can be at once 'sepulchral' and 'founded on her mother's' (677) and Mortimer Lightwood is 'but the double of the friend [Wrayburn] on whom he has founded himself' (470). Everything and everyone is undecidably *modelled* – parasitical and contaminated – subject at once to 'a catechizing infection' (348) and to 'an infection of absurdity' (817).

The asocial chorus of *Our Mutual Friend* is perhaps most darkly evoked by the acoustic image of many children endlessly 'repeating the word Sepulchre' (264) or by Jenny Wren's singing 'Come back and be dead, Come back and be dead!' (334). But for all its emphasis on self-destruction, the novel is not merely delineating a kind of social-world-as-death-drive. It does not simply figure 'the whole framework of society' in the way that Wegg does, namely as a 'human skelinton' (540). For if *Our Mutual Friend* gives comical as well as terrifying prominence to the active, generative power of death (a dead man's will), the productivity and financial value of dust, human corpses, dead birds and animals; if (to invert Catherine Gallagher's phrase) the novel presents us with a thanato-economics,[10] this has to be situated in terms that would no longer be reducible to an opposition of life and death.

In the dark

A spectropoetics. *Our Mutual Friend* disarticulates and disfigures any notion of living that would be ultimately separable from the ghostly and double. This novel is about living on, not as the triumph of continuing to live but as a movement of return or haunting which comes back, folds back from the beginning on what one might have wanted to call 'life' itself. There is no life in *Our Mutual Friend*, there is only the spectral elusiveness of living on. Life – to invoke once more a phrase cited (as if always already in quotation marks) in Maurice Blanchot's *Death Sentence* (1948) – is 'scattered like sand'.[11]

No doubt the notion of living on, playing dead, neither living nor dead, is most obvious in the case of Harmon/Handford/Rokesmith/the unnameable 'himself': 'like a Ghost' (257), this character's life is largely an experience of being dead. The opening pages of the bizarre chapter, 'A Solo and a Duett' (421–30), offer us the telepathised thoughts of a figure who can reflect on his death as one who has survived *and* on his life as one who is dead. Harmon/Handford/Rokesmith/the unnameable foreign body is no doubt 'the living-dead man' (430) par excellence. But this spectrality of experience is everywhere in *Our Mutual Friend*. It is figured in the death-in-life of both Jenny Wren and Betty Higden. The former's 'Come back and be dead' (334), like the latter's 'Have I been long dead?' (575), highlights a more general exploration of a sense of death-in-life that would no longer be an individual aberration (the effect for example of trauma or refused mourning), or a supplementation to simply 'living'. This is most *vividly* true of Rogue Riderhood and Eugene Wrayburn. In the case of Riderhood, thought to have drowned in the Thames but revived, 'the doctor declares him to have come back from that inexplicable journey where he stopped on the dark road, and to be here' (506). Wrayburn, on the other hand, thought to have been murdered by Bradley Headstone but kept alive, kept in suspense on the verge of death, announces in apparent delirium: '"I am wandering in those places – where are those endless places, Mortimer? They must be at an immense distance!"' (807). Living beyond living, inexplicably stopped on the dark road, errant in a kind of distanceless distance, Riderhood and Wrayburn could be said to figure both the nature of writing itself (its capacity for survival, its still-life effects, its strange telegraphics) and the condition of reading. For to read *Our Mutual Friend* is to have been drawn into the current of living on, swallowed up on the dark road of reading, as if repeatedly finding and losing oneself at an immense distance. Blurring and crossing the margins of having a character die or live, die *and* live, keeping 'character' itself in a suspension of being dead and living on, *Our Mutual Friend* cuts adrift, cuts us adrift, in the dark.

Everything but figure

The spectropoetic embraces corpses and dolls. It takes up and takes in taxidermy. In Jenny Wren's parlour, we read: 'there, in the midst of the dolls with no speculation in their eyes, lay Mr Dolls with no speculation in his' (801). As the play on 'dolls' as common noun and proper name suggests, the name is linked to death. Like a 'headstone', the name is structured to outlive its bearer: the name lives on. But the name (most dramatically, in *Our Mutual Friend*, the name of 'Harmon' or 'Rokesmith') never simply lives, it is always a kind of ghost. That is why the comparison between Jenny Wren's dolls and the corpse of Mr Dolls is a kind of spectro-hyperbole. For the dolls in *Our Mutual Friend* are not merely dead, lifeless, inanimate: they stare indifferently at the animate and inanimate, the living and the dead, the real and the fictional. Jenny Wren says of the fine aristocratic ladies on whom her dolls are modelled:

> When they go bobbing into the hall from the carriage, and catch a glimpse of my little physiognomy poked out from behind a policeman's cape in the rain, I dare say they think I am wondering and admiring with all my eyes and heart, but they little think they're only working for my dolls! There was Lady Belinda Whitrose. I made her do double duty one night. (496)

Lady Belinda does 'double duty', unconsciously offering herself as a model for two different dolls in one evening. But this 'double duty' is itself doubled: the dolls are subordinate to or dependent on the ladies but the ladies are also subordinate to the dolls, working only for them. Jenny Wren's reversal of the original over the copy here is woven into a more pervasive characterisation of dolls as uncanny, not because they are corpse-like but because they are neither living nor dead. In this respect it is perhaps not coincidental that, as Stephen Gill notes (909), the description of the dolls and Mr Dolls having 'no speculation' in their eyes recalls Macbeth's addressing a ghost (Banquo): 'thy blood is cold, / Thou hast no speculation in those eyes' (III.iv). As elsewhere in the novel, we could suggest, 'speculation' is haunted by the spectral.[12]

What does Mr Venus's shop figure? Henry James's celebrated pooh-poohing of the novel as 'nothing but figure' might be overturned here.[13] For perhaps the singularity of Mr Venus's shop consists in the fact that it does not figure anything: with all its crammed figures and forms of sus-pended animation and taxidermic productions, it makes the very space of figuration tremble and crack. It figures, as it were, the dissolution of reading, at once a figure and disfiguring of reading. Mr Wegg ends his first visit:

> Mr Wegg, looking back over his shoulder as he pulls the door open by the strap, notices that the movement so shakes the crazy shop, and so shakes a momentary flare out of the candle, as that the babies – Hindu, African, and British – the 'human warious', the French gentleman, the green glass-eyed cats, the dogs, the ducks, and all the rest of the collection, show for an instant as if paralytically animated. (130)

If to paralyse is 'to deprive of the power of action' (*Chambers*), the phrase 'paralytically animated' is an oxymoron. As such, it comports with the play the novel makes on the notion of articulation. Venus is an articula-tor of human bodies in a double sense. As he tells Mr Wegg:

> 'Mr Wegg, if you was brought here loose in a bag to be articulated, I'd name your smallest bones blindfold equally with your largest, as fast as I could pick 'em out, and I'd sort 'em all, and sort your wertebrae, in a manner that would equally surprise and charm you.' (128)

Impossible surprise, the surprise of the impossible: to be articulated and to have your articulator articulate the articulation in your presence, for your benefit. The charm of this impossibility is also the charm of *Our Mutual Friend* – a text at once offering and withholding figuration and articulation, a text of 'shivers and smithers' (847), paralytically ani-mated.

Of an anal character

To conclude on a slightly different note, we could suggest that *Our Mutual Friend* is a heap of shit, a great heap of dirt, or several or many heaps: a phantasmagoric landscape and riverscape of dirty magical mounds and rivers.[14] As Eve K. Sedgwick remarks, '*Our Mutual Friend* is *the* English novel that everyone knows is about anality'. She then qualifies this: '*Our*

Mutual Friend is the only English novel that everyone *says* is about excrement in order that they may *forget* that it is about anality.'[15] Sedgwick offers a brilliantly provocative account of the novel in terms of homosocial desire (the relations between Lightwood and Wrayburn – those 'muppets', as she nicely calls them – and the relations between Headstone and Charley, Headstone and Riderhood, Wrayburn and Headstone, etc.), focusing in particular on images of male rape in the novel. In this way she reiterates her broader argument that the nineteenth-century English novel is about what is going on *between men*, and not really about women at all. Thus with the triangle of Wrayburn, Lizzie Hexam and Headstone, Sedgwick observes: 'far from loving her as *he* imagines he does, the violent rival is really intent on using her as a counter in the intimate struggle of male will that is irrelevant and inimical to her'.[16] If Sedgwick provides a good sense of the anality of Dickens's novel in terms of the erotism and murderous rivalry between men, she gives less attention to the relation between anality and money and leaves 'wholly abstracted' (to borrow her own, perhaps inadvertent, witticism)[17] the relations between anality and writing as such.[18]

To write is doubtless to engage with the desire to give, and this desire is doubtless linked up with shit. As Freud observed, faeces are the baby's first gift to the world.[19] The anal character of *Our Mutual Friend* is complex and multiple: it has to do both with thematisations such as male rape, the meaning of waste, the value of dirt, 'moral sewage' (63), the links between anality and sadism, and with the 'orderliness, parsimoniousness and obstinacy' which Freud distinguishes as the most distinctive traits of the anal character and which of course clearly apply to a number of the characters in Dickens's novel.[20] But it is also a question of the enigma of writing as such.

Ours is a copreous as well as copious language. As such, it is inseparable from the question of remains, remnants, traces. A youngish sallowish gentleman with spectacles and a lumpy forehead searches his lumps in vain before Podsnap (or, we might say, Bowelbreak) turns the conversation to more faecal matters:

> the gentleman with the lumpy forehead having for the time delivered himself of all that he found behind his lumps, spake for the time no more.
>
> 'I Was Inquiring,' said Mr Podsnap, resuming the thread of his discourse, 'Whether You Have Observed in our Streets as We should say, Upon our Pavvy as You would say, any Tokens – '
>
> The foreign gentleman, with patient courtesy entreated pardon; 'But what was tokenz?'

'Marks,' said Mr Podsnap; 'Signs, you know, Appearances – Traces.'
'Ah! Of a Orse?' inquired the foreign gentleman.

'We call it Horse,' said Mr Podsnap, with forbearance. 'In England, Angleterre, England, We Aspirate the "H," and We Say "Horse." Only our Lower Classes Say "Orse!"'

'Pardon,' said the foreign gentleman; 'I am alwiz wrong!'

'Our Language,' said Mr Podsnap, with a gracious consciousness of being always right, 'is Difficult. Ours is a Copious Language, and Trying to Strangers. I will not Pursue my Question.' (178–9)

The copious and copreous nature of *Our Mutual Friend* consists in the fact not only that this text is 'about anality' in the thematic sense that Sedgwick suggests, but more radically that it is *about* the relations between anality and language, anality and writing. The novel is at once a kind of textual coprolith and a discourse *on* the coprolith.

Coprolithology: writing as quasi-fossilised, encrypted, monumentalised (like a headstone), *and* as bountiful, overflowing, potentially illimitable. Like Dickens's head, chopped off, profiled on today's English ten-pound note.

Notes

I would like to thank Timothy Clark and Grahame Smith for their stimulating and helpful comments on an earlier version of this chapter.

1 Bill Readings, *Introducing Lyotard: Art and Politics* (London: Routledge, 1991), p. xxi.
2 Richard T. Gaughan, 'Prospecting for Meaning in *Our Mutual Friend*', *Dickens Studies Annual: Essays on Victorian Fiction*, 19 (1990), 241.
3 Garrett Stewart, *Reading Voices: Literature and the Phonotext* (Berkeley: University of California Press, 1990), p. 228.
4 *Ibid.*, p. 229.
5 *Ibid.*, p. 228.
6 Patrick O'Donnell, '"A Speeches of Chaff"': Ventriloquy and Expression in *Our Mutual Friend*', *Dickens Studies Annual: Essays on Victorian Fiction*, 19 (1990), 247–79: see p. 248.
7 Cf. Ned Lukacher's interesting speculations on what he calls Freud's 'Dickensian style' in his *Primal Scenes: Literature, Philosophy, Psychoanalysis* (Ithaca: Cornell University Press, 1986). Lukacher concludes his book with a claim similar to that being advanced in the present chapter: 'In the culture of psychoanalysis, Dickens has always been the figure of both its prehistory and its future' (p. 336).
8 Roland Barthes, *The Pleasure of the Text*, tr. Richard Miller (Oxford and Cambridge, Mass.: Basil Blackwell, 1990), p. 47.
9 J. Hillis Miller, *The Form of Victorian Fiction* (Notre Dame: University of Notre Dame Press, 1968), p. 41.

10 See Catherine Gallagher, 'The Bio-Economics of *Our Mutual Friend*', in *Fragments for a History of the Human Body*, Part Three, ed. Michel Feher with Ramona Naddaff and Nadia Tazi (New York: Zone Books, 1989), pp. 345–65.

11 Maurice Blanchot, *Death Sentence*, tr. Lydia Davis (Barrytown, New York: Station Hill, 1978): see p. 30.

12 See Mary Poovey's essay, 'Reading History in Literature: Speculation and Virtue in *Our Mutual Friend*', in *Historical Criticism and the Challenge of Theory*, ed. Janet Levarie Smarr (Urbana: University of Illinois Press, 1993), pp. 42–80. Poovey does not deal specifically with the ghostly but her exploration of 'the economic and representational systems that *Our Mutual Friend* simultaneously participates in and resists' (69), for example, could certainly be linked to the sort of logic proposed here as spectropoetic.

13 Henry James, 'Our Mutual Friend', in *Selected Literary Criticism*, ed. Morris Shapira (Cambridge: Cambridge University Press, 1963), p. 9. Of course James's review is in many respects wonderfully acute and certainly his proposition that the novel is 'nothing but figure' can be productively aligned with his acknowledgment of how 'intensely *written*' (6) it is.

14 By this we do not of course mean to elaborate on some (mistaken) notion that the dust heaps of the novel 'literally' included excrement, human or otherwise. For a succinct discussion of the 'literal' contents of the dust heaps around London in the mid nineteenth century, see Michael Cotsell, *The Companion to 'Our Mutual Friend'* (London: Allen & Unwin, 1986), pp. 30–4.

15 Eve Kosofsky Sedgwick, *Between Men: English Literature and Male Homosocial Desire* (New York: Columbia University Press, 1985), pp. 163–4.

16 *Ibid.*, p. 181.

17 This paronomasia is evoked in the title of an essay by Monika Rydygier Smith, though not further developed in the course of the essay itself: see her 'The W/Hole Remains: Consumerist Politics in *Bleak House, Great Expectations*, and *Our Mutual Friend*', *Victorian Review*, 19:1 (summer 1993), 1–21.

18 It is indeed a striking feature of Sedgwick's account that it almost completely elides discussion of questions of language. The chapter she devotes to Dickens's novel, 'Homophobia, Misogyny and Capital: The Example of *Our Mutual Friend*' (161–79) seems to us limited in other respects as well: the issue of sadism goes largely unelaborated (perhaps because it would threaten the gender-specific focus on the rivals Wrayburn and Headstone), and there is little or no discussion of various women characters (presumably, again, because this would call into question the implicit gender-separatism of Sedgwick's argument: the question remains, for instance, what is going on in the relationship between Bella and Lizzie? Is it 'the same' as what obtains in the muppet-show between the likes of Wrayburn and Lightwood?).

19 See, for example, Sigmund Freud, 'On Transformations of Instinct as Exemplified in Anal Erotism', tr. James Strachey, in *On Sexuality*, Pelican Freud Library, vol. 7 (Harmondsworth: Penguin, 1977), p. 299.

20 See Sigmund Freud, 'Character and Anal Erotism', tr. James Strachey, in *On Sexuality*, Pelican Freud Library, vol. 7 (Harmondsworth: Penguin, 1977), pp. 209–15.

4

Pure Oliver: or, Representation without agency

RICHARD DELLAMORA

In the final completed volumes of *The History of Sexuality*, Michel Foucault attempts 'to show how, in classical antiquity, sexual activity and sexual pleasures were problematized through practices of the self, bringing into play the criteria of an "aesthetics of existence"'. The pleasures that Foucault has in mind usually occur between a male citizen and an adolescent on the threshold of the privileges and responsibilities of citizenship. Foucault observes that in neo-Platonic ethics and early Christian asceticism both these contexts are lost. Instead, purity becomes of central importance; and this paradigm is gendered not as male but as female:

> At a certain moment, the problem of an aesthetics of existence is covered over by the problem of purity, which is something else and which requires another kind of technique. In Christian asceticism the question of purity becomes more and more important; the reason why you have to take control of yourself is to keep yourself pure. The problem of virginity, this model of feminine integrity, becomes much more important in Christianity. The theme of virginity has nearly nothing to do with sexual ethics in Greco-Roman asceticism. There the problem is a problem of self-domination. It was a virile model of self-domination and a woman who was temperate was as virile to herself as a man. The paradigm of sexual self-restraint becomes a feminine paradigm through the theme of purity and virginity, based on the model of physical integrity. Physical integrity rather than self-regulation became important. So the problem of ethics as an aesthetics of existence is covered over by the problem of purification.[2]

From the eighteenth century onwards, the 'feminine paradigm' became an important aspect of novels by men. Consider, for instance, the passage near the end of *David Copperfield* in which David appeals to his second wife: 'My lamp burns low, and I have written far into the night; but the dear presence, without which I were nothing, bears me company. Oh Agnes, oh my soul, so may thy face be by me when I close my life indeed; so may I, when realities are melting from me like the shadows which I now dismiss, still find thee near me, pointing upward!'[3] David's Agnes is the angelic mediator who connects the life of the mid-Victorian writer with another, higher order of existence. She smooths over disruptions in family history and the religious doubts liable to attend a Victorian man of intellect. As his 'soul', Agnes is David's imaginary counterpart, a disembodied essence protected from the weaknesses and humiliations to which the body is subject. Fulfilling this multifaceted role requires purity but virginity only before marriage. Agnes becomes an angel by virtue of being inscribed within marriage, an institution by which, in British law, she became a legal minor.[4] Her elevation depends upon contractual subordination to her husband.

In *David Copperfield*, the importance of female physical integrity is signalled in the novel's preoccupation with the seduction of Little Em'ly and in David's disgust at the thought that Uriah Heep might succeed in forcing Agnes to marry him. It is worth keeping in mind, however, that while 'the problem of purity' is, as Foucault says, 'something else', the terms of male mentorship and induction into citizenship that frame 'the problem of an aesthetics of existence' do not cease to exist. Rather, they are 'covered over'. As a result, readers of Dickens lack a context in which to consider a number of questions. What is the connection between masculine desire and citizenship? How is male–male desire configured within the processes whereby younger males achieve parity with male adults? And how should relations of desire between men and boys in Dickens's novels be characterized?

In this chapter, I address these questions in the context of the man who writes far into the night. In 1837 Dickens the novelist was in process of being born or, in a more apt figure, of being constituted through serial publication, publishers' contracts, and reviews that appeared in contemporary newspapers and journals with each succeeding number. When Dickens began publishing *Oliver Twist* in 1837, it was not clear that it would become a novel.[5] Only after the text was specifically contracted as a novel did Dickens address generic questions whose answers would determine how male relations were to be represented. Decisions about how to represent male relationships occur within the context of a dramatic shift from the production of books as petty commodities.[6] In the earlier phase, writers retained ownership of their texts even when booksellers published them; in the latter, literary creativity was converted into a form of surplus value for publishers through the alienation of ownership through copyright. In this way, a writer like Dickens came to be in the same sort of legal relationship to his publisher as any other worker contracted to an employer.[7] The new mode of production had other effects as well. Through serial publication, large new markets could be created. Moreover, these markets had a particular class character, not popular or plebeian but bourgeois.[8] These factors constitute, in turn, the possibilities of representation so that generic choices need to be construed within the context of the mode of production. When humanist critics of Dickens assert that 'political comment was no essential part of his purpose', they ignore the politics of economic production. They also ignore the politics of masculine representation, which are not dissociable from the issues of citizenship that shaped English politics during the decade.[9] The Chartist struggle for universal manhood suffrage was based on concerns about the ownership of the product of one's labour that Dickens knew immediately in his complicated dealings with publishers. But the form in which these concerns could be addressed to a new public that included Chartists and their supporters was encoded within a new mode of production that shapes the radicalism that motivates *Oliver Twist.*

Foucault argues that Christianity demands an 'austerity . . . linked to the necessity of renouncing the self and deciphering its truth'.[10] In the second half of *Oliver Twist*, Dickens endorses 'austerity' by removing Oliver from the creatural satisfactions afforded by Fagin's den and by insisting that he demonstrate his 'true' self. This truth is not religious but socio-economic. For Oliver, 'the problem of purification' focuses on his mysterious origin, out of wedlock. From where, or more properly from what class, does he come? It focuses likewise on his relation to the bodies of lower-class men and boys. The integrity of a *boy's* body can be affirmed only by removing him from the possibility of violation by these others. In the world of crime and poverty that Dickens portrays, the contamination of young male bodies is usually described in terms of eating and drinking. Within the novel, the sociable indulgence that once characterised lower-class life as festive and oppositional in character is relegated to the underworld of the *lumpenproletariat*. To cross over into this world or to be seized into it, as Oliver is, exposes the body to violent abuse and, ultimately, to annihilation.

While the character of *Dickens's* investment in Oliver's physical integrity requires attention, I have already indicated that this investment is constituted in relation both to the mode of production of the text and to contemporary political debates. Investments in Oliver are both psychological and sociological. As Jacqueline Rose has pointed out, these are usually removed from the field of inquiry by confining the analysis of desire in children's literature to a study of the author's intentions, avowed or implicit. This focus covers over the character of 'the adult's desire for the child' represented or to whom a text is addressed. Rose emphasises that this desire can be eroticised without necessarily being sexualised. 'I am using desire to refer to a form of investment by the adult in the child, and to the demand made by the adult on the child as the effect of that investment, a demand which fixes the child and then holds it in place.'[11]

The phantasmatic body that needs to be defended, violated and restored is metamorphic. Not only a child's body, it is the social body whose integrity is threatened. The word 'body' is especially pertinent because in the early nineteenth century the island of Great Britain was a body of land under threat of foreign invasion, literal and ideological. The constitution of British subjects as a unified people, i.e., a national body, was one consequence of efforts to ward off this danger. This incorporation joined together ethnic and economic groups in new ways that emphasised both unity and a new and powerful sense of difference among particular groups. For a generation after 1815, the regulation of this new body became a focus of aggravated anxieties but likewise of democratic and egalitarian dissidence. In the mid-1830s, as a disciplinary structure in its own right, the mass circulation of fiction in the form of serial publication over an extended period of months helped bring into existence a cross-class readership.[12] But just as patriotism simultaneously prompted an awareness of specific variations, the creation of a reading public made possible not only the dominant mode of reading and writing but also a variety of oppositional modes.

Dickens parodies male mentorship at the opening of *Oliver Twist* in the relation between the boys of the parish workhouse and the beadle, Mr Bumble.[13] In the first illustration, 'Oliver asking for More' (plate 1), George Cruikshank represents the relationship through the shocked gaze of Mr Bumble as he stares at Oliver. Dickens connotes gender inversion in the name of 'Mrs Mann', who manages the workhouse. Cruikshank supplements this suggestion with the connotation of perversity. He draws an oversized spoon directed at a forty-five degree angle from Oliver's crotch to the open mouth and popping eyes of Bumble. Standing behind him, Mrs Mann is a stick figure, open mouth and eyes. She 'sees' the scandalous abuse of workhouse children by those who are supposed to be their legal protectors. Michael Steig refers to the

1 George Cruikshank
'Oliver asking for More', Chapter 2

Richard Dellamora

illustrations to Dickens's novels as 'an iconographic counter-text', but Cruikshank's text is counter only to the humanistic responses, appearing in contemporary reviews, that emphasise the humour, pathos or satire of the verbal text at the expense of covering over its expression of class anger.[14]

Resort to the iconography of radical protest is characteristic in the novel. For instance, the sale of Oliver to Mr Sowerberry, the parochial undertaker, recalls the abuses condemned by Richard Oastler, 'the fiery Yorkshire industrial reformer'. His attack on working conditions for children employed in the Bradford textile mills 'inaugurated the Ten Hours Movement and ignited a general controversy over factory labor in the 1830s and 1840s'.[15] In 1832, Oastler condemned 'Slavery at Home'. Similarly, Chartist writers, disillusioned with the Reform Bill of 1832, declaimed ironically against their status as supposedly 'FREE LABOUR-ERS' under a 'FREE GOVERNMENT'.[16]

The opening chapters of the novel are full of ominous warnings about the sexual abuse of children. Oliver, for example, is consigned to Sowerberry 'to do what he likes with' (71). These threats render less occluded the relations of desire between adults and children that Rose finds to be characteristic of children's writing. The usual negation of desire in these relationships determines what Rose calls 'the impossibility of children's fiction', a phrase by which she means that it is impossible to address children in literature precisely because the constitution of 'the child' either as a literary protagonist or as a reader is withdrawn from the field of inquiry. This withdrawal makes it possible to represent the child as pure while ignoring the impurities, sexual and otherwise, that attend it. Purity becomes an aspect of textuality in yet another way in the sense that, in writing for children, 'the child and the adult' become 'one at the point of pure identity'.[17] Identification depends on withholding from consideration the character of the author (and other adults') investment in the representation.

Dickens's novel provides a more complicated example since there is little doubt about many impurities in which Oliver is implicated. The contrast between the degeneracy of his keepers and his purity puts that purity in question, even more so because of the extraordinary lengths to which Dickens and Oliver's middle-class benefactors must go to prove him 'pure'. The truth of purity, which the plot equivocally discloses, is impossible. Dickens stands on both sides of this dilemma, proving Oliver's moral purity while confirming the illegitimacy of his birth. The same legal document, his father's will, makes both points.

Rose's argument helps explain a number of silences in *Oliver Twist*, including silence about male working-class agency. Because the threat of working-class insurgency in the 1830s was real, the character of such agency mattered. Dickens ushers Oliver on stage as a young representative of his class. This start implies a progress toward emancipation or, to use a Foucauldian term, 'definitive status'.[18] In the context of popular agitation, this status means achieving civil status, which was denied at the time to children, women and most men. Young Oliver's demand for 'more' partakes in this effort since Chartists wanted the vote in order to correct economic abuses.

But, of course, Oliver does not grow up to become a *big* working-class hero. This outcome is excluded from the generic possibilities available to the novel in the 1830s. The English novel at this time includes paradigms for protagonists from the *lumpen* but not for successful working-class spokesmen. A protagonist from the lower orders can be represented only if he is denied agency as a representative of popular reform or revolt. Dickens gains civil status for Oliver by plotting his rise out and away from the class among whom he is born. Doing so, however, promises to confirm the bourgeois (and generic) biases that diminish the humanity of the lower classes in the first place and justify their exclusion from the vote. The complicated plotting that Dickens resorts to in the second half of the novel has long been criticised for aligning moral integrity with class origin.[19] The ideological constraints of a serial publication for a rapidly increasing readership limit his vision. But the constraints of political economy and aspects of ethnic, racial and class bias likewise inhabit radical outlooks themselves. As Peter Stallybrass has shown, proponents of the working class such as Marx and Engels are none the less ambivalent. They tend to bifurcate the lower classes between the proletariat, with whom they identify and who are destined to become the subjects of history, and the contaminated riff-raff known as the *lumpenproletariat*. Dickens represents Oliver as a junior version of a working-class hero at the same time that his imaginary counterparts, Jack Dawkins, Bill Sikes and Fagin, parody what John Forster, Dickens's biographer, refers to as 'lower life'.[20]

By insistently representing Fagin *as a Jew*, moreover, Cruikshank and Dickens participate in the tendency of writers like Marx and Engels to 'use *lumpenproletariat* as a racial category'.[21] Anxieties about purity in the novel have a major focus in Fagin's attempts to corrupt Oliver. This anxiety is at once extravagantly anti-Semitic and anti-bourgeois since to be deracinated is to be despeciated and thereby to confirm the conservative political view that the lower classes threatened the very survival of the human species. Dickens resists this view by taking as his protagonist a boy from the very bottom of the social order. Doing so, he challenges ethical/demographic distinctions drawn, on the one hand, between gentlemen and labourers and, on the other, between the decent working poor and the criminal *lumpen*. He makes it clear that the representation of the poor as a non-human other is an ideological construct of their class enemies. Further, in a blow at the pretences of liberal reform following passage of the reform Bill of 1832, he sets the novel within the reformed workhouses of the mid-1830s, an instrument of demographic regulation that reform had made possible. The New Poor Law was a Whig measure, but it was motivated by a reactionary animus against the people that was lodged in Robert Malthus's widely held axioms about the dangers posed by excess population.

(An alternative genre open to Dickens is that of the Newgate or criminal novel. Oliver's cognomen, 'Twist', plays on this possibility by combining the associations of early, violent death with those of excessive consumption and what Malthus refers to as 'unnatural passions'.[22] 'To twist is to hang, and represents an all-too-likely end for a parish boy.' To twist also means 'to eat heartily; . . . a twister is a very hearty eater'. The word also connotes 'perversion'.[23] In representing Sikes, Dickens adopts the kind of narrative contained in books like the 'history of the lives and trial of great criminals' (196) that Fagin gives Oliver to read. In this way, Dickens conforms to novelistic expectations. But by parodying them he invites readers to laugh at the rules of genre together with the moral and social assumptions that they encode. Conversely, Dickens refuses to plot for Oliver the route upward into the middle class that could be signalled by the novel's subtitle, 'The Parish Boy's Progress'. Oliver is no Dick Whittington. The claim to Oliver's humanity rests elsewhere than in upward mobility)

A speaking face

Who is the purest boy in Victorian literature? One is likely to answer 'Oliver', the little boy in *Oliver Twist*, who has the chutzpah to ask for 'more'. Doing so, he unwittingly confirms a principle of political economy, namely the tendency of the poor to consume an excessive amount of resources. If someone does not say 'no' to Oliver and the other poor boys who crowd Cruikshank's illustration, population will grow unchecked with the results of 'epidemics, wars, plague, and famine' that Malthus predicts in his study, *An Essay on the Principle of Population*.[24] It needs to be remembered that this principle is scientific. 'The causes of population and depopulation', as he says, 'have probably been as constant as any of the laws of nature with which we are acquainted'.[25] Oliver's plea is consistent with natural law, but it also exceeds the natural order since it implies a threat to the survival of others.

⌐The opening chapter of *Oliver Twist* both acknowledges and challenges political economy. First of all, it recognises Malthus's principle of 'Necessity, that imperious all-pervading law of nature, [which] restrains . . . [population] within the prescribed grounds'.[26] Second, Dickens represents an institution shaped in deliberate accordance with this principle: a workhouse reformed under the terms of the 1834 act. Malthus, who died in 1834, had long argued against the provisions of the old Poor Law on the grounds that the right of the poor to parish relief tended to promote 'vice and misery' by encouraging population growth. In line with this view, the law of 1834 segregated workhouse residents by sex and mandated a low diet to discourage paupers. Dickens satirises this operation of knowledge/power.⌐

In Cruikshank's illustration, the gaze that Bumble directs at Oliver's spoon belongs to him as representative of the bureaucratic oversight of poor relief. His gaze is the gaze of Enlightenment institutions as Foucault describes them in texts such as *The Birth of the Clinic*.

> Clinical experience – that opening up of the concrete individual, for the first time in Western history, to the language of rationality, that major event in the relationship of man to himself, and of language to things – was soon taken as a simple unconceptualized confrontation of a gaze and a face, or a glance and a silent body; a sort of contract prior to all discourse, free of the burdens of language, by which two living individuals are 'trapped' in a common, but non-reciprocal situation.[27]

This 'confrontation', however unconceptualised, is beset with a political unconscious that fantasises the lower-class penis as a huge spoon – a phallus that consumes as well as spends. It is excessively productive in contrast to the genuine productivity of manual labour.

In the language of Malthus, 'man' is 'impelled to the increase of his species' by a 'powerful instinct'. Unchecked by 'reason',[28] this instinct produces over-consumption. Humanity is threatened by cannibalism, at first metaphorical, later literal, as some eat the resources that are necessary to the survival of the species. Eighteenth- and nineteenth-century discourse about sexual perversity follows a homologous course. Spending/taking semen outside the normal circuit of (re)production 'threatens because of its seeming *limitlessness*'.[29] These discussions are carried on in the midst of a continuous struggle over the allocation of

Richard Dellamora

resources. Malthus explains how the stresses that accompany demographic pressures result in increased concentrations of capital, higher productivity and falling real wages.[30]

Malthus first produced the *Essay* in 1798 as 'a polemic against radical egalitarianism' in contemporary French and English thought.[31] He had been educated, however, in the very tradition against which he reacted. He regarded his efforts as consistent with the Enlightenment project of improvement and with Christian theodicy since the need for prudence forced human beings to develop their moral and intellectual capacities.[32] Committed to educating the general population in the necessity of delayed marriage and reproductive prudence, he was 'convinced that nothing would so powerfully contribute to the advancement of rational freedom as a thorough knowledge, generally circulated, of the principal cause of poverty'.[33] This view was at odds with radical thinking in the 1830s, within which the difficulties faced by 'the lower classes of society' were much more likely to be regarded as resulting from the denial of citizenship. The fact that most men and all women and children in Great Britain were denied the vote was at once a practical and a symbolic sign of their lack of full civil status. The demand for 'more' is a demand for citizenship – with all that implies in terms of empowerment and a share of resources.

Oliver is 'the small rebel' (56) chosen by lot by the other boys to ask for more gruel. His innocence threatens Bumble just as it later threatens the police-magistrate, Mr Fang, and as it threatens Fagin. Dickens dramatises the scene so as to parody Malthus's grim view of nature:

> Oliver Twist and his companions suffered the tortures of slow starvation for three months: at last they got so voracious and wild with hunger, that one boy, who was tall for his age, and hadn't been used to that sort of thing . . . , hinted darkly to his companions, that unless he had another basin of gruel *per diem*, he was afraid he might some night happen to eat the boy who slept next him, who happened to be a weakly youth of tender age. He had a wild hungry eye; and they implicitly believed him. (56)

However much Dickens contests the political implications drawn by Malthus, he does accept a number of his principles. In the preface to the 1850 cheap edition of the novel, for example, he calls for rebuilding London's slums because otherwise 'those classes of the people which increase the fastest, must become so desperate and be made so miserable, as to bear within themselves the certain seeds of ruin to the whole community'.[34] Consumption in Malthus's *Essay* and the novel signifies social, moral and economic disorder. The absence of a sense that positive aspects of plebeian culture continued to exist into the early Victorian period and that they had significant connections with the self-conscious-ness of the Chartists skews in negative ways lower-class representation in the novel. The omission correlates with the absence of agency in the rep-resentation of Oliver. On both counts, the novel is contradictory, moti-vated by radical perspectives but excluding constructive oppositional practices and radical political agency.

The place of the people in British society changed for ever as a result of the mass mobilisation of men during the Napoleonic Wars. Motivated by fear of invasion, the landed élites, together with their allies in the gov-ernment, press and Church, encouraged the development of a militant patriotism. This weapon, however, was double-edged since 'by summon-ing men from all classes, all political opinions, all parts of Great Britain and all religious denominations to its defense . . . , by treating them indis-criminately as patriots, the authorities ran an obvious risk of encourag-ing demands for political change in the future'.[35] By the early 1830s, many of the one-third of a million men demobilised during the economic depression of the decade after Waterloo had been radicalised, especially around the issue of universal manhood suffrage. The limits of the Reform Bill of 1832, which excluded 80 per cent of adult males from the fran-chise, bitterly disappointed these men. The Act belied the language of 'patriotic union' that the Whigs had invoked in campaigning on its behalf. 'Anger among the excluded was immense.'[36] These men possessed the numbers, the vigour, and the organisational skills to threaten the stability of the reformed Constitution. According to Linda Colley, this was the one generation of British men in the nineteenth century who could conceiv-ably have led a mass insurrection.[37]

Dickens lodges middle-class anxieties about aggressive lower-class men in the figure of Sikes, thief and murderer, whose life ends in what is, in effect, the exemplary spectacle of public execution. When first intro-duced, he is accompanied by 'a white shaggy dog, with his face scratched and torn in twenty different places' (136). But in the following illustration, the dog becomes a mongrel bulldog. For his part, Bill acquires negroid features. Further on, after Fagin consigns Oliver into Sikes's hands for a break-and-entry, Sikes becomes drunk and falls into 'most unmusical snatches of song, mingled with wild execrations' (193). This behaviour parodies characters in the novels of Sir Walter Scott such as Madge Wildfire in *The Heart of Midlothian* (1818), though an even more apt com-parison might be with the Whistler, a young Highland brigand who is sold to a planter in Virginia, kills his master in an uprising and is ultimately forced to take refuge among a tribe of 'wild Indians' (Chapter 52).

Creating a nation of Britons to fight Napoleon meant downplaying ethnic differences, yet the string of associations that can be played on the word 'savage' indicates the counter-tendency to project ethnic and class others as racially inferior. Malthus, for example, contends that 'if America continue increasing [in population] . . . , the Indians will be driven further and further back into the country, till the whole race is ultimately exterminated'.[38] In making this observation, Malthus does not endorse the extermination of the Indians, but, in describing it as a natural process rather than as a de facto result of national policies, he provides the grounds of an apology for annihilation.

Oliver's arrival in London adds the reminder of the additional threat posed by the cityscape of the 'great towns' criticised by Malthus.[39] Oliver sees with a demographer's eyes: he

> could not help bestowing a few hasty glances on either side of the way, as he passed along. A dirtier or more wretched place he had never seen. The street was very narrow and muddy, and the air was impregnated with filthy odours. There were a good many small shops; but the only stock in trade appeared to be heaps of children, who, even at that time of night, were crawling in and out at the doors, or screaming from the inside. The sole places that seemed to prosper amid the general blight of the place, were the public-houses; and in them, the lowest orders of Irish were wrangling with might and main. Covered ways and yards, which here and there diverged from the main street, disclosed little knots of houses, where drunken men and women were positively wallowing in filth; and from several of the door-ways, great ill-looking fellows were cautiously emerging, bound, to all appearance, on no very well-disposed or harmless errands. (103)

But if Irish urban squalor, crime, excess reproduction and intoxication represent one set of inhumanities, the Jew Fagin poses a yet more threatening one. Oliver's bodily integrity is threatened with racial contamination.

Cruikshank's representations of 'The Jew' belong to a tradition of caricature by printmakers such as Hogarth and Thomas Rowlandson that dates to mid-eighteenth-century Parliamentary debates over the naturalisation of Ashkenazic Jews.[40] The images indicate how alien to British nationality Jews were reckoned to be. The tradition continues in the representation of Ikey Solomon, Fagin's real life prototype, by 'Phiz' (Hablôt Browne), in *The New Newgate Calendar* (1841) (plate 2).[41] Entitled 'Doing a Jew', the illustration shows Solomon having his beard pulled by a Bill Sikes look-alike, who happens to be accompanied by a terrier ripping at the Jew's coat. These representations capitalise on contemporary ambivalence

2   Hablôt Browne ('Phiz')
'Doing a Jew', in *The New Newgate Calendar* (1841)

about Jews. Following passage of the Catholic Emancipation Act in 1829, a similar measure was proposed on behalf of Jews. Introduced a second time in 1833, the Jewish Emancipation Bill passed the House of Commons. Despite this fact and the admission of Jews to municipal offices, the Bill 'was consistently rejected by the Lords in one session after the other'.[42]

Cruikshank's representation of Bumble staring at Oliver implicitly draws attention to the gaze that the novel's illustrations and texts direct at him. Both Dickens and Cruikshank associate their judgements with the moral wisdom that Hogarth tries to capture in his engravings. This wisdom does not, however, exist in a universal moral discourse set apart from the Enlightenment project of general education. Rousseau and Bentham both imagine 'a transparent society' in which virtue would be immediately evident. Dickens's journalistic scrutiny is in the service of this 'universal visibility'. Such seeing is itself a mode of power, dominating the objects represented and readers of the text. Significantly, Hogarth's friend and ally, John Fielding, whom Dickens emulated, was not only a novelist but also a London magistrate. In imitating Fielding's moral realism, Dickens makes himself the subject of a juridical gaze. Seeking to illuminate, he shows instead how resistant individuals and institutions are to rational benevolence. What remains most compelling are social and psychic 'zones of disorder'.[43]

Cruikshank's plate 'Oliver introduced to the Respectable Old Gentleman' (plate 3) is a diptych to 'Oliver asking for More'. The workhouse boys have been replaced by four preternaturally aged boys smoking at a table. Fagin, grinning, looks at Oliver. In contrast to Mr Bumble, he holds the handle of a pan of (pork?) sausages cooking over a fire. In his hand, he holds a toasting-fork pointing upward to the broadside of a public execution, an image of Oliver's likely future under Fagin's care. As in the earlier illustration, Oliver carries an object at an angle, not a spoon this time but a walking stick acquired on the way to London. Fagin provides the creatural satisfactions denied at the workhouse. But details of Dickens's description of Oliver's introduction to Fagin (the epithet, 'the 'spectable old genelman', the toasting-fork, Fagin's red hair) are drawn from the iconography of the devil.[44] Dawkins, who stands as intermediary, is 'one of the queerest-looking boys that Oliver had ever seen. . . . He had about him all the airs and manners of a man' (100). What, apart from theft, smoking, and gin-drinking accounts for this liminal state of man/boy? What secret ties the boys so closely to Fagin that they dare not 'peach' on him even after arrest? Why does he periodically arrange for them to be caught, tried, convicted, and sometimes hanged? What motivates the extreme guilt he evinces before his own hanging? Why does Oliver yearn for release from

3   George Cruikshank
'Oliver introduced to the Respectable Old Gentleman', Chapter 8

his bodily self while in a hypnagogic state the morning after he arrives at Fagin's?[45] Could the answer be sexual abuse?

In a well-known essay, 'Who is Fagin?', Steven Marcus implies as much, beginning with a comment on 'Alec Guinness's lisping, asthmatic, and vaguely homosexual Fagin', and later referring to Dickens's dependence on Bob Fagin, a fellow worker at the blacking warehouse where he worked as a boy while his father was in prison for debt. Marcus refers to Dickens's friendship with Fagin as 'a companionship or affection which is at once needed and intolerable'. The ambivalence suggests the 'profound attraction of repulsion' that Dickens exhibits in the opening chapters of *Oliver Twist*. While these comments suggest the simultaneous existence of homosexual attraction/repulsion in writer and child, Marcus heterosexualises Dickens's dis-ease by insisting that what Oliver sees after his first night at Fagin's 'corresponds' with a primal fantasy of parental coitus.[46] Yet the Oedipal construction of the primal fantasy is only one possible construction.[47] Since Oliver, who has never met his parents, last remembers being given 'a glass of hot gin and water' by Fagin, then being 'gently lifted on to one of the sacks' (106) and falling asleep, other fantasies are more likely. Of course, an unmentionable act may be concealed in the darkness of Fagin's den. Whether sexual abuse literally occurs or not, Dickens's intense gaze prompts the thought.

Cruikshank hints at perversity again later when Oliver, having briefly been rescued from the gang, is kidnapped and returned to Fagin. In both the text and the plate, 'Oliver's Reception by Fagin and the Boys' (plate 4), the recaptured boy's new trousers receive a lot of attention. Fagin still grins, open armed while holding an open O of a cap. 'Delighted to see you looking so well, my dear' (163), he says. The phantasy of introjection (Fagin's address recalls that of the Grimms' wolf) is exacerbated by Dickens's suppression of the domestic side of Fagin/Solomon as reported in *The New Newgate Calendar*.[48] Solomon, whose criminal career ended in 1831, was a family man who made a good living first in London, then in New York City, and eventually in Hobart. His loyal wife once helped him escape legal custody. He also set up his son in business. By excluding relations of this sort from *Oliver Twist*, Dickens exacerbates the intensity of Fagin's relationship with the boys.

A queer kind of chap

Oliver uses an idiom of stagy innocence that belies his environment. The contrast to the Cockney slang of characters like Jack Dawkins, 'The Artful Dodger', could not be more marked. Oliver pretends to find

4   George Cruikshank
'Oliver's Reception by Fagin and the Boys', Chapter 16

thieves' cant incomprehensible. This refusal is a necessary ruse since, if he were to show that he does understand the grammar and syntax of the dangerous classes, he would be capable of choosing to act as they do. William Cohen points to a scene in the novel in which Dickens shows Oliver unable to understand either the language of theft or the language of boyish perversity. Cohen emphasises the play on the name *Master Bates*, but the insertion of foreign objects into the boys' mouths during the scene suggests the act of fellatio: *png*)

> [The Dodger] looked down on Oliver, with a thoughtful countenance, for a brief space; and then, raising his head, and heaving a gentle sigh, said, half in abstraction, and half to Master Bates:
> 'What a pity it is he isn't a prig!'
> 'Ah,' said Master Charles Bates; 'he don't know what's good for him.'
> The Dodger sighed again, and resumed his pipe: as did Charley Bates. They both smoked, for some seconds, in silence.
> 'I suppose you don't even know what a prig is?' said the Dodger mournfully.
> 'I think I know that,' replied Oliver, looking up. 'It's a th—; you're one, are you not?' inquired Oliver, checking himself.
> 'I am,' replied the Dodger. 'I'd scorn to be anything else.' Mr. Dawkins gave his hat a ferocious cock, after delivering this sentiment, and looked at Master Bates, as if to denote that he would feel obliged by his saying anything to the contrary. (181)

Cohen comments: 'The gloss on "prig" that Oliver is incapable of uttering is presumably "thief," yet the persistence with which the term goes undenoted throws us deliberately back upon the signifier – where, with the alacrity of any English schoolboy, we might take the usual phonemic detour from a bilabial to a fricative and detect a "frig" (Victorian slang for manual stimulation of the genitals).'[49] Oliver's silence has a confessional aspect. It is not that he *can't* say the word, it is that he won't because acknowledging what he knows might suggest that he knows too much. (The boys are lecturing him about how important it is not to 'peach' on one's fellows.) Oliver's silence is complicitous but also (self-)resistant, a way of saying 'not me' by saying 'you are'.

After Dickens's death, Cruikshank claimed that he had suggested to him the possibility of a more suitable collaboration upon a different Oliver. Cruikshank wanted to 'make Oliver a nice pretty little boy' so that 'the public – and particularly the ladies – would be sure to take a greater interest in him'.[50] Disagreement on this point caused Dickens to reject a late plate, 'Rose Maylie and Oliver' (plate 5). Cruikshank also wanted a different story.

5   George Cruikshank
'Rose Maylie and Oliver', rejected plate for *Oliver Twist*

> I suggested to Mr. Dickens that he should write the life of a London boy,
> and strongly advised him to do this, assuring him that I would furnish him
> with the subject and supply him with all the characters, which my large
> experience of London life would enable me to do. My idea was to raise a
> boy from a most humble position up to a high and respectable one – in
> fact, to illustrate one of those cases of common occurrence, where men of
> humble origin by natural ability, industry, honest and honourable conduct,
> raise themselves to first-class positions in society. And as I wished particu-
> larly to bring the habits and manners of the thieves of London before the
> public . . . , I suggested that the poor boy should fall among thieves, but
> that his honesty and natural good disposition should enable him to pass
> through this ordeal without contamination, and after I had fully described
> the full-grown thieves (the 'Bill Sikes') and their female companions, also
> the young thieves (the 'Artful Dodgers') and the receivers of stolen goods,
> Mr. Dickens agreed to act on my suggestion, and the work was com-
> menced, but we differed as to what sort of boy the hero should be. Mr.
> Dickens wanted rather a queer kind of chap.[51]

Oliver is 'queer' because he is not one of those 'men of humble origin'
who succeed in raising themselves into positions of respectability, afflu-
ence, and influence. Lacking this class interest, the pure boy is suspect as
a protagonist.

In its second half, the novel is overtaken by an awkward mystery, in
debt to the Gothic novel, that ultimately produces an Oliver whose
parents are gentlefolk. This outcome is usually seen as in craven compliance with the expectations of middle-class readers.[52] Yet the one
thing that Dickens does not offer at the end of the novel is a representation of a conventional nuclear family. The fraternity of Brownlow, Mr
Grimwig, Mr Losberne and Oliver with which the novel ends is too
obviously an inverse image of Fagin's fraternity not to have something
odd about it. Cruikshank conveys the sense of something askew in the
illustrations – as Henry James remembered from his experience of
reading the novel as a youngster. In *A Small Boy and Others*, James writes
that *Oliver Twist*

> seemed to me more Cruikshank's than Dickens's; it was a thing of such
> vividly terrible images, and all marked with that peculiarity of Cruikshank
> that the offered flowers of goodnesses, the scenes and figures intended to
> comfort and cheer, present themselves under his hand as but more subtly
> sinister, or more suggestively queer, than the frank badnesses and horrors.
> The nice people and the happy moments, in the plates, frightened me
> almost as much as the low and the awkward.[53]

James experienced attraction–repulsion not only to the dangerous world of the boys but to the 'solution' of Oliver's problems through his adoption by a ring of bachelors.

When Cruikshank refers to Oliver as 'a queer kind of chap', he uses the word in its primary signification of 'strange, odd, peculiar, eccentric, in appearance or character'. James supplements these meanings with the sense of 'uncanny'. The word also signifies sexually perverse, including homosexual though without the full panoply of medical and juridical meaning that 'homosexual' acquired during James's lifetime. James uses the word in this sense in a letter where he speaks of 'the queer Beckford'.[54] A wealthy and accomplished musician and writer, William Beckford was forced into exile in 1785 after being accused of having sexual relations with a sixteen-year-old named William Courtenay.[55] The significations overlap in a sentence that the *OED* cites from *Dr Jekyll and Mr Hyde* (1885): 'The more it looks like Queer Street, the less I ask.' The *OED* locates this quotation in the context of 'cant' or thieves' argot, citing writers of the 1820s with whose work Dickens was thoroughly familiar. In cant, the word signifies 'bad' or 'worthless', especially with reference to counterfeit or forged coinage and currency. Dickens exploits the indeterminacy to provoke anxieties by uttering what remains unspeakable.[56]

Brownlow and Co. fill the role of good fairies that Jacqueline Rose associates with an especially pernicious aspect of contemporary Tory ideology: the elevation of 'the principle of the good fairy – "little people who grant wishes and do good deeds around the world" – into a social law' that excuses government in abdicating its responsibilities.[57] Rose argues that this form of benevolence subjectifies its practitioners as well as their objects.[58] She quizzes the meaning of both agency and good intentions. Describing similar operations at work in the guise of nineteenth-century Tory benevolence, Dickens shows the instability of the innocence that the 'good fairy' model projects on to both benefactors and child.

The word 'gentleman' provokes similar disturbances in the text. Dickens plays up the analogy, present in *The New Newgate Calendar*, between commerce and crime. The redundant use of 'gentleman' works similarly to suggest the possibility of comparing respectable male relations with Fagin's travesty of them. In the overworld of bourgeois gentlemen like Brownlow, who eventually adopts Oliver as his son, the perverse suggestiveness of Fagin's relationship with the boys is effaced. But how can the spirit of Oliver's deceased aunt adequately account for and contain the desires that bind Brownlow, the boy, and Edward Leeford, Oliver's dead father, who was at one time Brownlow's closest friend?

Once disclosed, the mystery about Oliver's origins negates his innocence. Though he is renamed, it is not as Leeford. His illegitimacy likewise mars the memory of his sainted mother. Nor can a father be exonerated who permitted himself to be forced into a 'wretched marriage' motivated by 'family pride, and the most sordid and narrowest of all ambition' (435). The face of Oliver's half-brother, Monks, is disfigured by a 'hideous [*read* venereal] disease' (439). This barbarous history turns against the upper classes the complaint that Malthus had charged against the lower ones. The Gothic plot demystifies the allegedly superior values of the 'country gentlemen' to whom Malthus appealed against popular unrest as 'the appointed guardians of British liberty'.[59] Instead, Oliver's birth demonstrates Malthusian principle against the grain:

> When a general corruption of morals, with regard to the sex, pervades all the classes of society, its effects must necessarily be to poison the springs of domestic happiness, to weaken conjugal and parental affection, and to lessen the united exertions and ardour of parents in the care and education of their children; effects which cannot take place without a decided diminution of the general happiness and virtue of the society; particularly as the necessity of art in the accomplishment and conduct of intrigues, and in the concealment of their consequences, necessarily leads to many other vices.[60]

Together with the absence of the plot of upward mobility envisaged by Cruikshank, the Gothic narrative of *Oliver Twist* shows how strongly disidentified with middle-class certification Dickens was in 1837.

And yet the transformation of *Oliver Twist* from a series of sketches into a novel was a crucial incident in the production of 'Charles Dickens' as a household name and professional writer. The upward mobility ratified by *Oliver Twist* is Dickens's. At the same time, he was involved in a continuing struggle to claim his name and career. Serial publication of the novel had begun under the pseudonym of 'Boz', author of the *Sketches* of Cockney and criminal life that first brought Dickens to notice as a writer of 'serial fiction'. *Oliver Twist* became a novel definitively only after Dickens proposed it to fulfil the terms of a contract signed a year earlier to provide Richard Bentley with two (unnamed) novels. By September, his new friend and legal adviser John Forster was puffing the serial as promising 'to take its place among the higher prose fictions of the language'.[61] Bentley retained copyright to the magazine serial of *Oliver Twist* as well as, for three years, the book version. In the meantime, Dickens continued to struggle with Cruikshank over who should determine the general shape and specific details of the text. This dispute originated again in the commodity-character of Dickens's early fiction.

Dickens's first contracted 'novel' focuses on a legal document that seeks to establish an equivalence between the monetary and moral worth of an individual. In making his name as an author, Dickens was doing the same. Within this context, 'purity' – of form, of motive – can exist only on an ever receding horizon of expectations. While writing the novel, Dickens established agency – as a husband, a father, a money-maker, and a professional writer. But he had no way at hand of turning 'the orphan of a workhouse' into a man who could convert purity into respectability while continuing to represent the classes among whom he had been born.

Notes

I would like to thank Jo-Ann Wallace, whose paper 'Technologies of the Child', presented at the Human Sciences in the Age of Theory conference, at the University of Western Ontario, 3 April 1993, stimulated many of the reflections pursued in this essay.

1 Michel Foucault, *The Use of Pleasure*, volume 2 of *The History of Sexuality*, tr. Robert Hurley (New York: Vintage, 1986), p. 12.
2 Michel Foucault, 'On the Genealogy of Ethics: An Overview of Work in Progress', in *The Foucault Reader*, ed. Paul Rabinow (New York: Pantheon, 1984), pp. 365–6.
3 Quoted by Alexander Welsh, *The City of Dickens* (1971; rpt Cambridge, Mass.: Harvard University Press, 1986), p. 180.
4 Lee Holcombe, 'Victorian Wives and Property: Reform of the Married Women's Property Law, 1857–1882', in *A Widening Sphere: Changing Roles of Victorian Women*, ed. Martha Vicinus (Bloomington: Indiana University Press, 1977), p. 3.
5 Although Kathleen Tillotson avers that Dickens may have had the novel in mind as early as 1833, by her own account, he had not thought of Oliver before January 1837 (Charles Dickens, *Oliver Twist*, ed. Kathleen Tillotson (Oxford: Clarendon Press, 1974), pp. xv, xix). For the development of the serial into a novel, see Kathryn Chittick, *Dickens and the 1830s* (Cambridge: Cambridge University Press, 1990), pp. 61–91.
6 Norman Feltes, *Modes of Production of Victorian Novels* (Chicago: University of Chicago Press, 1986), p. 3.
7 Feltes, pp. 7–8.
8 *Ibid.*, p. 103 n. 50.
9 Tillotson, in Dickens, *Oliver Twist*, p. xvii.
10 Foucault, 'On the Genealogy of Ethics', p. 366.
11 Jacqueline Rose, *The Case of Peter Pan or The Impossibility of Children's Fiction* (Philadelphia: University of Pennsylvania Press, 1993), pp. 3–4.
12 D. A. Miller is the most significant proponent of the concept of the novel as a disciplinary structure within nineteenth-century liberal culture (*The Novel and the Police* (Berkeley: University of California Press, 1988), pp. vii–xiii).
13 Richard Dellamora, 'Male Relations in Thomas Hardy's *Jude the Obscure*', *Papers on Language and Literature*, 27 (fall 1991), 455; for Magwitch's interest in Pip, see William Cohen, 'Manual Conduct in *Great Expectations*', *ELH*, 60 (1993), 242–4.
14 J. Hillis Miller quotes Steig in *Illustration* (Cambridge, Mass.: Harvard University Press, 1992), p. 96; Chittick, p. 76.

15 Local boards were empowered under the Poor Law Amendment Act of 1834 to indenture orphans to factory-owners.

16 Catherine Gallagher, *The Industrial Reformation of English Fiction: Social Discourse and Narrative Form 1832–1867* (Chicago: University of Chicago Press, 1988), pp. 3, 27, 32.

17 Rose, p. 5.

18 Foucault, *The Use of Pleasure*, p. 194.

19 Arnold Kettle, *An Introduction to the English Novel* (1951: rpt New York: Harper, 1960), p. 131.

20 John Forster, *The Life of Charles Dickens*, new ed., rev. (New York: Dutton, 1969), 1.90.

21 Peter Stallybrass, 'Marx and Heterogeneity: Thinking the Lumpenproletariat', *Representations*, 31 (summer 1990), 70.

22 Thomas Robert Malthus, *An Essay on the Principle of Population*, selected and introduced by Donald Winch (Cambridge: Cambridge University Press, 1992), p. 24. Winch reprints the edition of 1803. Subsequent references in the notes, unless otherwise indicated, are to this edition.

23 Robert Tracy, '"The Old Story" and Inside Stories: Modish Fiction and Fictional Modes in *Oliver Twist*', *Dickens Studies Annual*, 17 (1988), 2.

24 Thomas Robert Malthus, *An Essay on the Principle of Population . . .*, ed. Antony Flew (Harmondsworth: Penguin, 1970), p. 23.

25 Malthus, p. 32n.

26 Malthus, p. 14. Unless otherwise cited, subsequent references to the text are to this edition.

27 Michel Foucault, *The Birth of the Clinic: An Archaeology of Medical Perception*, tr. A. M. Sheridan Smith (New York: Vintage Books, 1975), pp. xiv–xv.

28 Malthus, p. 14.

29 Cohen, p. 256 n. 26.

30 Malthus, p. 28.

31 In particular, in William Godwin's *Enquiry concerning Political Justice* and the Marquis de Condorcet's *Sketch for a Historical Picture of the Progress of the Human Mind*. Gareth Stedman Jones, *Languages of Class: Studies in English Working Class History, 1832–1982* (Cambridge: Cambridge University Press, 1983), p. 105n.; Malthus, *Essay on Population*, p. vii.

32 J. M. Pullen, 'Malthus' Theological Ideas and Their Influence on His Principle of Population', in *Thomas Robert Malthus: Critical Assessments*, ed. John Cunningham Wood (London: Croom Helm, 1986), 2.213–14.

33 Malthus, p. 243.

34 Dickens, *Oliver Twist* (ed. Tillotson), p. 382.

35 Linda Colley, *Britons: Forging the Nation 1707–1837* (New Haven: Yale University Press, 1992), p. 318.

36 Colley, p. 349.

37 Colley, pp. 361–3.

38 Malthus, p. 18.

39 Malthus, p. 23.

40 Miller, 'The Fiction of Realism: *Sketches by Boz, Oliver Twist*, and Cruikshank's Illustrations', in *Dickens Centennial Essays*, ed. Ada Nisbet and Blake Nevius (Berkeley: University of California Press, 1971), p. 136.

41 Camden Pelham, *The Chronicles of Crime; or, The New Newgate Calendar* (London: Miles & Co., 1887), facing page 241; Tracy, p. 17.

42 *Encyclopaedia Judaica* (Jersualem: Keter Publishing House Ltd.), 6.755.

43 Michel Foucault, 'The Eye of Power', in *Power/Knowledge: Selected Interviews and Other Writings, 1972–1977*, ed. Colin Gordon (New York: Pantheon Books, 1980), p. 152.

44 Lauriat Lane, Jr, 'The Devil in *Oliver Twist*', *The Dickensian*, 52 (summer 1956), 132–6.

45 Steven Marcus, *Dickens from Pickwick to Dombey* (New York: Simon & Schuster, 1968), p. 371.

46 Marcus, pp. 359, 367, 369, 374.

47 Jean Laplanche and J.-B. Pontalis, *The Language of Psycho-Analysis*, tr. Donald Nicholson-Smith and intro. Daniel Lagache (New York: Norton, 1973), pp. 335–6; cf. Lee Edelman, 'Seeing Things: Representation, the Scene of Surveillance, and the Spectacle of Gay Male Sex', in *Inside/Out: Lesbian Theories, Gay Theories*, ed. Diana Fuss (New York: Routledge, 1991), pp. 95–6.

48 Laplanche, p. 230.

49 Cohen, p. 218.

50 Tracy, p. 12.

51 Cited in Tracy, p. 13.

52 See, for example, John Sutherland, *The Stanford Companion to Victorian Fiction* (Stanford: Stanford University Press, 1989), p. 478.

53 Quoted by Miller, p. 128. James's description suggests that he read a text with the illustration as retouched for the 1846 edition. The crudely touched-up plates exaggerate Cruikshank's grotesquerie. It is these images that I reproduce from the novel.

54 Cited by Adeline Tintner, 'Henry James, Orientalist', *Modern Language Studies*, 13 (fall 1983), 128.

55 Louis Crompton, *Byron and Greek Love: Homophobia in 19th-century England* (Berkeley: University of California Press, 1985), pp. 118–20.

56 *The Oxford English Dictionary*, 2nd edition (Oxford: Clarendon Press, 1989). In a phobic exclusion of their own, the editors claim that the signification of 'homosexual' originated in the United States in the twentieth century. The interweave of proper and cant meanings indicates, however, that the word connotes/denotes sexual perversity at least from the early nineteenth century.

57 Rose, p. x.

58 Thomas Flynn, 'Foucault as Parrhesiast: His Last Course at the Collège de France (1984)', in *The Final Foucault*, ed. James Bernauer and David Rasmussen (Cambridge, Mass.: MIT Press, 1988), p. 103.

59 Malthus, pp. 247, 245.

60 *Ibid.*, p. 23.

61 Chittick, pp. 58, 81, 82, 84.

5

The avuncular and beyond:
family (melo)drama in *Nicholas Nickleby*

HELENA MICHIE

About half-way through Scott Turow's recent best-selling detective novel *The Burden of Proof*, the attorney hero, Sandy Stern, ponders his relationship with his most difficult client who is also, not coincidentally, his brother-in-law: ' "My brother-in-law," thought Stern, alone in the tiny room. "Brother. In. Law. What kind of peculiar term was that?" '[1] In the process of Stern's meditation, the familiar and familial term becomes de-familiarised, fragmented into its component parts, revealed, even, as oxymoronic: 'brother' would seem to express a natural biological relation, 'law' a social and constructed one. 'Brother-in-law', then, becomes a legal fiction.

The term 'brother-in-law' in Turow's novel is of course rendered more complex and more evocative by the fact that Sandy is in fact Dixon's lawyer; their relation is a legal one in the most obvious and – to Sandy, who suspects Dixon of criminal activity – disturbing sense. By representing Dixon and becoming implicated in his crimes, Sandy becomes a brother both in and outside of the law.

There are no pairs of brothers-in-law in *Nicholas Nickleby* until they are fashioned by the double wedding at the end, a fact only surprising when we realise how many different kinds of familial, quasi-familial and metaphorically familial relationships there are in the novel. The novel may in fact be read as an exploration of the complexity and capaciousness of what I am calling the familial idiom – the system of terms which transforms what might at first seem non-familial relations into familial ones. The phrase 'in-law' has a special place in this idiom, transforming as it does people who are not related by blood into relations marked by the always qualified signs of the nuclear family: 'father', 'mother', 'brother', 'sister'.

When Nicholas and his uncle Ralph pay Mr Squeers their initial visit at the end of which Nicholas is hired to work at Dotheboys Hall, Mr Snawley appears with two boys whose relation to him is the subject of comic negotiation within the idiom of family. Snawley is obviously intending to dispose of the boys for as long as possible; Squeers and Snawley form a pact based on a shared understanding of the familial idiom:

> Squeers: 'Let us understand each other; I see we may safely do so. What are these boys; – natural children?'
> 'No', rejoined Snawley, meeting the gaze of the schoolmaster's one eye. 'They ain't.'
> 'I thought they might be', said Squeers coolly. 'We have a good many of them; that boy's one.'
> 'Him in the next box?' said Snawley.
> Squeers nodded in the affirmative, and his companion took another peep at the little boy on the trunk, and turning round again, looked as if he were quite disappointed to see him so much like other boys, and said he should hardly have thought it.
> 'He is', cried Squeers. 'But about these boys of yours; you wanted to speak to me?'
> 'Yes', replied Snawley. 'The fact is, I am not their father, Mr Squeers. I'm only their father-in-law.'
> 'Oh! Is that it?' said the schoolmaster. 'That explains it at once.' (95)

To 'understand' this scene as Squeers and Snawley come to 'understand each other', we as readers must be conversant, of course, with the fact that 'natural' is a euphemism for 'illegitimate' and that 'father-in-law' in Dickens's time was used as 'stepfather' would be today. 'Natural' in this case means literally outside the law, outside the legal institution of marriage. 'In-law', on the other hand, suggests a relationship completely defined by marriage; Snawley becomes a father-in-law by contracting to become husband, not, as he insists, by becoming – in any sense – a father. Further complicating the relation between the legal and the biological lexicons of family is the fact that what Snawley wants to do is his legal right although the novel presents it as both unnatural and potentially – given the legal reform of Yorkshire schools argued for by Dickens – against the law.

An interesting feminist reading of this scene might begin with the observation that this is a scene between two men in which they contract within the law for the disposal of a woman's biological offspring. Such a reading might focus on the laws that made such a contract possible – which made stepchildren into the property of the father, which made the husband, quite literally, the father-in-law. The reading would take further strength from the Lacanian notion of 'law of the father', which suggests not only that the father is privileged by the law but that he in fact represents it: his 'no' is the law that shapes and delimits the lives of all children. I would enjoy doing this feminist reading, but for the purposes of this chapter I am more interested in exploring how the familial idiom, the lexicon of family in *Nicholas Nickleby*, allows us to think about different kinds of relations and how these relations, in turn, allow us to rethink the distinction between law and nature which makes the familial idiom so rich and so powerful. Because this novel is so full of characters exploring, naming and renaming their relation to each other, *Nicholas Nickleby* allows us to see, on the one hand, how 'family' is a social construct infinitely bound up in the cultural process of naming and, on the other, how powerful cultural appeals to 'nature' can be in obfuscating the constructedness of social arrangements.

Nicholas Nickleby seems both critical of and wedded to appeals to nature as the ground of familial definition: its nervousness about the tension between social and natural constructions of the family surfaces in two kinds of discourses employed throughout the novel: the legal, as I have mentioned above, and the performative or the theatrical. If the conflict between nature and culture in the realm of the legal leads to questions of inheritance and the rights of children, tensions in the realm of the theatrical lead directly to questions of affect or feeling. If the questions which animate debate within the lexicon of the legal have to do with the natural, then those that arise within a theatrical context have to do with sincerity. Issues of nature and sincerity, on the one hand, and culture and performance, on the other, are explored in *Nicholas Nickleby* through a complicated network of familial or quasi-familial relations which extend outward from the nuclear family and into a number of different registers including the comic, the sentimental and the melodramatic. The different sections of my chapter – 'Natural and unnatural fathers', 'The avuncular', 'Mother-in-law jokes', 'The tantular', 'Brothers and sisters', 'Family melodrama', and 'Two marriages' – attempt provisionally to name some of these relationships, to establish them within a dominant family idiom and to outline the tensions between the legal and the natural, the sincere and the performative, as they are articulated within a particular instance of family relation.

Natural and unnatural fathers

If Snawley appears as a father-in-law at the beginning of the novel, he returns as a natural father two-thirds of the way through the book. His claim that he is Smike's father is based on a series of documents so official-looking as to convince Nicholas of their validity:

> There was nothing about them that could be called into question. The certificates were regularly signed as abstracts from the parish books, the first letter had a genuine appearance of having been written and preserved for some years, the hand-writing of the second tallied with it exactly. (683)

Snawley's paternity is, of course, false: an illegal legal fiction. It would be easy at this point to oppose this fiction, depending as it does on papers and technicalities, to some benign discourse of natural feeling. Interestingly, however, the novel does not quite make this move – it makes another marked by the reappearance of the word which ratified the initial implied contract between Snawley and Squeers: 'understand'. When Squeers is thrown bodily from the Nickleby house, he himself uses what might first appear to be the language of feeling as he accuses *Smike* of hardheartedness:

> 'He never loved nobody', bawled Squeers, through the keyhole. 'He never loved me; he never loved Wackford, who is next door but one to a cherubim. How can you expect that he'll love his father? He'll never love his father, he won't. He don't know what it is to have a father. He don't understand it. It an't in him.' (685)

This is a passage full of ironies, the most obvious of which are directed characterologically towards Squeers. His 'he don't know what it is to have a father' is, in this reading, both a pathetic statement of fact and a self-accusation. Other ironies, however, complicate the direction and efficiency of the first; these are focused not so much or not only on Squeers as they are at the idea of 'natural' parenting itself. Oddly – or perhaps predictably – this cynical critique of parenting is most clearly articulated by the novel's figure of innocent benignity, Charles Cheeryble, in his only textualised moment of bitterness:

> The same mistake presents it to me, in one shape or other, at every turn. . . . Parents who never showed their love, complain of want of natural affection in their children – children who never showed their duty, complain of want of natural feeling in their parents – law-makers who find both so miserable that their affections have never had enough of life's sun to develop them, are loud in their moralizings over parents and children too, and cry that the very ties of nature are disregarded. (687)

Charles is arguing here for nothing less than the constructedness of 'natural' ties; although later in his tirade he does extol natural affections as the greatest of God's gifts, these are natural affections that are not, it seems, given naturally to everyone. Interestingly enough, Charles does not portray culture here as thwarting or distorting natural instincts; it is the 'law-makers' who coerce in the name of the natural.

Charles's critique of natural affection allows us to visit, as it were, the scene of Smike's paternity with a more jaundiced eye. We can now read through Squeers's tears – these are paradoxically real enough, although they are not of course caused by love of Smike – to the traces of his initial contract with Snawley, to the word 'understand' which signifies a shared lexicon, a shared relation to the familial idiom. What Squeers understands, then, is that all parenting is parenting-in-law, that being a parent is a matter of a specifically legal authority to own, to punish, to beat and even to sexually abuse children. This law is, as we have seen earlier, a gendered one; children are the property of their fathers, whether these fathers be 'natural' or 'legal'. The issue of legality is gendered of course in yet another sense; feminist historians have suggested that patriarchal law is itself compensatory for the fact that paternity is no more than a 'legal fiction'. Children are the property of their fathers precisely because they cannot be biologically proved to be their children. We can then set in motion a chain of anxieties at once spectacularly displayed and repressed in this novel: all paternity is legal; all paternity a legal fiction; all paternity fiction; all fiction writing about the recovery of paternity.

The novel's anxieties do not stop there; one more turn of the screw offers us a new and newly horrifying possibility. What if the child-as-property is a daughter? The marriage plot, that staple of nineteenth-century fiction, offers us part of the answer: the legal fiction which constructs and authorises paternity also authorises a contract between men for a daughter. It is Madeline's father who literally contracts for her marriage; it is a contract based on metaphor, that is the substitution of one thing (the father's authority, the father) for another (the husband's authority, the husband). At the climactic moment of her father's death, Madeline is completely absent from the scene enacted by four men: the man she thinks is going to be her husband, the man who will be her husband, the uncle of the man who will be her husband and, not coincidentally in this scene of triumphant coincidence, not accidentally in this scene of spectacular accident, her father. It is only after his death that Nicholas gestures away from the battle of men in which he has been engaged towards the comfortingly female presence of his sister.

The law of this father dies with him; the law of Nicholas's own father does not. The law of Nicholas senior is all the more powerful because it is feminised, because it does not appear as a law at all, but, significantly enough, as nature. Since the entire novel takes place after the death of Nicholas senior, we know him only through the traces he leaves on his family: these take the form of proscriptions (his wife, despite an active interest in matters erotic, will, the narrator assures us, not betray the husband's memory by marrying again) and prescriptions (Nicholas and Kate will keep his memory green, will return to the rural – read 'natural' – scenes of their happy childhood to raise their families). I want to make clear here that I do not think Nicholas senior's pro-scriptions and prescriptions were ever articulated as such: the prescription to imitate his father, to constitute the metaphoric or sub-stitutive metaphor on which paternity depends – it is not for nothing that Nicholas bears his father's name – is the inevitable law of pater-nity, not this quite gentle and incompetent father's individual paternal acts. Nicholas senior is one of a series of financially incompetent Victorian fathers like Mr Bennet in *Pride and Prejudice* and Dr Madden in *The Odd Women* who shape their children's lives precisely by failing to act as a father should. Their passivity none the less gets inscribed as law in the form of inheritance; their weak wills, as it were, become the law for their children. Active proscription is left to the uncle – and to the avuncular.

The avuncular

Eve Sedgwick, in her reading of *The Importance of Being Earnest*, turns from the law of the father to the law of the aunt and uncle, from the paternal to what she calls the 'avunculate' or the 'avuncular'.[2] In her reading, the avuncular suggests a possible place for the depiction of adult non-repro-ductive sexuality, for non-coercive familial relationships, for homosexual-ity that is not divorced from but an expansion upon the traditional definition of the family. Sedgwick's uncles and aunts are loud, funny, playful and ultimately benign. Her notion of the avuncular is close in spirit to its connotative popular meaning: uncles are kind. It is also tonally linked to what might be called the avuncular fantasy against which this book is written and which Mrs Nickleby, that great articulator of cultural fantasy, delineates for her daughter:

'Your uncle has taken a strong fancy to you, that's quite clear; and if some extraordinary good fortune doesn't come to you after this, I shall be a little surprised, that's all.' With this, she launched out into sundry anecdotes of young ladies, who had had thousand pound notes given them in reticules, by eccentric uncles; and of young ladies who had accidentally met amiable gentlemen of enormous wealth at their uncles' houses, and married them, after short but ardent courtships. (302)

Like all of Mrs Nickleby's fantasies, which routinely dissipate under the weight of narrative irony, this one can be thought of as a fantasy of the culture at large; it is also, of course, a fantasy which this novel ultimately cannot cordon off. With the sudden appearance of the Cheerybles and their consistently avuncular interventions in the lives of an ever-increasing adoptive family, *Nicholas Nickleby* ultimately concedes power to the very imaginings it ironises. It is vitally important, however, that the Cheerybles are not, in fact, the biological uncles of anyone but Frank. The avuncular, like the paternal, is metaphoric; natural feeling is separate from and, indeed, usually opposed to biology. The biological uncle turns the avuncular on itself, producing a spectrum of unnatural desires.

The issue at the heart of the novel is, of course, not the individual evil of a particular uncle, Ralph Nickleby, but of the authority invested in him as uncle. This authority is not, I want to point out, strictly speaking legal, although it is derived, like much of the authority in this novel, from a series of wills. As an uncle, Ralph has no legal responsibility to provide for his nephew and niece. Even more ambiguous in Victorian culture than the relation between uncles and nephews and nieces was the relation between brothers- and sisters-in-law. Attempts to describe and to codify this relationship appear in discussions about the Deceased Wife's Sister's Act of 1835, which made it illegal for a widower to marry his late wife's sister. Although this act applied only to widowers and there was no law and little discussion having to do with men marrying their dead brothers' wives, the issue of the relation between brother- and sister-in-law was a current and provocative one at the time of the writing of *Nicholas Nickleby*. The question, of course, was a sexual one: are brothers- and sisters-in-law relations, and are sexual relations between them then incestuous? I linger on this issue, this obscure law, precisely because it asks the question posed by the avuncular in this novel. Which relations are sexual and which are not? What happens when the two get confused?

One way of reframing the avuncular is as an alternative to the paternal. After all, the Nicklebys place Ralph in the position of the paternal – again through a process of metaphor and substitution – by coming to London at the beginning of the book to ask for his financial advice. On one level, the fact that Ralph is an uncle and not a father allows for the cordoning off of paternal ineptitude; the critique of the father hinted at in the first chapter becomes displaced as we come to know the evil of the uncle. The figure of the uncle, then, allows us to critique the father but to do so safely without investigating or challenging paternal law. It is because the uncle is so evil that we can participate in the Nicklebys' nostalgia for the father; at the same time we can see and critique the operations of patriarchy. The evil uncle assures the father a safe space – tellingly enough, that space is projected away from the action of the novel in both a chronological and a geographical sense. The space with which we are left for the operation of paternal law is Golden Square and the space of the avuncular.

Golden Square and its urban bleakness, its 'gardens' where nothing grows, are contrasted throughout to the more bucolic delights of the nuclear family, both as it was embodied before the death of the paternal Nickleby and as it is re-embodied in the riverside cottage with which mother, brother and sister are rewarded by the Cheerybles. If the uncle is identified with barrenness, however, he is even more importantly affiliated with specifically unnatural increase: although the novel will not name what Ralph does for a living, he clearly lends money at interest. Ralph's unprofessed but all-absorbing profession of usury links him to another figure in the Victorian avunculate: the pawnbroker, often referred to by his clients in Victorian times as 'uncle'. If the uncle does not produce children, he does produce money; if children traditionally serve as capital and labour, the uncle produces interest. His reproduction is, in the economy of the family idiom, sterile, selfish, self-reflexive: paternity, or at least the fantasy of paternity, is generous and other-directed.

Ralph's accumulation of interest and the control over others that this steady engendering of wealth makes possible parallel another and more sinister form of 'interest': his unnameable attraction to and interest in Kate. The most horrifying abuse in this novel, the one most obviously outside what we might call in collapsing the binary with which we began 'the law of nature', is of course incest. Much critical work on *Nickleby* has treated incest as the novel's empty centre, the unspoken and probably unconsummated act which none the less shapes all others. On the surface, incest is uncomfortably but definitively situated within the avuncular. Ralph's procuring of Kate for Mulberry Hawk and Lord Verisopht is, of course, a sexual act in itself: Ralph's status *vis-à-vis* the marriage plot is consistently figured as that of a procurer and a voyeur. There is more than a hint, however, of a slippage between his pandering to other men's desires and his own.

It is for this reason that so many readers associate the violations not with the infamous dinner party scene but with the scene that sets the stage for it: Ralph and Kate's initial walk through the London streets to visit Mme Mantalini:

> It was a curious contrast to see how the timid country girl shrunk through the crowd that hurried up and down the streets giving way to the press of people, and clinging closely to Ralph as though she feared to lose him in the throng; and how the stern and hard-featured man of business went doggedly on, elbowing the passengers aside, and now and then exchanging a gruff salutation with some passing acquaintance, who turned to look upon his pretty charge with looks expressive of surprise. . . . But it would have been a stranger contrast still, to have read the hearts that were beating side by side; to have laid bare the gentle innocence of the one, and the rugged villainy of the other. (187–8)

This is one of the many street scenes in *Nickleby*; perhaps it is not too much to call this one a streetwalking scene, as Ralph displays and transforms Kate's innocence through this public journeying. The 'contrast' which serves as the narrative framing for the scene is, of course, a contrast of idiom. Kate, the 'simple country girl', sees the avuncular, reads the term 'uncle' within the private lexicon of feeling; for Ralph the term 'uncle' means something literally more public. The term 'charge' in this passage is itself doubly charged; in the idiom of feeling it means something like ward or responsibility; in Ralph's lexicon it means – as everything comes to mean – simply money and the legal or extra-legal processes by which that money is made. Kate clings to her uncle because she cannot read the avuncular as sexual; the narrator begins in this scene to make a place for the sexual in the avuncular.

This making a place for the sexual within the family suggests the shifting boundary between the familial and the non-familial, a boundary both the good and the evil characters seem constantly working to break down. The other side of making strangers into uncles, as the Cheerybles do, is the making of uncles into strangers: uncles can be both uncaring and sexual. Incest, because of its lack of respect for boundaries, is contagious; it breaks down barriers of all sorts. If uncles can be procurers and rapists, then so can fathers: if the law of the avuncular can be abused, so can the law of the father – or, as we will see later, the law of the brother. Even the most sacred familial relations are not free of the erotic and the violent. In the novel's most charged throwaway line, the narrator compares Gride's situation on the morning of his wedding to that of a young man in a 'legend' who, 'not having before his eyes the fear of the canons of the church for such cases made and provided, conceived a passion for his grandmamma' (806), which brings us to women and to their multiple relational position.

Mother-in-law jokes

Every mother-in-law, to adapt the abortive children's rhyme about ducks, is somebody's mother. The mother who involves herself in the marriage plot of her children, who schemes and plans for them as Jane Austen's Mrs Bennett does, is guilty primarily of trying to become a mother-in-law. And this, of course, is part of the joke. It is a critical commonplace to notice that most mothers in Victorian fiction are dead; their death makes possible, among other things, the independent development of their children, particularly their daughters, and propels those daughters into the marriage plot. Mothers who want to become mothers-in-law do the same thing, only more messily, more loudly than their dead sisters.

One disadvantage of the mother who is alive is that she can figure in the marriage plot another way: as a sexual rival or competitor. While the narrator's reassuring comments about Mrs Nickleby's monogamy contain our fears of maternal competition with the daughters, there are several places in the text where Mrs Nickleby inserts herself into the marriage plot not as mother-in-law but as potential wife. Mrs Nickleby's structural rivalry with her daughter is sometimes a matter of pronominal slippage; when Mrs Nickleby tells Kate that Frank has been 'very attentive', Kate, of course, thinks that her mother means that Frank has been attentive to her – the pronominal slippage infects my attempts to make sense out of this – I mean that Kate thinks Frank has been attentive to *Kate*. Even when Mrs Nickleby realises that Frank is in love with Kate, she tries to get him to declare himself through a series of strategies which can only be described as flirtatious or seductive:

> At one time she was all cordiality and ease, at another, all stiffness and frigidity. Now she would seem to open her whole heart to her unhappy victim, and the next time they met receive him with the most distant and studious reserve, as if a new light had broken in upon her, and guessing his intentions, she had resolved to check them in the bud. . . . At other times . . . the worthy lady would throw out dark hints of her intention to send her to France for three or four years, or to Scotland for the improvement of her health, impaired by her late fatigues, or to America on a visit, or anywhere that threatened a long and tedious separation. Nay, she even went so far as to hint obscurely at an attachment entertained for her daughter by the son of a neighbour of theirs, one Horatio Peltirogus (a

young gentleman who might have been at that time four years old, or thereabouts) and to represent it indeed as almost a settled thing between the two families. (825)

In this series of manoeuvres Mrs Nickleby acts a part – or parts – that Kate cannot; she takes over the workings of the marriage plot, the mechanics of plotting. This work, what Austen calls the 'business' of Mrs Bennet's life, leaves the daughter free to disassociate herself from the marriage plot and, indeed, from desire itself. We should not forget, however, the inevitable alignment between the plotting mother and the plotting author, between the maternal function of getting her daughters well married and the authorial function of providing a happy ending for each of his or her heroines.

While Mrs Nickleby's other ventures into the marriage plot are not explicitly framed as competitions with Kate, they do depend on an assumed analogy between them. Sir Mulberry Hawk and Lord Verisopht know they can get to Kate through flattering the mother; they depend on the analogy between mother and daughter to ensure maternal complicity in their designs. And when the man in small clothes comes down the chimney and begins to make advances towards Miss La Creevy, Mrs Nickleby is sure that this is a case of mistaken identity and that she herself remains the object of the madman's desires. She works out her rivalry with Miss La Creevy with explicit reference to Kate: '"I am sure . . . that it's a great relief under these trying circumstances, to have someone else mistaken for me . . . and it's a circumstance that never occurred before, although I have several times been mistaken for my daughter Kate"' (744).

The scenes with the man in the small clothes, especially this second one, are scenes of humiliation for Mrs Nickleby; this humiliation is part of a narrative strategy of matrophobia which is articulated and deployed not only against Mrs Nickleby but also against other women in the novel who act younger than they are. If matrophobia is not only the fear of the mother but the fear of becoming like the mother and, more specifically, the repulsion towards the maternal body, this is a text filled, despite Kate and Nicholas's kindness to Mrs Nickleby, with matrophobia. Indeed their kindness – ironic in Nicholas's case and a symptom of Kate's patience in his sister's – itself aligns the reader against the mother and with the narrative matrophobia.

In the matrophobic world of *Nicholas Nickleby*, the sister comes to stand for the mother: not in the sense which Mrs Nickleby so desires in her comments about the similarity between mother and daughter, but in a way which highlights the fantasy of the brother, not the fantasy of the mother. For Nicholas, Kate serves as the mother he never had; more maternal, in the good sense, than her mother, Kate provides Nicholas with food, clothing and uncritical nurture. To all intents and purposes, Kate is Nicholas's mother, not, of course, his biological mother but a mother constructed by cultural norms – finally, a mother-in-law.

If fathers-in-law are suspect because they are not 'natural' fathers, mothers are suspect because they foreground biology. The novel – and Nicholas and Kate – must come to terms with the paradox of maternity: that it is constructed as asexual but that it depends for its existence on sexuality. If one is uncertain about one's father or one's paternity, one is only too certain about one's mother: psychoanalytic theory suggests that we distance ourselves from our origins in our mothers' bodies in order to become independent selves, in order to come to terms with our own sexuality. Kate and Nicholas enter the marriage plot over the body of the mother, and it is a body which the text repeatedly defamiliarises and renders grotesque. The grotesque also governs the representation of all mature women in the text; anxieties about female bodies are negotiated by what we might call, by analogy to the avuncular, the 'tantular'.

The tantular

I coin this term at a gap in the English language and use it here to describe not only 'an aunt-like role' but all female relations for which there is no name or for which there are too many. At two important moments in *Nickleby* the text seems to fumble in the naming of a female relative. It is no accident, as I meant to imply in the mother-in-law-jokes section, that these are textual locations not only of naming but of humour – and specifically of gynophobic humour directed against the female body. The novel's first scene of the tantular is a mirror-image of the one between Squeers and Snawley in which Snawley establishes himself as a father *in law*. In this second scene, Squeers is reading an 'affecting' letter from one of the children's aunts; the narrator intervenes to tell us, 'It was affecting in one sense, for Graymarsh's maternal aunt was supposed, by her more intimate friends, to be no other than his maternal parent' (159). While the pun on 'affecting' suggests acting and deceit – which, as we shall see later, although seemingly opposed to family life are always a part of it – the term 'maternal parent' insists, through its redundancy, on biology. If all fathers are fathers in law, all mothers are mothers in body; their authority derives from literal, not metaphoric, parenting. The phrase 'maternal aunt' functions as a denial of the body and of the natural tie between parent and child. The second joke which seeks to articulate a metaphorical female relation is one of many in which the narrator indulges at the expense of older women and the process of female ageing. When Miss Knag declares that she has a 'singular' 'sisterly interest' in Kate, the narrator intervenes to set things straight: 'Undoubtedly it was singular, that if Miss Knag did feel a strong interest in Kate Nickleby, it should not have been the interest of a maiden aunt or grandmother, that being the conclusion to which the difference in their ages would have naturally tended' (287). While I will discuss the problem of women's ages in more detail later on, I want to point out here that even metaphoric relations are governed by the narrator's need to arrange women according to generation and to a literal biological potential for reproduction. The 'maiden aunt' metaphor, which the narrator suggests as more appropriate, cuts across generations to suggest the presence of a 'tantular', a female relation marked of course by deceit and female competition, since Miss Knag has no real affection for Kate. While the novel does not worry about the ages of uncles in its struggle for accuracy within the familial idiom, it does divide women against each other vertically by generation.

'Aunt', like 'uncle', is an unstable term. The 'maternal aunt' of the first scene is revealed to be a mother after all; the novel reveals Uncle Ralph to have been a father all along. The collapsing of the tantular into the maternal takes one overdetermined sentence; the collapsing of the uncle into the father is a legal mystery surrounded by illegal actions; it stands, moreover, for the telos of the book.

Brothers and sisters

In a world of uncertain fathers and all-too-certain mothers; of paternal, avuncular and maternal complicity in rape; of aunts and mothers who turn out to be sexual rivals; of relationships mediated by laws, wills, documents and crime, safety would seem to reside in the brother–sister relationship. This is conduct-book writer Sarah (Mrs) Ellis's prescription for such a relationship:

> Brothers and sisters are so associated in English homes, as materially to promote each other's happiness, by the habits of kindness and consideration which they cultivate; and, when a strong friendship can be formed between such parties, it is perhaps one of the most faithful and disinterested of any which this aspect of human life presents. A young man of kind and social feelings is often glad to find in his sister, a substitute for what he afterwards ensures more permanently in a wife; and young

women are not backward in returning this affection by a love as confiding, and almost as tender, as they are capable of feeling.[3]

The relation between brother and sister serves in this explicitly developmental model as a dress rehearsal for marriage. Young men solicit their sisters' love as a 'substitute' for that of a wife, but there is no textualised account of the transition from the substitute to what we can only imagine as the real thing. The word 'afterwards', as in 'a substitute for what he afterwards ensures more permanently in a wife', papers over some difficult cultural work which is given some textual representation in *Nicholas Nickleby*. It is only one of a series of words in Ellis's description having to do with time; time itself seems to be the agent of change and transition: the move from sister to wife is a natural one unmarked by friction or resistance.

It is important, I think, that Ellis's description of the relation between brother and sister, like her – and other Victorian writers' – description of marriage, is an asymmetrical one in which the man's love is chronologically prior to the woman who is coyly 'not backward' in 'returning' his affection.

Like *Nicholas Nickleby*, Ellis's *Women of England* is deeply invested in the sincerity of the brother–sister relation and, like the novel, it opposes sincerity to the language of melodrama, specifically to melodramatic gesture. Ellis warns, in what might almost be a gloss on the novel:

> let the sister possess all that ardour of attachment which young ladies are apt to believe they feel, let her hang about his neck at parting, and bathe his face with her tears; if she has not taken the trouble to rise and prepare his early meal, but has allowed him to depend upon the servant . . . it is very questionable whether her brother could be made to believe in her affection.[4]

Ellis's warning protects the brother–sister relation from the insincerity of the outside world; according to her a good brother–sister relationship is one in which gestures mean fully, in which gesture and intention are unmediated by convention or law. This makes the relationship, in the idiom of *Nicholas Nickleby*, anti-theatrical.

Family melodrama

Despite its repeated recourse to tropes of sincerity, Kate and Nicholas's relationship also participates in the language of melodrama, a language of gesture and hyperbole. When Nicholas returns to London from his travels with Crummles's theatre company, Kate, like the hypothetical sister of Ellis's example, 'fall[s] . . . on his neck'; if she does not 'bathe his face in tears' she 'burst[s] into tears' and threatens that if he leaves her where she is she will 'die of a broken heart' (502). Nicholas's melodramatic gestures are larger, more public and more violent; like the hero he plays in his theatrical debut, he too 'quarrel[s] with [an]other' (actually many other) 'gentlem[e]n about [a] young lady'; like many a melodramatic hero he violently upholds his sister's honour and ends up making the fortunes of his impoverished family. Kate and Nicholas both speak, at moments of crisis, in lines from classic melodrama, from Kate's 'unhand me sir, this instant!' to Nicholas's 'I am the brother'. These instances of the melodramatic idiom and others too numerous to mention here should signal that something funny is going on. After all, this is a text with a fully articulated critique of melodrama and particularly of stage families.

Before we can seek to resolve that apparent contradiction, it is important to look at the opposition between family, on the one hand, and theatre, on the other. If we look hard enough, that opposition dissolves into what I am calling family theatre. The Crummleses, after all, are a family company; their relations to each other are as orchestrated as their productions on stage. Crummles's admiration of his wife and his amazement at the talents of the Infant Phenomenon are of course part of his repertoire. Similarly, the 'theatrical wedding' that joins Lillivik and Miss Petowker suggests a continuum between married life and theatre; indeed, many of the marriages in this text are performances *à deux*: the Mantalinis go through their rituals of debt, threat and attempted suicide, and the Wititterlies each have their complementary roles. Even the more benign Kenwigses stage their family dramas where literal melodramatic performances (Miss Petowker's rendering of the Blood Drinker) slip into family entertainment (Miss Petowker and Mrs Kenwigs 'settle to have a little pressing on both sides, because it looked more natural').

The performances of the minor characters might be read narratively as comic relief or characterologically as personality flaws if it were not for the infectiousness of family melodrama; even Kate and Nicholas cannot resist the novel's dominant idiom. Their deployment of melodrama should not be read characterologically either; it is not a 'flaw' that they posture, gesture and declaim – it is emphatically not a sign of their insincerity. Indeed the collapsing of melodrama and insincerity is itself a fundamental misreading of melodrama and particularly of melodramatic gesture. For a post-Stanislavskian audience, acting begins with feeling: to play, say, a frightened heroine or an evil uncle, you must first feel like a frightened heroine or an evil uncle. Melodramatic acting, with its roots in eighteenth-century theatre, has historically worked through an opposite relation between affect and gesture: as Michael Booth explains,

> The eighteenth century believed that the major passions – joy, grief, anger, fear, jealousy, etc. – expressed themselves in a universal language of gesture, movement, and facial expression. By the very assumption of these outward forms, it was argued, the actor would then feel the appropriate passion.[5]

In this account, feeling follows upon and is indeed created by gesture; gesture is not so much an expression of feeling as a catalyst for it. Melodramatic gesture cannot then be properly accused of insincerity; by referring forward instead of backward it embodies the possibility of an emotion. Strangely enough, then, this eighteenth-century style has more in common with postmodern than with modern notions of affect; like postmodern accounts of feeling, melodrama insists that emotion is constructed and celebrates that construction.

Moreover, melodrama anticipates another postmodern notion: namely, that the body is a language or a series of codes readable only because a culture has been taught to understand them. *Nicholas Nickleby* is filled with references to such codes: Mrs Crummles takes on 'a beautiful attitude of despair'; Mr Lenville gives Nicholas two looks, an upward one and a downward one, 'which . . . as everybody knows, express defiance on stage'; Mrs Kenwigs clasps her daughters 'to her bosom, with attitudes expressive of distraction'. Melodramatic gestures infect and inflect so-called 'real life', recasting our notions of the real and the theatrical. Perhaps this is nowhere more complexly rendered than in Dickens's description of Nicholas teaching Smike to act:

> As soon as he began to acquire the words pretty freely, Nicholas showed him how he must come in with both hands spread out upon his stomach, and how he must occasionally rub it, in compliance with the established form by which people on stage always denote they want something to eat. After the morning's rehearsal they went to work again, nor did they stop, except for a hasty dinner, until it was time to repair to the theatre at night. (407)

Smike, who has felt hunger all his life, must learn to enact hunger through 'compliance' with 'an established form'; 'compliance', of course, hints at a system of rules and punishment bound up in the idiom of the law. Smike's real hunger, the pain that he knows so well in real life, would be unreadable on stage, unreadable without legible marks on his body.

Dickens's own novelistic portrayals of hunger, love, anger, despair and other emotions are also, however, written upon the body. We watch Smike for signs of consumption, Kate for blushes, Nicholas for bodily expressions of anger.

Nicholas Nickleby, then, depends for its legibility upon the very melodramatic conventions it parodies in its descriptions of the theatre. The narrative melodrama becomes most visible in the context of the brother–sister relationship; here gesture seems strangely protected from narrative irony. Perhaps this is because the text is in some sense aware that family relations can also be thought of as family drama. In our post-Freudian culture the canonical family drama has only three players: the father, the mother and the (usually male) child. Dickens's novel extends the possibilities and perils of family drama to a more horizontal, and ultimately more extended, notion of family.

Two marriages

I have already suggested that the 'theatrical marriage' of Miss Petowker suggests a possible link between problematic marriages and performance. But what can we make of the presumably happier marriages with which the novel ends? Certainly, on the level of narrative, marriage serves as the ultimate 'readable' gesture, the 'established form' with which characters and authors must comply. Other endings to domestic novels are almost literally unnarratable in D. A. Miller's sense: they are beyond cultural and textual imagining.

Nicholas Nickleby does, however, briefly imagine another ending which does not comply with the marriage plot: the brother–sister idyll where Kate and Nicholas would share a cottage and grow old together. Perhaps predictably, this idyll, this narrative possibility, is never realised in the text. The marriage plot is too powerful, too efficient, to let the idyll stand for more than a perfunctory 'some weeks':

> Some weeks had passed. . . . Madeline had been removed; Frank had been absent; and Nicholas and Kate had begun to try in good earnest to stifle their own regrets and to live for each other and for their mother . . . when there came one evening, an invitation from the Brothers to dinner. (908)

Like Ellis, Dickens relies on time to transform the brother–sister relation into marriage; he is apparently even better at producing its effects: this change takes place in a few weeks and one sentence. The Cheerybles themselves rush to conclude their quasi-authorial performance: as Tim

Linkletter 'archly' reminds them, 'You didn't keep em in suspense as long as you said you would.' The speed with which what might be called the firm of the Dickens Brothers moves to complete the marriage plot foregrounds its status as form and gesture. Like the gestures in melodrama, the authorial gesture of marriage is designed to produce the very feelings it enacts.

The production of feeling through the gesture of marriage brings us to the novel's foundational gender asymmetry. Hitherto when I have spoken of the 'brother–sister plot', I have treated the novel as though its title were something like *Nicholas and Kate*; I have paid no attention to the asymmetries of narration and power which make this novel into *Nicholas Nickleby*. Predictably, Nicholas and Kate have very different relations to marriage and the marriage plot: one of these differences gets played out in terms of affect. Nicholas falls deeply in love long before he can enter the marriage plot; indeed much of the second half of the novel is devoted to redescription of his feelings for Madeline. Kate's feelings are less spectacular, less prone to expression in large gesture. If we read them at all we do so as practised readers of the small gestures of novels, not of the spectacular bodily movements of melodrama. The reason for Kate's silence, of course, has much to do with the strictures of normative Victorian femininity: young women were not supposed to feel desire for men before they were proposed to – in some accounts, perhaps not even until they were married. For women, then, the relation between marriage and affect, marriage and desire, can be described in terms of the telos of melodrama. If they were not allowed melodramatic gesture, their feelings took, or were supposed to take, the temporal *style* of melodrama. For both Nicholas and Kate, then, marriage is 'theatrical'; for Nicholas, marriage feeds on and is shaped by large gesture; for Kate, the narrative time of the marriage plot is also the dramatic time of theatrical convention.

Nicholas Nickleby ends, then, with gestures that work simultaneously as sincerity and performance, as legal and natural. Marriage brings together these supposed opposites, marries them, even, partly so that they can be revealed not as opposites but as styles that can be articulated together.

Notes

1 Scott Turow, *The Burden of Proof* (New York: Macmillan, 1992), p. 216.
2 Eve Kosovsky Sedgwick, 'Tales of the Avunculate: *The Importance of Being Earnest*', in *Tendencies* (Durham, NC: Duke University Press, 1993), pp. 52–72.
3 Sarah Stickney Ellis, *The Women of England* (1845), p. 65.
4 Ellis, p. 67.
5 Michael R. Booth, *Theatre in the Victorian Age* (Cambridge: Cambridge University Press, 1991), p. 120.

6

Nobody's fault: the scope of the negative in *Little Dorrit*

PATRICIA INGHAM

In some way negation allows us to construct new propositions out of old.
Fogelin[1]

Little Dorrit (1857) takes negation as its medium visually, verbally and structurally. Its visual framework depends on the contrast of negatives and pos-
itives. The 'Sun and Shadow' of Marseilles in the first chapter contrasts
the staring whiteness in the blazing sun with the prison darkness entomb-
ing the criminals Rigaud (alias Blandois) and Cavalletto (alias Baptist,
alias Altro). In the final chapter the newly married Clennam and Amy
Dorrit pass along 'in sunshine and shade'.[2] But the negatives predominate
in the central locations of the Marshalsea debtors' prison and Mrs
Clennam's tomb-like house. Night comes more often than day in this narrative.

In the language of a world of darkness the negative mode is the most
natural form. The only manifestation of national power and government
is dedicated to it and to the stasis it brings:

> It is true that How not to do it was the great study and object of all public
> departments and professional politicians all round the Circumlocution
> Office. It is true that every new premier and every new government,
> coming in because they had upheld a certain thing as necessary to be
> done, were no sooner come in than they applied their utmost faculties to
> discovering How not to do it. It is true that from the moment when a
> general election was over, every returned man who had been raving on
> hustings because it hadn't been done, . . . and who had been asserting that
> it must be done, . . . began to devise, How it was not to be done. It is true
> that the debates of both Houses of Parliament . . . uniformly tended to the
> protracted deliberation, How not to do it. It is true that the royal speech

at the opening of such session virtually said, My lords and gentlemen, you have a considerable stroke of work to do, and you will please to retire to your respective chambers, and discuss, How not to do it. It is true that the royal speech, at the close of such session, virtually said, My lords and gentlemen, you have . . . been considering with great loyalty and patriotism, How not to do it, and you have found out; . . . All this is true, but the Circumlocution Office went beyond it. (145–6)

The effect of this negation is to seal off the governing classes from those they are supposed to govern. The separation symbolises what the historian Crossick calls 'the absence of a public and formal conception of the social order' in Victorian liberal ideology.[3] This refusal to see social groups as interrelated suggests an anomic society with no common set of social values and standards. Only a mixture of stasis and chaos is publicly on offer. It is the state of affairs also described by Carlyle in *Chartism* (1839) in answer to his own questions 'How an Aristocracy, in these present times and circumstances, could . . . set about governing the Under Class? What should they do . . . ?' Doing something, he declares, is 'far, very far indeed, from the "usual habits of Parliament," in late times; . . . had the mischief been looked into as it gradually rose, it would not have attained this magnitude. That self-cancelling Do nothingism and *Laissez-faire* should have got so ingrained into our Practice, is the source of all these miseries.' This leaves society 'full of difficulty, savagery, almost of despair'.[4]

The Circumlocution Office, dedicated to the maintenance of this state of affairs, depends for its existence on the withholding or refusal or denial of information. This is illustrated repeatedly by Arthur Clennam's attempts to procure information that will allow him to clear William Dorrit's debts and release him from prison; and to establish the rights of the distinguished inventor, Daniel Doyce. But withholding communication is a disease that spreads widely to individuals outside the Office. Mrs Clennam withholds from Arthur the secret of his and her past; Miss Wade and Rigaud will not reveal the whereabouts of the stolen paper which tells the secret; Miss Wade will not disclose Harriet Beadle/Tattycoram's whereabouts when she runs away from the Meagles; Mr Casby will not tell what he knows about Miss Wade.

In other instances, communications offered are refused: ears are shut. Amy Dorrit will not listen to protestations of affection from John Chivery, son of the keeper of the Marshalsea lock. Her sister Fanny at first evades similar attention from Edmund Sparkler, stepson of the great financier Merdle. Other, more elaborate resistance is practised. Miss Wade, her perceptions distorted by a sense of shame, reads all positive expressions of approval as ironic statements of negative feelings of contempt and condescension; Henry Gowan, a well-connected but impoverished artist, similarly interprets any visible good in society negatively – as a sham, as not-good. When, ultimately, crucial information is conveyed it is negative: Miss Wade is not legitimate; Casby is not benevolent; Merdle is not a financial genius; Mrs Clennam is *not* Arthur's mother. A textual preoccupation with negatives is easy to illustrate.

But linguistically negation is not a simple matter. Its range is wide. Child language acquisition studies show that its uses cover statements of non-existence, of rejection, of refusal to comply and of denial. These are all semantic areas crucial to *Little Dorrit*. Each might be the figure for a central character: Amy Dorrit, Mrs Clennam, Miss Wade and Arthur Clennam respectively. But there is more to negation than this. It is complicated by the question of scope: the identification of that part of a sentence structure which is negated by the insertion of a negative form. The concept can be crudely illustrated by a comparison of two verbally similar sentences which vary as to the scope of what is negated and so differ greatly in meaning: *I do promise not to assassinate the Queen* and *I don't promise to assassinate the Queen*. The first makes a negative promise, the second makes no firm promise at all. So, in handling the negative in Dickens's novelistic language, it becomes necessary to discuss not merely its frequency but also its logical scope. The question raised by the latter is, since *Little Dorrit* is written in a negative mode, how radically is the text affected by it? How far-reaching are its negatives?

In assessing the scope of the negative in a sentence its syntax must be made clear so that the negated area can be clearly defined. The equivalent in a novel is the narrative structure/syntax. Is it linear like *Robinson Crusoe* or centrifugal like *Bleak House*? This becomes a particularly interesting question in a novel where the Circumlocution Office figures a chaotic, anomic society. The linear or picaresque structure asserts the value of a resourceful individual journeying through the obstacles society places in her or his way and largely evading or overcoming them. It is a structure potentially assertive of the importance of the individual over the social group as a mechanism for social order. The centrifugal structure on the other hand can naturally assert the value of the social group – in this period the family – over the individual to whom it gives identity and support. If either is outside the scope of the novel's negative force, then that structure is the affirmative meaning of the text.

Critics offer two accounts of the narrative structure of *Little Dorrit*. The first accepts the direction of the published title to take a female character as central, for the only time in a Dickens novel. The implication is that she gives coherence to the text; that she is in a sense its explanation. Though she never became what Collins calls a 'cult-figure', she was seen by critics like Lionel Trilling[5] as holding things together in a way that asserts the virtue that lies in the familial group centring on a woman, with all the ideological implications as to gender construction that this idea carries. On this reading she is a womanly figure who, like Cordelia in *King Lear*, affirms such values through the perfection of womanly silence and self (ab)negation.

The alternative account of narrative structure as linear derives from an earlier title used during the writing of the first three serial episodes – 'Nobody's Fault'. Four titles of chapters in the published work, 'Nobody's Weakness' (16), 'Nobody's Rival' (17), 'Nobody's State of Mind' (26), and 'Nobody's Disappearance' (28) identify Clennam as now (though not originally) the Nobody in question. Before he acquires this strange alternative name Arthur arrives in picaresque fashion from China to encounter whatever obstacles may face him after an absence of twenty years. He moves from group to group (his mother, the Marshalsea prisoners, the Bleeding Heart Yarders, the Casbys, the Meagleses, Henry Gowan, Mrs Merdle, Miss Wade, Cavalletto and the rest). Certainly in this obvious way he is the string on to which the beads of the narrative are threaded. His presence may be supposed to lend it coherence. A representative of those who think it does claims that 'Despite Dickens's title, it is not Little Dorrit but Arthur Clennam who occupies the novel's structural center'.[6] For such critics his activity as an itinerant makes him the hero. Thus, considering the scope of the negative, the reader is faced with alternative structures, one linear with Clennam as its Tom Jones, one centrifugal with Amy as its unifying centre. So, how much of each lies within the scope of the negative?

It is the linear structure which offers itself first to the reader, despite the published title. It is Arthur who initiates the narrative on his arrival in England by revealing that he has a quest. What he is searching for is something that will link his present to his past and so confirm a positive and continuous identity essential to the functioning of the individual and so of society. This continuity is initially impossible because of his recognition that a dark secret hangs over his past. In search of a revelation he visits his mother to question her about the mystery that involves her, his dead father and himself. He finds no answer but stasis as complete as that of the Circumlocution Office: a once active woman now paralysed on 'a

black, bier-like sofa' (73). The paralysis figures her refusal of communication in answer to his question as to whether his father had 'unhappily
wronged anyone, and made no reparation' (87). Is there a negative in the
past that can be made positive by atonement? Hand on Bible, she denies
him the facts and refuses to reopen a relationship:

> I only tell you that if you ever renew that theme with me, I will renounce
> you; I will so dismiss you . . . that you had better have been motherless from
> your cradle. I will never see or know you more. And if, after all, you were
> to come into this darkened room to look upon me lying dead, my body
> should bleed, if I could make it, when you came near me. (90)

This leaves Arthur disconnected from his past and from her. Far from
allowing reparation to repair his sense of self, she increases the burden of
unfocused guilt he feels obliged to carry. She breaks the supposed continuity of the linear narrative, leaving it a brittle affair, dependent only on
his moving from one group to another. In doing this he unexpectedly
encounters an important figure from his past – his sweetheart Flora (now
the widow Casby) from whom his mother forced him to separate twenty
years earlier. Apparently, like Crusoe on his island, he has cherished a
secret treasure during that time:

> In his youth he had ardently loved this woman, and had heaped upon her
> all the locked-up wealth of his affection and imagination. That wealth had
> been, in his desert home, like Robinson Crusoe's money; exchangeable
> with no one, lying idle in the dark to rust, until he poured it out for her.
> Ever since that memorable time . . . he had kept the old fancy of the Past
> unchanged, in its old sacred place. (191)

But the reality that confronts him bears so little resemblance to the past
as to make him doubt whether it ever really existed. His 'lily' has not only
become an overblown 'peony', but 'Flora, who had seemed enchanting
in all she said and thought, was diffuse and silly' (191). The sight of a fat,
posturing, garrulous, middle-aged woman not only presents him with the
negation of the Flora he remembers but causes him to wonder whether
he misread her all along: 'Was it possible that Flora could have been such
a chatterer in the days she referred to? Could there have been anything
like her present disjointed volubility in the fascinations that had capti-
vated him?' (193). This meeting, like that with his mother, breaks a link
and further erodes his sense of his own identity.

Turning from the past to the present he acquires through a chance
encounter on his journey home a new attachment to Minnie/Pet, the

only child of the wealthy lower-middle-class Meagleses. This hope for the future is, however, something he denies even to himself. Picaresque heroes may construct themselves positively out of the adventures they consume. Clennam completes his negative self-construction with the description of what might be a new love affair. As Freud points out in his essay on 'Negation', negative statements made by certain individuals may, in areas relating to strong emotions, contain a positive assertion. It is, he asserts, a way of 'taking cognizance of what is repressed'. He tells of an 'obsessional neurotic' patient who may say: ' "I've got a new obsessive idea, . . . and it occurred to me at once that it might mean so and so. But no; that can't be true, or it couldn't have occurred to me." What he is repudiating . . . is, of course, the correct meaning of the obsessive idea.' Therefore, says Freud, 'In our interpretation, we take the liberty of disregarding the negation and of picking out the subject matter alone of the association. It is as though the patient had said: "It's true that my mother came into my mind as I thought of this person, but I don't feel inclined to let the association count".'[7]

Clennam turns out to be a suitable case for this Freudian treatment through the period of his (non-)hopes that Pet Meagles (who eventually marries Gowan) will return his love. He watches unfolding events without taking part in them. His only action is to process the episode in his mind so as to preclude a positive outcome for himself. This is done by a skilful use of the subjunctive mood (of non-fact). Through this device his love for Pet is translated into something which might have happened but didn't. The four chapters already listed above are characterised by thoughts in which Clennam systematically denies his own feelings.

Visiting the Meagleses' house his thoughts run on the lines of Freud's patient's:

> Suppose that a man . . . who had been of age some twenty years or so . . . were to yield to the captivation of this charming girl, and were to persuade himself that he could hope to win her; what a weakness it would be! . . . Why should he be vexed or sore at heart? *It was not his weakness that he had imagined.* It was nobody's, nobody's within his knowledge; why should it trouble him? And yet it did trouble him. (244: my italics)

Whereas Gowan's pursuit of Pet is accepted as present fact to be described in the indicative mood, Clennam's silent pain is always treated as the hypothetical anguish of 'Nobody's Rival': 'If Clennam had not decided against falling in love with Pet; if he had had the weakness to do it; . . . he would have been, that night, unutterably miserable . . . As it was, the rain fell heavily, drearily' (254).

As the courtship proceeds before his eyes, he makes no intervention, shows no resourcefulness, except in a skilful use of negatives and subjunctives. Using the latter he converts the present into a past in which he has already lost Pet and so describes 'Nobody's State of Mind':

> if his heart had given entertainment to that prohibited guest, his silent fighting of his way through the mental condition of this period might have been a little meritorious . . . But, after the resolution he had made, of course, he could have no such merits as these; and such a state of mind was nobody's – nobody's. (356–7)

Though convinced that Gowan is a villain, he accepts the news of Pet's engagement to him without opposition and the chapter 'Nobody's Disappearance' completes his identification as Nobody: 'At that time, it seemed to him, he first finally resigned the dying hope that had flickered in nobody's heart so much to its pain and trouble' (383).

Arthur, the supposed hero who links the separate groups and figures in the text, has now established a dual identity: the minimally positive one known to the world and a powerfully negative *Doppelgänger*. Talking to Gowan, already discontented with Pet and her money, he shows signs of recognising this as he begins to fear that the man 'would always be a trouble to him, and that so far he had gained little or nothing from the dismissal of Nobody' – now capitalised as his proper name – 'with all his inconsistencies, anxieties, and contradictions' (453). Faced with this psychological burden he decides to cut short his own story. Already in 'Nobody's State of Mind' he has become 'from that time . . . in his own eyes, as to any similar hope or prospect, a very much older man who had done with that part of life' (383). No more sexual love for Nobody. Since the past and present have failed him, he negates and erases the future and at forty describes himself as an old man whose life is nearly over. He elaborates on this later to Amy Dorrit when she is already the object of a love of which he has suppressed all knowledge:

> forgetting . . . how old I was, and how the time for such things had gone by me with the many years of sameness and little happiness that made up my long life far away, . . . forgetting all this, I fancied I loved some one . . . Being wiser, I counted up my years and considered what I am, and looked back, and looked forward, . . . I found that I had climbed the hill, . . . and was descending quickly. (432)

A feature of the picaresque hero is that he should progress by luck or resourcefulness or a capacity to survive and so provide a positive narrative dynamic. This would symbolise the ability of the individual to overcome the chaos and disconnectedness of society for himself. Clennam does the reverse of this. He subverts all progress by ruling it out in advance and resists or denies all positive impulses. He makes his own bad luck. Since he cannot progress, he circles aimlessly from group to group, trapped in his own abbreviated story. He sees himself at one stage as a criminal 'chained in a stationary boat on a deep clear river, condemned, whatever countless leagues of water flowed past him, always to see the body of the fellow-creature he had drowned lying at the bottom, immovable and unchangeable, except as the eddies made it broad or long, now expanding, now contracting its terrible lineaments' (742).

Anchored by this awful burden of displaced guilt, he cannot accept that he loves Little Dorrit and so create a trajectory of desire through the narrative. He resists the knowledge that might fuel a progression until it is forced on him by John Chivery in a scene that is the apotheosis of both withholding and resisting communication. The infatuated Chivery finds it almost impossible to utter the positive statement that Amy loves Clennam, even when he wishes to comfort him for his imprisonment in the Marshalsea after the Merdle crash. Oblique hints evoke Clennam's claim not to know what he means. Chivery takes this denial as an insult to his own feelings. But Clennam only reiterates 'I don't understand it . . . I don't understand it . . . I do not understand you . . . I do not understand you' (795–6). When the truth is uttered Clennam feels he has been dealt 'a heavy blow' (797). His negative persona is damaged by the news that the woman he loves returns his love. He resists this intrusion of the positive: 'Your fancy. You are completely mistaken' (797). He finds the new state of affairs 'More bewildering to him than his misery, far' (798). His struggle with Nobody is painful and confused. Subjunctives only turn into questions, a halfway house to the positive:

> In the reluctance he had felt to believe that she loved any one; . . . in a half-formed consciousness he had had that there would be a kind of nobleness in his helping her love for any one, was there no suppressed something on his own side that he had hushed as it arose? Had he ever whispered to himself that he must not think of such a thing as her loving him . . . (799)

Nobody asserts himself with the conclusion that 'Happily, if it ever had been so, it was over' (801). Any possible projection into a happy future is thus cancelled and the present is again negatively coded with the old skill. He has already previously cut short his own life story; he can now merely add a full stop. Everything in 'its perspective led to her innocent figure' and 'Looking back upon his own poor story, she was its vanishing-point' (801–2). She is in positive terms the point at which parallel lines in the story appear to meet and in negative terms the point of complete disappearance. By this doublethink he temporarily and effectively deletes her. The effectiveness derives partly from the aptness of his description to a woman so self-effacing that her entry into the narrative is revealed only retrospectively by Clennam's question to Affery Flintwinch: 'It was a girl, surely, whom I saw near you – almost hidden in the dark corner?' Affery's reply confirms the willed invisibility: 'Oh! She? Little Dorrit! *She's* nothing' (80). In this way the linear structure is devalued by Clennam's verbal negation of the self, which should sustain its thrust. For it is upon the resilience of the self that the triumph of individualism over circumstance depends. The individual alone, so this structure declares, cannot overcome the chaos of a disordered society.

The narrator, however, claims a different meaning for Little Dorrit's self-erasure. For him it is the essence that enables her to act as the focal point of the alternative centrifugal structure. She is supposed to hold it together and so provide a model for the rest of society, strong and affirmative. As usual in Dickens's texts, the model is a familial group, assumed by domestic ideology to give society coherence, order and stability. It depends on the contemporary construction of femininity. This represents 'woman's' natural qualities, when properly schooled, as creating figures like Little Dorrit who will guard morality in general and sexual purity in particular by perfect service at the domestic hearth. Complementary masculinity then falls into place: self-interested, competitive and assertive. Most exponents of feminine value like Florence in *Dombey and Son* or Lizzie Hexam in *Our Mutual Friend* are marginalised. But for the narrator (and some critics) Little Dorrit is the unfolding centre of the text, not the vanishing point, despite her public self-effacement. Such a view is repeatedly stressed by an unrelenting strain of narratorial approval that follows her from the age of eight. Its insistence on her feminine value and radiating beneficence seem to be what lead Trilling into reading her as an overriding positive in an otherwise gloomy narrative. However, he too clearly had doubts to suppress: 'Her untinctured goodness does not appall [*sic*] us or make us misdoubt her as *we expect it to do*' (my italics).[8] If this Clennam-like suppression is avoided, the negatives in the text surface and reveal that their scope is extensive. They are both verbal and, crucially, structural.

Little Dorrit on this reading is the prime example in Dickens's work where a negative subtext reveals the contradictions which underlie both the contemporary construction of gender and the ideological representation of the family unit as an ideal. The latter ideal, if evoked as valuable, would remove the responsibility for a chaotic inequitable society from the governing classes. The negation of the idea offered by Arthur's wanderings that individual progress is the answer to social ills could be a preliminary to the eulogising of the family in that role. However, the eulogy itself is so dismantled as merely to provide yet further evidence of the state of affairs represented by both the Circumlocution Office and Arthur's (non-)success. The dismantling is effected by the inclusion within the text's negative scope of two areas essential to the affirmation of the value of the family group: Little Dorrit's own character and her influence over others.

The central and apparently positive constituent of Little Dorrit's character, like that of other nubile girls in Dickens's novels, is disinterested kindness. This quality is identified in Sarah Stickney Ellis's contemporary conduct books for women as the one for which 'woman' is 'most valued, admired and loved'. Female examples of it in the past are identifiable because they overcame 'every impediment that intervened between them and the accomplishment of some great object', provided that it 'was wholly unconnected with their own personal exaltation or enjoyment, and related only to some beloved object whose suffering was their sorrow, whose good their gain'.[9]

For Dickens this is 'femininity' in its perfect form, and Little Dorrit embodies it. Femaleness was something different: a biologically determined set of characteristics of a non-intellectual, intuitive, reactive kind. Unchecked, these produced unreasonable, emotional, demanding and often insanely garrulous monsters like Mrs Nickleby, Mrs Skewton, Mrs Joe Gargery, Mrs Wilfer, and others.[10] The magic ingredient that turns the female into the feminine is the very one that Little Dorrit has in abundance: plasticity when faced with the needs of others. Upon this the creation of feminine value depends. That is why Little Dorrit is to be so highly valued: because she is able to transmit her power from the centre to others, in the form of long-sufferingness, compassion and affection. She is supposedly able to do this because she stands in a parental role to those around her. It is significant that for Dickens a 'true' woman, as opposed to a female in her natural state, is necessarily 'a mother'. Not in a biological sense, for such people either by typical carelessness die prematurely or, lacking plasticity, turn to self-nurturing like Mrs Clennam. 'True' motherhood is most frequently found in innocently nubile girls who achieve it in a surrogate fashion which also turns them into virginal wives. In the nineteenth century the frequency of maternal death in or soon after childbirth often led to a daughter or a wife's sister taking on the chief domestic burden of a family. As Davidoff and Hall point out,[11] strong bonds frequently grew up between widower and housekeeper. She became a kind of substitute mother and partner. Hence the necessity, given the incest taboo, for a prohibition on marriage with a deceased wife's sister, which persisted until 1907.

This is, in practical terms, the kind of role that Little Dorrit moves into after the early death of her mother. Narratorial eulogy wraps it round with a particular air of sanctity. Her ability to nurture is supposedly demonstrated by arranging, under great difficulties, for her sister Fanny to train as a dancer, and by finding her brother Tip/Edward a string of jobs to lose and a chance of emigration to throw away. Most of all, the satisfaction of her father's needs is figured as religious: 'She filled his glass, put all the little matters on the table ready to his hand, and then sat beside him while he ate his supper. Evidently in observance of their nightly custom, she put some bread before herself, and touched his glass with her lips' (122). Her domestic services take on a sacramental tone that in a mid-Victorian text is faintly blasphemous in giving her even a minor priestly role.

However, Little Dorrit – like Clennam – has an alternative persona and, like his, it functions through verbal negation. In this guise she may be conveniently referred to as Amy. As Little Dorrit she possesses, for instance in the Clennam house, what some regard as a Cordelia-style capacity for womanly silence. As the secret Amy she shows herself a perfect liar – often by not speaking. Even her skill in meeting her father's domestic needs is surpassed by her skill in pandering to his obsessions. Thanks to her, he is able to sustain even in the debtors' prison a fantasy that he has a special dignity and social standing, and a special respect and affection from those around him. Silence is here her chief tool. She does not tell him the truth about his son's distressing profligacy, nor her own grinding work as a seamstress, nor Fanny's as a dancer. She conceals the fact that the devoted brother Frederick, whom he has absent-mindedly ruined, is earning a meagre living in a shabby theatre orchestra. As Godmother of the Dorrit Mafia she manipulates all those involved into colluding with the code of silence. With his fantasy secure, Dorrit can also be prevented from knowing that his moderate comfort is achieved at the expense of others. He can wound well-meaning onlookers like Chivery and Old Nandy without paying any penalty. Little Dorrit's capacity in this particular area of concealment, denial and lying by silence makes the genteel Mrs General's skill in 'varnishing' look amateurish. All the latter does, to much derision from the narrator, is to 'varnish':

> Mrs General was not to be told of anything shocking. Accidents, miseries, and offences, were never to be mentioned before her. Passion was to go to sleep in the presence of Mrs General, and blood was to change to milk and water. The little that was left in the world, when all these deductions were made, it was Mrs General's province to varnish . . . she dipped the smallest of brushes into the largest of pots, and varnished the surface of every object that came under consideration. The more cracked it was, the more Mrs General varnished it. (503)

Amy goes beyond this to deny the existence of realities altogether. Further, there are indications that Amy's disinterested kindness is not so disinterested after all. The subservient relationship to her father takes on a new implication when on three occasions she displays sexual jealousy towards him. These occur when the question of a sexual partner for one or other of them occurs. In the first she is mildly harassed by the attentions of John Chivery who has become infatuated with her. She regards her father's encouragement of him and hints to her to string him along as little less than pimping. Her 'O dear, dear Father, how can you, can you, do it!' (261) is more suited to a wife than an unmarried daughter. Similarly, she responds inappropriately to the lover's kiss that Clennam gives her after the news that her father is to be free and inherit a fortune. She reacts as though he were her father: 'As he kissed her, she turned her head towards his shoulder, and raised her arm towards his neck; cried out "Father! Father! Father!" and swooned away' (465).

A later episode makes it plain that Amy will brook no rival for her father's affections when he becomes enamoured of his daughters' companion. Fanny Sparkler (née Dorrit) is against a match with Mrs General on financial grounds but Amy refuses to recognise what is happening. The truth is forced on her only by her father's suggestion that she should do as Fanny did:

> 'Amy . . . your dear sister, our Fanny, has contracted – ha hum – a marriage, eminently calculated to extend the basis of our – ha – connection, and to – hum – consolidate our social relations. My love, I trust that the time is not far distant when some – ha – eligible partner may be found for you.' (669)

The expression of her repugnance is characteristically minimal but its motive is very different from Fanny's. It springs from a jealous sense of betrayal, cast in the hypothetical subjunctive mood that Clennam favours, and denied (like Clennam's love) even as it dawns: 'If the thought ever entered Little Dorrit's head that night, that he could give her up lightly now in his prosperity, and when he had it in his mind to replace her with a second wife, she drove it away. Faithful to him still, . . . she drove the thought away' (670). There is a literal truth in the idea that Mrs General would be William Dorrit's second wife, replacing Amy's mother; but the girl's own phrase 'replace her' referring to herself makes *her* the faithful wife who is to be displaced. The insistence on driving out, even the thought of another wife, indicates a picture too horrible to contemplate of herself supplanted, betrayed, in effect divorced.

Sadoff argues away the incestuously sexual overtones of these scenes. She reads William Dorrit as a mere surrogate from whom in due course love is transferred to the 'real' lover, Arthur Clennam:

> When I use the term 'incestuous' with regard to Dickens' fathers and daughters, I mean they create a community built on familial structures of desire yet also purified of desire and perfected through idealized love. The figure of the daughter draws to herself the father and the lover – the father as lover, the lover as father – and also redeems the desire that calls this incestuous structure into being.[12]

This is all very well as an abstract argument but is vitiated by the fact that, by contrast with Amy's jealousy of her father, her relationship with Clennam in the text remains sexless on both sides.

He thinks of her always as 'Little Dorrit' not Amy, his 'delicate child', his 'adopted child'. After Chivery's revelation that she loves him he has to try in his 'stunned' state, to transform her in his mind into a normal adult woman: 'He had been accustomed to call her his child, and his dear child, and to invite her confidence by dwelling upon the difference in their respective ages, and to speak of himself as one who was turning old. Yet she might not have thought him old' (798). His struggle is to free himself from an ingrained practice of denial and from any sense that sexual love for her would be paedophiliac. Her response to him involves an easier transition to the role of mother. When they become recognised lovers while he is imprisoned in the Marshalsea, 'drawing an arm softly round his neck, [she] laid his head upon her bosom, put a hand upon his head, and resting her cheek upon that hand, nursed him as lovingly, and G O D knows as innocently, as she had nursed her father in that room when she had been but a baby, needing all the care from others that she took of them' (825). She *has* grown into an adult woman but simultaneously turned into the mother he has never had, not a sexual partner. Her image of him has long been visually negative and non-sexual: 'the shadow' whom, in her tale to Maggie, the 'tiny woman' treasures in a secret place until she dies and it disappears (339–43).

Her long nursing of her father, on the other hand, is figured as less 'innocent' than this. Its eroticism is irrevocably crystallised in the image of Amy as 'the Roman Charity'. This was a familiar icon in pictorial art from the Renaissance on and frequent in the Victorian period (plate 6). Its most cited classical source is evidently Valerius Maximus.[13] It appears when William Dorrit throws a fit of histrionic self-pity to evade the consequences of his mean part in the Chivery affair. His daughter responds heroically:

> There was a classical daughter once – perhaps – who ministered to her father in his prison as her mother had ministered to her. Little Dorrit, though of the unheroic modern stock and mere English, did much more, in comforting her father's wasted heart upon her innocent breast, and turning it to a fountain of love and fidelity that never ran dry or waned through all his years of famine. (273–4)

What Amy offers her father is endless mother's milk, in the apotheosis of her nurturing function. The circumlocutory nature of the reference to breast feeding, the appeal to the respectability of classical authority and the hypothesising inference of 'perhaps' cannot take away from the shock of a young female endlessly suckling an adult male.

The eroticism of such an action is evident from the pictorial version of the scene such as plate 6. The disturbing effect in the novel is increased by the dual identity of the woman. Amy is woman enough to suckle a man but Little Dorrit is 'a child'. Her pre-pubertal appearance is implicit in her nickname which has been so insisted upon, even by Clennam. She is 'little' or 'slight in appearance/asexual-looking': 'A woman, probably of not less than two-and-twenty, she might have been passed in the street for little more than half that age' (93). This early description has been constantly kept in mind by her name and pinned to the masthead of the novel as its title. It has been underlined also by the contrast with the overgrown and retarded woman Maggie, child in mind but woman in body. There is a moment when the text registers an unexpected awareness that what the narrator is offering as the stable centre of the centrifugal structure, an example of the womanly ideal perfectly achieved, is monstrous in her duality. This is when a prostitute, who has mistaken Amy for a child out too late at night and Maggie for her careless nurse, realises her mistake as she kisses the child's' cheek: '"Why, my God!" she said, recoiling, "you're a woman!"' (218). This horrified reaction to a child–woman is structurally negated and dissociated from by being put into the mouth of a non-person, a prostitute. But the gratuitousness of the episode, which has no bearing on any event in the novel, enforces a reading of the passage as emphatic: a Little Dorrit/Amy, a child–woman, is a manifest horror. This is only further compounded by the canonisation of the child–woman as the Roman Charity. No eulogy from the narrator can disguise the doubly incestuous nature of the scene in which the female figure is indistinguishably daughter, mother and lover.

These confusions, rather than a sense of social order and fulfilment for individuals, speak out through the centrifugal structuring of the text. Consequently the proper roles of the other members of the Dorrit family are unclear to them. Tip and Fanny oscillate between submissiveness towards a parent and resentment towards a younger sister. Tip becomes overdependent on the maternal figure of Amy, Fanny strikes out to find an independent identity for herself in another family group by marrying the rich idiot, Edmund Sparkler. There is no positive outcome for either: Tip deteriorates into a moral/physical illness through which his younger sister nurses him to an early death; Fanny finds that, after the Merdle crash, her rich idiot is no longer rich. The wealth and social position, which were dependent on it, have disappeared. She must live for ever, bosom by bosom, with Sparkler's hated mother, Mrs Merdle, and 'fight it out in the lists of Society, sworn rivals' (874). Total destruction, however, is the lot of the father/child/husband in whom Amy has invested most of her nurturing milk. Thanks to her careful protection of his fantasies which transformed his prison life into a kingdom, William Dorrit cannot deal with the reality of life even in the shape of untold wealth and social prestige. With her help, he accommodated to prison life, but he cannot accommodate to the real world. His public breakdown at a Roman banquet is a retreat into the old comfortable fantasy as Father of the Marshalsea. Amy too has accommodated herself to the domestic life in prison with her father. She takes no pleasure in the sights of Italy and speaks of a terrible 'home-sickness' (610), presumably for the only home she has ever known, the debtors' prison. The ruins of Rome are for her 'ruins of the old Marshalsea – ruins of her own old life . . . ruins of its loves, hopes, cares, and joys' (671). When her father's delusion scatters the Roman dinner party, she returns with relief to that narrow and crippling past. Its destructive nature is evident as it kills both William Dorrit and that other dependent child of hers, his brother Frederick. Yet she is at ease with herself as grieving mother in a way that she never was as a jealous partner to a rich man.

Deßinne et Gravé par J.Saunders, d'après l'original de Carlo Sirani, dans la Galerie de Son Altesse le Prince Borboerville. 1799.

CHARITÉ ROMAINE.

6   Andrea Sirani
'Roman Charity' (1630–42), engraving by J. Saunders (1799)

Thus Little Dorrit/Amy herself is ultimately a contradictory and disruptive figure who sustains nothing more than a sadly dysfunctional family. The narrator, however, averts his eyes from the fact and insists on a conventionally eulogistic reading of her. Like the linear structure, the centrifugal one based on the family group as a model of social harmony is negated, not merely verbally but structurally through the workings of the plot. Consequently the scope of the negative in *Little Dorrit* is comprehensive: both solutions to a society without order or common values are put under the sign of negation. No reading of society can be found that offers hope for its reform. Only the chaos remains, as the pictorial summation of the novel on the cover of the serial number of the text shows (plate 7). This presents a jumbled procession of characters shambling in a pointless and disorderly circle. *Little Dorrit*, far from offering a picture of the family as a harmonious and benign unit on which society can model itself, reveals it – despite narratorial approval – as manipulative and destructive.

The counterview to conventional domestic ideology was expressed by a few individual voices even in the mid nineteenth century. One was that of Florence Nightingale in a work written in 1852 that appeared only as an interlude in a religious volume privately printed in 1860. In it she says outrageously:

> The family? It is too narrow a field for the development of an immortal spirit . . . The family uses people, *not* for what they are, not for what they are intended to be, but for what it wants them for – for its own uses . . . This system dooms some minds to incurable infancy, others to silent misery.[14]

In Dickens's text the conventional view and the outrageous are in conflict. It is only under the safety of negation that the contradictions inherent in the contemporary construction of gender are exposed. This is the first step in a popular mainstream writer towards a recognition of what ideology suppresses. The image of the Circumlocution Office makes a strong assertion that a society consisting of governors and underclass is necessarily anomic. The only alternatives offered by the text as possible counters to this view, individualism or family groupings, are invalidated by the negative form in which they appear. This invalidation is of course covert and surreptitious. As Freud says in his essay on 'Negation', 'the function of judgement is not made possible until the creation of the symbol of negation has endowed thinking with a first measure of freedom from the consequences of repression'.[15] In the language of *Little Dorrit*

No. III.   FEBRUARY.   Dex 280 PRICE 1s.

LITTLE DORRIT

BY

CHARLES DICKENS.

WITH

ILLUSTRATIONS BY H. K. BROWNE.

LONDON: BRADBURY & EVANS, BOUVERIE STREET.

AGENTS: J. MENZIES, EDINBURGH; MURRAY AND SON, GLASGOW; J. M'GLASHAN, DUBLIN.

☞ The Author reserves the right of Translation.

7   Hablôt Browne ('Phiz')
cover design for the serial (1856)

115

negation releases underlying contradictions in the construction of gender and social class that offer some such freedom of expression.

Notes

1 R. J. Fogelin, *Wittgenstein* (London: Routledge & Kegan Paul, 1976), p. 139.
2 See E. Showalter, 'Guilt, Authority and the Shadows of *Little Dorrit*', *Nineteenth Century Fiction*, 34 (1979), 20–40.
3 G. Crossick, 'From Gentlemen to Residuum: Languages of Social Description in Victorian Britain', in P. J. Corfield (ed.), *Language, History and Class* (Oxford: Blackwell, 1991), p. 160.
4 T. Carlyle, *Selected Writings*, ed. A. Shelston (Harmondsworth: Penguin, 1986), pp. 197–8.
5 P. Collins, *Dickens: The Critical Heritage* (London: Routledge & Kegan Paul, 1971), p. 357; see L. Trilling, *The Opposing Self: Nine Essays in Criticism* (London: Secker & Warburg, 1955).
6 M. Squires, 'The Structure of Dickens's Imagination in *Little Dorrit*', *Texas Studies in Literature and Language*, 30 (1988), p. 50.
7 S. Freud, The Standard Edition of *The Complete Psychological Works of Sigmund Freud*, vol. 19 (London: Hogarth Press, 1961), p. 235.
8 Trilling, *The Opposing Self*, p. 65.
9 S. S. Ellis, *The Women of England, Their Social Duties and Domestic Habits* (London: Fisher, 1839), pp. 63–4.
10 See P. Ingham, *Dickens, Women and Language* (Hemel Hempstead: Harvester Wheatsheaf, 1992).
11 L. Davidoff and C. Hall, *Family Fortunes: Men and Women of the English Middle Class, 1780–1850* (London: Hutchinson, 1987), p. 346.
12 D. Sadoff, *Monsters of Affection: Dickens, Eliot and Brontë on Fatherhood* (London: Johns Hopkins University Press, 1982), p. 55.
13 M. Meisel, *Realizations: Narrative, Pictorial and Theatrical Arts in Nineteenth Century England* (Princeton: Princeton University Press, 1983), p. 305.
14 F. Nightingale, *Cassandra*, ed. M. Stark (New York: City University Feminist Press, 1979), p. 37.
15 Freud, *Complete Psychological Works*, vol. 19, p. 239.

7

Literary careers, death, and the body politics of *David Copperfield*

LINDA M. SHIRES

This same Man-of-Letters Hero must be regarded as our most important modern person.

> Thomas Carlyle, *On Heroes and Hero Worship*[1]

Capital is dead labor which, vampire-like, lives only by sucking living labor, and lives the more, the more labor it sucks.

> Karl Marx, *Capital I*[2]

But often, in the din of strife
There rises an unspeakable desire
After the knowledge of our buried life.

> Matthew Arnold, 'The Buried Life'[3]

In his most autobiographical fiction, written directly after what John Forster has termed the 'turning point'[4] of his career, Charles Dickens exposes the killing fields and the self-commodification of bourgeois literary authorship. This chapter examines death, bodies, and literary careers in *David Copperfield*, within a context of three other 1849–50 texts, Alfred Lord Tennyson's *In Memoriam, A. H. H.*, Charlotte Brontë's 'Editor's Preface' to the 1850 edition of *Wuthering Heights* and her 'Biographical Notice of Ellis and Acton Bell', included in the reissue of her sister Emily's *Wuthering Heights* and Anne's *Agnes Grey*. I will propose a way of thinking about biography, secrets, established authorship and specific literary texts in the mid-century marketplace. In the ensuing analysis, moreover, I hope to avoid equalising or opposing personal and cultural elements; instead I shall emphasise negotiations at differing levels between them.[5]

As many critics have noted, David Copperfield opens his tale by holding out a possibility with an unknown outcome: 'Whether I shall turn out to be the hero of my own life, or whether that station will be held by anybody else, these pages must show' (49). Dickens's phrasing serves to open a gap, both epistemological and interpretative.

Perhaps, most interestingly, the gap opens a space for irony and questioning. The gap suggests that although there may be a hero of David's life other than David, there may, in fact, be no hero at all. Even more radical, there may be no 'I' at all – indeed the gap itself may become the hollow ground of the text. *David Copperfield* will count the cost of self-division serving as the ground of heroism. At the same time, it will do everything possible to establish that 'I' as heroic. For what is at stake, finally, is the heroism of Charles Dickens, author, before his readership.

'Subduing my desire': biography, secrets, narrative[6]

Reproducing the split between the exterior and interior selves character-istic of bourgeois subjectivity, especially acute in the nineteenth century and after, most biographers locate a secret at the heart of their subject's life, which they delight in claiming as somehow 'responsible' or 'explana-tory' for much else that occurs in that life. Whatever it is – incest, indul-gence in pornography, homosexuality, pederasty, epilepsy, clinical depression, class shame or a major loss of some kind – it is said to shape and colour the life. When the secret of an author's life is revealed, it is often traced to or made identical with what is termed an originary trauma. As John Sutherland recently pointed out, competing biographies of Tennyson, of Larkin, or other literary lives, often seem to rise or fall on how the public responds to the nature and importance of the secret chosen.[7] We similarly gauge the power of celebrities of the 1990s, such as Michael Jackson, O. J. Simpson, the Royal Family or Woody Allen, according to how much a secret exposed and magnified by the press can damage or leave intact a figure's popularity. Locating such secrets in a famous life, whether they are actually defining experiences or not, helps sales, since narrative enjoyment is structured by the discovery and reve-lation of secrets. The public thrives on being entertained with such secrets. Perhaps even more to the point, many people tend to ground their own lives in terms of originary traumas and defining moments in order to express mastery over them, provide drama to ordinary lives, or explain failures and success.

But what of Dickens? In writing the life of Dickens, it is difficult for a biographer to avoid a shaping provided by the author himself in the auto-biographical fragment and subsequent novel. It has also proven standard for critics to note that Dickens introduces unwieldy personal materials in his Christmas books, especially *The Haunted Man*, and works through these materials in the novel which best articulates them and which persistently inscribes the name and persons of himself and his family – from DC/CD initials reversed to Mr Micawber to Mr Dick.

Yet in his recent study *From Copyright to Copperfield* Alexander Welsh astutely redirects our attention away from the blacking house incident as originary trauma. Nor does Welsh adopt Steven Marcus's revisionary explanation that the blacking house incident itself is a screen memory for some earlier trauma. Welsh does not support the notion of originary trauma, which he believes to be an incorrectly imposed, 'modern' idea. Indeed, he reacts against the grain of the Victorian/modern hermeneutics of secrecy and surveillance.[8]

Instead, Welsh asks us to regard authors' lives, indeed all lives, in terms of stages of development punctuated by what Erik Erikson terms 'mora-toria'.[9] By way of example, Welsh labels Dickens's late twenties and early thirties a moratorium of protracted adolescence. He argues that, although Dickens was overjoyed by his unprecedented early success, the popular author still betrayed doubts about his vocation. The moratorium was a time of confusion before a reaffirmation.

During the early 1840s, a time of personal upheaval, Dickens took leave of Chapman & Hall for a year, made a trip to America, shopped for another career upon his return and wrote a seemingly differently motivated prose with the Christmas books. Welsh argues that the three novels *Martin Chuzzlewit*, *Dombey and Son* and *David Copperfield* 'repre-sent a beginning-over-again as a determined novelist'.[10] The period is unique in Dickens's life up to that time for its inward reflectiveness. The moratorium comes to an end with Dickens's new assurance about his vocation, expressed in his personal correspondence.

Welsh's resistance to a Victorian hermeneutics of secrecy and his capacious view of a life – its hesitancies, displacements, reorganisations, blockages, redirections – causes him to 'deny that a trauma in childhood provides the best ground for biographical criticism'.[11] Referring to Dickens's twenties and thirties, Welsh argues that the incident at the blacking warehouse 'explains relatively little about this epoch; the journey to America, I believe, explains a great deal'.[12] I would agree.

Yet I am not convinced that the experience in America, when a young and famous English author was stripped of what he felt was his identity in order to be treated as a mythic figure, is that fundamentally different in its emotional resonances from the painful warehouse incident, in spite of all the differences of actual situation. This is not to argue that one or the other incident was more important in Dickens's life. Nor is it to claim, with Welsh, that a model of 'development' or 'stages' is more correct than a model of 'originary trauma', since I don't believe in either except as heuristic devices. Rather, I'm stressing that a certain kind of situation has predictable effects of crisis for Dickens's psyche and that such a situation is not only personal but cultural. Dickens clearly felt as exposed in America as he had felt in the blacking warehouse window. Celebrity status in America, as much as working in a factory window, dehumanised him.

Two of the same elements figure in both episodes: the effacement of what Dickens understands as a private self and a loss of class hierarchies. So while I agree with Welsh at many points of his argument, I would argue for a theoretical model even less purely psychological and more responsive to interactions between the psyche and social life. Such a model would consider how interior states (psychic or social, i.e. nineteenth-century domestic – in both private and national senses) are reoriented towards and by a changing public sphere. How would this work?

I cannot argue that the social sphere determines Dickens's psychic responses by insidious infiltration and possession or through a common root of identity. In other words, I am not setting up an opposition (psyche versus culture) or an affinity (psyche and culture). Rather, events in Dickens's early life and sets of his feelings, desires and needs, whether erotic, aesthetic or economic (including their repressions, displacements, condensations), bear important if shifting relations to social changes in the early- to mid-Victorian period.[13]

In particular, Dickens is conditioned to react (and overreact) to situations which appear to threaten or do threaten a sense of his value as a self. What causes such anxiety is certain kinds of display, humiliation and specularity. Dickens is born at a time when the understanding of selfhood undergoes an important change, a change which is both an effect and producer of capitalism, the introduction of the notion of personality. A cult of personality differs in at least four ways from the eighteenth-century view of natural character through its emphasis on appearances, the potential instability of personality, the private realm as something which must be secret, and self-consciousness as inhibiting a spontaneity of expression.[14] Dickens's mid-Victorian psyche has been threatened by being exposed to the marketplace, at home and abroad, both its surveillance and its specularity. Yet Dickens's very sensitivity, both conscious and unconscious, to the challenges of these combined social and social/psychological changes does not merely have negative effects in his life.

The trip to America, which both Welsh and Marcus rightly emphasise, forced Dickens to confront a nation which, unlike England, paid lip-service to individuality while promoting homogenisation. Although Dickens blamed American democracy for levelling distinctions between people, thereby encouraging homogenisation, it is clear that he bought into one of America's own myths: the classless society. What Dickens noted and fervently criticised, what so forcefully struck him, that the private life of the individual was being made more and more public and politicised, was not, however, a trait of nationhood or political system. In America, Dickens thought he saw a 'new kind of social authority' which, in Marcus's words, could 'convert the private self into public property and into something wholly externalized – an externalization accompanied by reckless, aggressive self-inflation'.[15] The self which Dickens saw emerging from this social situation proved to be a substanceless, un-critical, mass-produced, monotonous self. He feared becoming such a self. The trip to America thus seems to have fomented a crisis in Dickens about identity and spectacle which, given his hard-won success, impinged for him on issues of vocation and career.

To be estranged or feel dehumanised is for Dickens to be dead. The dead boy infant in *David Copperfield* is, like so many Dickens children, a self-image. The story of David is the narration of the self which survives to tell the tale. As author of the reparation fiction, Dickens needs to play the roles of survivor and agent of death, instead of the role of victim. In his construction of David Copperfield, a writer who undergoes a school-ing, regeneration and a self-disciplining, Dickens attempted doubly to counter what he labelled as defective in America. Having been unable to complete his autobiography, Dickens let the novel form serve as the (replacement) site for his (transmuted) revelations. Further, he constructs a hero who, moderately famous, wishes to be known for himself, not his works.

Yet the Victorian literary marketplace preserves a substantive, indi-vidual self no more than the 1990s rock, sports, political or film world. Not only are values of individualism inimical to a capitalism becoming more and more corporate-minded, they are inimical to dominant English social ideologies of the 1840s and 1850s. The problem Dickens perceives in America thrives in 1840s England, in spite of all the national differences. In a capitalist marketplace, commitment translates to aggres-sion, competitiveness and sales as much as to humility, self-reflection and substance. It would be Dickens's problem for the rest of his career to modify the relationship of the individual to the hostile society in which she or he lives, to support substance while critiquing institutions, in the hopes of somehow retaining moral standards. It would also be his problem to retain his popularity and increase his profits. To this end, the personal itself would have to become a commodity.

'I tell my secret? No, indeed, not I': self-expression, death, and authorial turning points at mid-career and mid-century[16]

The problem of the authorial self at mid-century – its desire to remain private and substantial yet its necessary commodification as spectacle – finds its way obliquely into fiction and poetry. Personal experience is externalised, dramatised if you will, as a strategy of control. This externalisation can bar as well as invite the sharing of what is presented as private. As in the Christina Rossetti poem 'Winter: My Secret' (1857), quoted above, flaunting the private does not necessarily mean revealing much, nor does it necessarily mean that there is much to reveal.

In characterising the emergent form of English fiction in 1848, Raymond Williams reminds us of the 'new stress on the imperatives of intense personal experience'.[17] But he carefully qualifies this generalisation by stressing that intense personal experience is often confided as if a secret. Moreover, he argues, the 1840s fiction does not ask us to identify with a single point of view but demands complex seeing. As part of its narrative structure, it thus sets up thick barriers which must be got through before any secrets can be revealed. Matthew Arnold's poem 'The Buried Life' (1852) may serve us as characteristic of an important strain of poetry at mid-century, what we could call the poetry of blocked sincerity. The barriers represented here are high and deep as well as thick. In Arnold's poem the speaker strongly desires to reveal what he names as 'the buried' and 'genuine' self, but complains that he can rarely do so. That self is bounded by limits, imposed and self-imposed, which dehumanise and even mechanise it most of the time. Moreover, neither willpower nor close friends can access what Arnold views as a 'genuine' core.

I have been noting characteristics which mark some of the most important fiction and poetry of mid-century. One could make a similar argument about non-fictional prose. However, I want to turn to a similar problematic of concealment/revelation at work in an author's life and career to indicate one intersection of cultural history, personal history and career history where meanings and strategies for practice get negotiated.

At some point in a mid-century Victorian writer's early career – it is most likely to occur when he or she is in the thirties or forties – depending on how long adolescence has lasted, on the career to date and on health and life-expectancy, an author writes a document which deals with deeply personal matters. Characteristically, the author reconceals them to stake out more social authority. These counter-Wordsworthian texts, which nevertheless depend heavily on a Wordsworthian matrix, work overtly to end a phase of life which is, from a sober, adult perspective, the least reputable, most disturbing and most narcissistic: childhood and adolescent subjectivism. Such a text may not always succeed in closing off the strong emotions of this or a prior period of life, or it may not be the only text deployed to do so in a career, but it works both to reveal and reconceal a set of strong emotions, usually those of private passion. For Charlotte Brontë, Alfred Lord Tennyson and Charles Dickens, the 'Editor's Preface' to the new edition of *Wuthering Heights* (1850) and the 'Biographical Notice of Ellis and Acton Bell', *In Memoriam, A. H. H.*, and *David Copperfield* perform this function.

In becoming notable public personae, that is: a woman novelist with whom all others had to reckon because of the achievement of *Jane Eyre*, a poet of tremendous talent worthy of consideration for Poet Laureate, and the most popular male novelist of his time, these three authors came face to face with a dilemma. Brontë, Tennyson and Dickens construct themselves and authorship, in the late 1840s and 1850s, somewhat similarly in this private/public regard. To different degrees and with different understandings, they note that the dramatisation of private life necessary to authorship in the nineteenth century means to them a concomitant loss of substance.

Further, all three try to reconcile public with private selves when confronted with loss: the deaths of Charlotte's sisters and the unpopularity of *Wuthering Heights*, Arthur Hallam's death and the death of substance noted by Dickens on his trip to America. These events are seemingly so very different in quality from each other that I will have more to say about each.

Appearing in 1850, the 'Preface', the 'Biographical Notice', *In Memoriam, A. H. H.*, and *David Copperfield* take part in a general trend which Carl Dawson has termed 'self-discovery through memory'.[18] All speak from a well of loneliness and melancholy. They evoke and silence passion, produce dead bodies and lead their readers to socialised, moderate views.

All function importantly in the further professional rise of Brontë, Tennyson and Dickens.

Charlotte Brontë, as Currer Bell, writes the 'Biographical Notice of Ellis and Acton Bell' and the 'Editor's Preface' to the 1850 revised, second edition of *Wuthering Heights* and *Agnes Grey* in order, ostensibly, to boost sales. She also stakes ground for herself as a mature, responsible editor of her dead sisters' works and as the shaper of their careers, as well as of her own. Referring to their use of pseudonyms, and the resulting confusion when critics attributed all their texts to one person, Charlotte Brontë tries again, as she did in the preface to *Jane Eyre*, to set the record straight. The obscurity surrounding the names Ellis and Acton, she says, should be done away with: 'The little mystery, which formerly yielded some harmless pleasure, has lost its interest; circumstances are changed. It becomes, then, my duty to explain briefly the origin and authorship of the books written by Currer, Ellis, and Acton Bell.'[19] In combining mystery, confusion of identity, origin and authorship, Brontë indicates more than she intends. For this explanation and the 'Preface' which follows serve to cover over and thus banish a secret which Charlotte cannot acknowledge publicly, or it would seem privately – namely, her incestuous feelings for her brother Branwell, a set of volatile emotions that Emily, in particular, had tapped, captured and memorialised in the lives and deaths of Catherine and Heathcliff.[20]

The surviving Brontë child is thus impelled to delete, edit, and construct her family of writers as she constructs the mid-Victorian audience to want them, rather than as they were. She claims and probably feels good intentions; that she is also one of the shrewdest and most ambitious female authors of her time can be gleaned from reading her revealing letters to her publisher's reader W. S. Williams.

In these documents of 1850 Charlotte works over the corpses of her family, promoting herself as distinctively different from her sisters in temperament, interests and authorial expertise. She deletes mention of Branwell entirely, except by a veiled reference to Acton's having witnessed 'near at hand and for a long time, the terrible effects of talents misused and faculties abused' (BN, 317). But she encodes the child Branwell and her moral revulsion to what he had later become in her evocation of the dead Heathcliff: 'unredeemed' from the moment the 'swarthy thing' falls out of the 'bundle' till the time when 'Nelly Dean found the grim, stalwart corpse laid on its back in the panel-enclosed bed, with wide-gazing eyes that seemed "to sneer at her attempt to close them"' (EP, 322). For Charlotte, a dominating male power, which seems to haunt her with its unrepentant gaze, is best remembered as a dependent child or a corpse.

Charlotte constructs herself as a wise, reasoning interventionist, who could not persuade her sisters to modify their outrageously unsoftened writings. 'The choice of subject', she writes of Anne's *The Tenant of Wildfell Hall*, 'was an entire mistake. Nothing less congruous with the writer's nature could be conceived' (BN, 317). Exposed to brutalities, Acton brooded over what she saw and, explains Charlotte, 'it did her harm' (BN, 317).

In order to dismiss the fierce emotions of arrested childhood and adolescence, explored in *Wuthering Heights*, Charlotte infantilises her sister Emily as an unambitious, reclusive, inexperienced author who, 'stronger than a man', was yet 'simpler than a child' (BN, 318) and who required an 'interpreter' (BN, 319) to convey reasonably to the Victorian audience the 'secret power and fire' of her brain (BN, 318). In her 'Preface', Charlotte sides with those characters whom she perceives to be mature and realistic: Lockwood, Nelly Dean and Edgar Linton. She successfully blinds herself to Lockwood's immaturity, Nelly's desires, and Mr Linton's stupidity as she condemns the 'creations' Heathcliff and Catherine, 'spirits so lost and fallen' (EP, 321). 'Having formed these beings', she writes, my sister 'did not know what she had done' (EP, 321).

In her discussion of the unrepentant Heathcliff on his way to 'perdition' (EP, 321), Charlotte reveals the key to the 'Preface'. She speaks primarily of Emily as a writer, but she shifts her rhetoric to the general in her discussion of writers and their materials: 'The writer who possesses the creative gift owns something of which he is not always master – something that at times strangely wills and works for itself' (EP, 322). It is precisely this 'something' which resists 'rules and principles' and which, startlingly Bertha-Mason-like, 'laughs' and 'refuses' its 'subjection' any longer. 'You', says Charlotte addressing herself, her dead siblings and other artists, as much as her readers, must be passive and take what praise or blame ensues. Charlotte knows that she speaks of an unconscious force; she knows, too, that the great Brontë subject is that of the interior life. However much she knows and feels this inspirational power, though, Charlotte strives to re-subdue it in her quest to write the reception of her sisters' novels and the authority of her own career.

In *Wuthering Heights* Emily Brontë tapped into the affectual centre of Charlotte Brontë: the desire for sustained intimacy with her male sibling. It was an intimacy that lay at the root of her imaginative and emotional life and it would be replaced, with Branwell's attraction to other women and his death, by a hatred of the male as well as by a continued desire for heterosexual, incestuous intimacy. Why does the poor sales record of *Wuthering Heights* force the issue for Charlotte? I would argue that

Charlotte both overidentifies with Emily and allows her as chief rival. Thus she must acknowledge her powers at the same time that she denigrates aspects of Emily's imaginative accomplishment by making her into an unschooled, unconscious adolescent. To be sure, Emily is also a stand-in for Branwell, towards whom Charlotte feels guilt and hatred, as well as desire.

Charlotte Brontë's use of her sisters' deaths in her promotion of their work, her malformation of their texts in the name of reason, and her ambivalent love/hate relation to the passionate male imagination and body differs significantly from Tennyson's attraction to dead bodies. In his early poetry, death is often associated with the female and her yearning for complementation by a sexual male, as in 'The Lady of Shalott' where viewing the male proves destructive. In its more positive association, death appears in the early poems as a Lethean forgetfulness, a drowsy mindlessness associated with the feminine, imagination, and/or with nature, as in 'The Grasshopper' or 'The Kraken'. But by the 1840s death and dead bodies assume more literal importance in the poet's work.

Elsewhere I have argued that dead or weakened male bodies often provide the *raison d'être* of a Tennyson text. The greatest of these texts is surely Tennyson's elegy for Arthur Henry Hallam who died suddenly in 1833 at at the age of twenty-two while visiting Vienna with his father. Tennyson had met Hallam at Cambridge five years earlier, where they had become inseparable friends. Perhaps even more importantly, Hallam had helped Tennyson recover from the harsh critical responses to *Poems Chiefly Lyrical* in 1830. In his role as poet-critic, Hallam had promoted Tennyson's work in a long review, published in *The Englishman's Magazine* in 1831. The review provided a conduit for Tennyson in which he and his intimate friend attempted to educate the Victorian readership to a new voice and style in poetry. Lastly, Hallam was engaged to Emily Tennyson, the poet's sister, and would soon enter the family. Confidante, editor, promoter, future brother-in-law, Hallam had been the repository of some of the most vulnerable feelings Tennyson bestowed in his early life. By winter 1833, he had undoubtedly commenced the lyrics which would eventually get collected for *In Memoriam, A. H. H.*, published in 1850.

In 1850, a banner year, Tennyson also married and was awarded the Poet Laureateship. With *In Memoriam* Tennyson invokes the homoerotics of his youth, as he mourns his friend. Hallam's father, who likened the poem to the love sonnets of William Shakespeare, resisted the greatness of the sequence. Tennyson himself wished his identity, and the identity of Arthur, to remain secret, as if he understood that critics, just like Hallam's father, would easily misinterpret, misunderstand and devalue the feelings

and memories he treasured. Thus, Tennyson published the poem anonymously, referred to his dead friend by initials only, and denied that the
elegy was a personal poem. Insiders knew the author and subject, but the
public would not have immediately known, except that Tennyson's name
was attached to the poem by a printer's error.

Besides Hallam, other dead men surface in the elegy. They are present
as part of the psychosexual deconstruction of identity which prompts and
structures the poem. The speaker adopts differing personae – he is a wife
who has lost her husband, he is a mother who has lost a son. Undoubtedly,
Tennyson believes that invoking these other losses universalises the experience. It substantially adds to the charged feelings centred on the death of
his friend. Moreover, the difficulty and challenge of representing a
male/male relationship in the mid-Victorian period is highlighted in the
poem precisely through the gender slippage involved in the speaker's
assumption of the roles of brother, lover, maiden, child, husband and wife
to Hallam.

But the feminine must be excluded, by ideological necessity, for the
male to be properly masculinised. To this end, the speaker calls on Time
and Sorrow (as wife) to school him against private fantasies about relations with the dead (sections 117 and 59). He renounces the female per-
sonification of knowledge which submits all to Desire in favour of
Wisdom which helps her know her place (114).

That dead male bodies act as sources of creativity for Tennyson seems
undeniable. Tennyson is both fascinated by and revolted by a sick or dead
man because it stimulates thoughts of vitality and weakness, mental and
physical, which marked Tennyson's life and his family's life. He had
watched brothers and father afflicted with epilepsy, madness and alco-
holism. He himself had received shock treatments for depression and was
given to trances. On the night of his father's death, he slept in the paternal bed, hoping to receive a ghostly visitation. It is arguable that for
Tennyson the whereabouts of the spirit of a dead man is just as important as the fact of cold flesh.

Certainly, the dead body of Hallam functions not as something which
must be discarded or used as a prop for self-affirmation, as the corpses
figure in the Brontë 'Biographical Notice' and 'Preface'. Indeed, we
rarely see the corpse of Hallam in the poem. It takes years of writing,
many lyrics and several textual burials to get Hallam buried, so much does
Tennyson desire his continued presence. Rather, Hallam must be loved,
reverenced and translated into an image of Godhead who can continue
to inspire (animate) Tennyson. Celebrating his friend even as he buries
him, Tennyson also bids farewell to his youth – to its type of poetry and

to its overcharged, male, erotic attachments. One might argue that this mode of farewell, so characteristic of Tennyson's early lyrics, becomes an ingrained habit in the 1850s as Tennyson works through his farewell to a childhood hero in *Ode on the Death of the Duke of Wellington* and his farewell to an early love, Rosa Baring, in *Maud*.

Yet while it may start a pattern, *In Memoriam* also marks the end of a phase of Tennyson's authorial career – that in which his poetry is regarded as merely mellifluous and unreflective and that in which death assumes a different face. In his long elegy for Hallam, Tennyson exposes his affectual centre – love for the male – but masks this gesture triply: by writing when Hallam is dead, by claiming that the poem is not personal and by translating secular love between man and man into religious devotion and into the heterosexual marriage of Edmund Lushington to Tennyson's sister Cecilia. Thus he makes palatable to himself and to his audience the homoerotic feelings of his youth. He does not, however, kill off the affectual centre of his writing as Brontë feels compelled to do out of decency. Male bonding, love for Arthur Hallam and fascination with the dead or dying male continue to be the major sources of his creativity.

Brontë, through non-fictional prose, and Tennyson, through elegy, work to reconstitute a fragmented bourgeois subjectivity. Both gain authorial strength through confronting the dead bodies of others. Both use those bodies as sites for displacement to discard aspects of their younger selves. Furthermore, they ground their increased authority on narratives of wholeness which accord fully with the ideologies of the male literary club they had joined.[21] They eliminate threats to that wholeness: sororal rivalry, incestuous love, homosocial love, all of which which appear to them to threaten their acceptance and promotion by their readerships. If Charlotte Brontë and Alfred Lord Tennyson ritualistically (and perhaps only temporarily) bury the others who were actual collaborators of their earlier imaginative productions, Emily, Anne, Branwell and Hallam, Charles Dickens confronts a different dilemma. Because he is writing a fiction, he must first create the stand-ins he then slays. Even more than the other texts considered, *David Copperfield* foregrounds the struggle and cost of gaining authority through discarding and decorporealising bodies.

'The writing being between us': decorporealisation, signification and bodies as objects in *David Copperfield*[22]

In the mid-century, mid-career text by Dickens which performs the same function as those by Brontë and Tennyson, we find an even greater emphasis on the double process of market culture: the disembodiment of individual persons and the embodiment of visible types of persons. In other words, we find a hollowing out of individual subjectivity. We also find a supplement of bodies used as objects: female bodies, lower-class bodies, corpses.

In both his 'Preface to the First Edition' (1850) and 'Preface to the "Charles Dickens" Edition', Dickens links his writing to the labour of embodiment and the process of physical reproduction. In the first preface, Dickens confides that he 'feels as if he were dismissing some portion of himself into the shadowy world, when a crowd of the creatures of his brain are going from him forever'. In the later preface Dickens goes so far as to call the book his 'favourite child'. Likewise, referring in organic metaphors to the serial method as producing an affective intimacy with readers, Dickens still bemoans a loss. The logic of self-possession and embodiment contends with the logic of abstraction and disembodiment. For Dickens's possession of David, which he is now giving up, also indicates a part of the self as property. This notion is reproduced in the text, of course, with the tale of David's caul and its economic fortunes. The market for which Dickens writes turns out to be a market in persons as much as in books. He is selling a part of himself.

The discourse in the prefaces appears to be direct and engaging, but it restrains a full telling because of a mental division in the author. Dickens states: 'My mind is so divided between pleasure and regret – pleasure in the achievement of long design, regret in the separation from many companions – that I am in danger of wearying the reader whom I love.' The statement opposes pleasure in labour with the labour market. Dickens hesitates to bother the reader with private affections or secret yearnings; after all, he maintains, 'all that I could say . . . I have endeavoured to say in it [the text]'. In other words, all authorial passion and desire, all labour and loss – all embodied impregnation and birth – are to be received in textual form.

Alongside the authorial hesitancy to confide in the reader directly, we find a strong flavour of censorship about this 'Personal History / Experience and Observation / of / DAVID COPPERFIELD / the Younger / of Blunderstone Rookery' with the subtitle: 'Which He Never Meant To Be / Published on Any Account' (my slashes reproduce the title as appearing on the wrapper of the first edition). The hesitancy about sharing private feelings and the unintentional aspect of the history provide barriers which the reader is forced to leap. Landing happily on the other side of them, with confidence that we are in possession of something beyond usefulness, but something of surplus value, we settle in.

129

Within the text itself, with the story of Richard Babley, Charles Dickens encodes not only a joke of self-inscription and a celebration and critique of youthful imagination but also a narrative about production and censorship. Mr Dick, suffering from the betrayal and absence of a just, paternal authority, is obsessed with Charles I, the sovereign overthrown and decapitated in 1649. Dick writes an appeal to the Lord Chancellor or any other Lord who can save him from his identity crisis. He cannot complete the appeal. It is quite right, as many critics following Stanley Tick have noted, that Charles Dickens identifies with the obsessional musings on family abuse of Mr Dick and that Mr Dick identifies with the self-absorption of Charles I (or I, Charles Dickens). Yet the headless king bears a greater meaning than self-absorption in a book about decorporealisation, a book where houses can appear like persons and persons can appear like ghosts, and where a scarred face can look like 'the writing on the wall' (353).

The problem set up by the figure of Mr Dick is that of the novel's project: how does one put back together a head and a body? The break between head and body represents a seventeenth-century split which is refracted somewhat differently in the nineteenth century. How can one re-attach reason to feeling and genuine life? Or, how can one feel whole again in a culture that has experienced the upheavals of both revolution and evolution? Moreover what Aunt Betsey refers to as an 'allegory' (Chapter 14) carries further meanings: how can one put together pieces of writing, some of which are constantly flying away, 'published' on a kite? This is not merely a joke about serial publication, or the craziness of writing, but an issue of engendering the self through writing. With the increasing failure of belief systems, the artist has lost the power of the paternal, authorising word. Dick is one of the 'lunatic figures for the writer who call into question self-origination' and the entire notion of embodiment in/through writing.[23] The only way finally to alleviate the split of Mr Dick is to provide him with two desks, one for public copying and one for private obsessional writing. The solution reproduces the split, but awards equal space to regulatory methods.

In the case of Charles I, the head of the sovereign has been cut off. Between the public staging of a murder spectacle in 1649, when the head of government is decapitated, and the writing of autobiography in 1849, the de-realisation of the body has occured. Individual bodies in *David Copperfield* are not displayed as exhibitions, whether whole or suffering. We have no severed heads, blindings, ugly corpses. The mark of violence is a facial scar. Dickens's textual bodies are reduced to parts; they brush against each other's surfaces; they lock eyes for an interplay of looks; they are classified as types, or killed off.

More specifically, *David Copperfield* uses bodies as part of its censoring devices. For the middle-class subject to succeed, David or Charles Dickens, he must excise passions. In part, then, *David Copperfield* writes the drama of the body's proximity to, but separation from, passions, whether hunger, sexuality or human relations of other kinds. These must be displaced or ended because they are all inextricably entwined with the economic, a connection which appears to degrade the subject. Uriah Heep, then, whose body is close to David except that they are 'divided by writing', when they first encounter each other at Mr Wickfield's, peeps over the paper to stare at his double.[24] He must be stereotyped and spurned. His body is ugly to touch and to see with its 'clammy hand' (281) and 'cadaverous face' (275) and 'sleepless eyes . . . like two red suns' (278). Driven by greed and economic necessity, Heep represents the male artist who must copy linguistic authority in order to gain class (social) authority. Likewise, he must steal Agnes away from her father and from David in order to gain full class position. He represents the vampiric element in David's own rise to success.

The women who fall, Emily and Martha Endell, act as further comments on the author's complicity with the marketplace. As persons who sell their bodies, they represent a hybrid form of physical capital, artefactual and physical at once, capital with a human face.[25] Other women in the text such as Rosa Dartle are emblematised as writing itself. She has experienced male violence unleashed on her body when Steerforth throws a hammer at her. For those who view her, her body becomes reduced to a mark, so that she is 'all edge' like a pen. Moreover, her identity has been reduced to a mark. When David sees her portrait minus the scar, he needs to restore it. Thus he becomes the oppressor like Steerforth and the writer who defaces and deforms out of a perverse misogynistic pleasure. Rosa's corporeality is transformed to signification, a disfigured face which will sell on the open market only if packaged with other figures.

Agnes, on the other hand, becomes an icon seemingly separated from physical desire and the marketplace. Yet of course she is merely the reverse of a coin, a human face which becomes capital. For David displaces on to her his passion and his self-censorship. She will regulate him so that he may succeed in the market, just as Wisdom regulated Tennyson. It has been argued, most persuasively by Mary Poovey, Alexander Welsh and Julia Swindells, that David is utterly dependent on Agnes in two related realms: as a guide to mature emotional life and as a reader of his writing.[26] The David we see last is unable to sustain emotional maturity or material success without Agnes; moreover the disciplining of his heart deprives him of desire.

Although the book does not trust male desire or domestic concord, with its series of failed relationships and marriages, it rewards David with happiness in the figure of Agnes, a replacement for the domestic felicity he once enjoyed with his mother. Thus the text serves the mid-Victorian ideology of the repression of transgressive passions into domestic harmony.

Even as Agnes serves David as his prime reader, so too she represents the ideologies of Dickens's readership. Thus Dickens's readership can take the place of his ideal mother – providing the chance for intimacy he can take for granted while he performs before her safely. The figure of Agnes serves to resolve anxieties of Dickens's about being received as a dehumanised celebrity. As mother, wife and audience, she knows David for himself through her understanding eyes.

The two men with the greatest energy in the novel and the two who elicit the greatest positive and negative passions from David, as aspects of his younger self, must be eliminated for this relationship with Agnes to occur. Steerforth and Uriah are, of course, rivals of David's for the love of Emily and Agnes respectively. But beyond that, both are implicated with David in homoeroticism. This is evidenced not only by physical contacts between Uriah and David but also through David's love for Steerforth, even in death. Both elicit from David a confused set of emotions which he cannot understand or regulate.[27] Finally, they both represent the author's vampiric tendencies – preying on women's bodies and men's dignity, stealing energy and sexual secrets.

It is significant that Uriah goes to jail where he becomes a model prisoner. For one suspects that he will soon be back at a copyist's desk searching for ways to improve himself at the expense of others. This element of ambition retains its freedom in the text although it is incarcerated. It is the residue of the struggle, the body which 'remains at the edge of visibility, troubling the space from which it has been banished'.[28]

'The savor of death'[29]

In the final paragraph of the text, David Copperfield calls forth his own death scene. He does not mean the death of his soul, which he has awarded already for safekeeping: 'Oh Agnes, Oh my soul' (950). But he calls forth the death of his consciousness and body, stressing the moment of loss of the substantial and corporeal, the final transition from subject to object. In this last moment, he hopes that he may savour what he thinks of as a woman's healing gesture, the awarding of presence and absence at the same time. 'May thy face be by me when I close my life indeed; so may I when realities are melting from me like the shadows [i.e. the characters whose destinies I have just narrated] which I now dismiss, still find thee near me pointing upward!' (950). As David closes his narrative and as we close the book, he describes a place of transition but also of continuity – he hopes to be located in a gap of presence and absence where one mixes with the other instead of where one is separated off from the other. This is the gap which opened up at the start of the narrative, with the constitution of the 'I' as both subject and object. David's hope for fusion has fuelled the project of the entire narrative, but language has been unable to produce it. His hope, the illusory dream of all liberal subjects, is that, out of the ultimate moment of absence, he may finally achieve presence to himself and for others. Yet at the end, intimate death seems more substantive than a life marked by estrangement.

Dickens, the author who professes his difficulty in letting go, seems able to end the text if it ensures a loving response from the audience he professes to love. The narrative strategy he adopts, consciously or unconsciously, does not guarantee such a response from his audience. However, it does promise a continuation of the authorial hope for a positive response, the very condition which makes the subject Charles Dickens at mid-career in mid-century continue to write at all.

Notes

1 Thomas Carlyle, *On Heroes and Hero Worship and the Heroic in History* (Lincoln: University of Nebraska Press, 1966), p. 155.
2 Karl Marx, *Capital: A Critique of Political Economy*, vol. I, tr. Ben Fowkes (New York: Random House, 1977), p. 2.
3 Matthew Arnold, 'The Buried Life', in Walter Houghton (ed.), *Victorian Poetry and Poetics* (Boston: Houghton Mifflin Company, 1968), p. 447, ll. 46–8.
4 John Forster, as quoted in Alexander Welsh, *From Copyright to Copperfield* (Cambridge, Mass.: Harvard University Press, 1987), p. 7.
5 For a stunning critical analysis of current practices of ideological critique, see Mark Seltzer, *Bodies and Machines* (New York: Routledge, 1992). Seltzer finely demonstrates how the 'romance of the market' has nostalgically and anachronistically entered many discussions and theories of capitalism, literary texts, separate spheres, and modernity generally. For a judicious critique of two major critical works on the marketplace and commodities, see Catherine Gallagher, 'Review Essay', *Criticism*, 29.2 (spring 1987), 233–42.
6 *DC*, 950.
7 John Sutherland, lecture at CUNY 'Victorian Lives' conference, May 1993.
8 Steven Marcus, *Charles Dickens: From Pickwick to Dombey* (New York: Norton, 1965).
9 Alexander Welsh, *From Copyright to Copperfield: The Identity of Dickens* (Cambridge, Mass.: Harvard University Press, 1987). Welsh admires Erikson's use of 'moratorium' to explain Luther's 'marking time' before arriving at a 'crossroads' of life. See Erik Erikson, *Young Man Luther: A Study in Psychoanalysis and History* (New York: Norton, [1958] 1962), p. 43 and pp. 99–104.

10 *Ibid.*, p. 13.

11 *Ibid.*, p. vii.

12 *Ibid.*, p. 12.

13 I am indebted here to Seltzer, *Bodies and Machines*, especially pp. 126–9.

14 For a working out of such differences, see Richard Sennett, *The Fall of Public Man: On the Social Psychology of Capitalism* (New York: Vintage, [1974] 1978) pp. 152–4, but all of Chapters 7 and 8 are particularly relevant.

15 Marcus, *Dickens*, p. 244.

16 Christina Rossetti, 'Winter: My Secret', in Houghton, *Victorian Poetry*, p. 602, l. 1.

17 Raymond Williams, 'Forms of English Fiction in 1848', in Francis Barker *et al.* (eds.) *Literature Politics and Theory, Papers from the Essex Conference 1976–84* (New York: Methuen, 1986), p. 7, although the entire essay is germane.

18 Carl Dawson, *Victorian Noon: English Literature in 1850* (London: Johns Hopkins University Press, 1969), p. 161.

19 Charlotte Brontë, 'Biographical Notice of Ellis and Acton Bell' and 'Editor's Preface' to the new edition of *Wuthering Heights* (1850), in William M. Sale, Jr and Richard J. Dunn (eds), *Wuthering Heights* (New York: Norton, 1990), pp. 312–22. Quotation from p. 313 of 'Biographical Notice'. Future references are coded with BN and EP before page numbers.

20 See U. C. Knoepflmacher, *Wuthering Heights, A Study* (Columbus: Ohio University Press, [Cambridge, 1989] 1994) pp. 5–10, 112–13, and, on Branwell, 99–105.

21 For Charlotte Brontë's courting of that male club, see the Preface to the 1847 edition of *Jane Eyre* and her letters to J .S. Williams. One can trace a growing rivalry with the most prominent male authors in her field as Brontë gains professional ground. For instance, she confides to Williams on 29 March 1848 that 'many doors of knowledge which are open for you are forever shut for me' and 'I must guess and calculate and grope my way in the dark, and come to uncertain conclusions unaided and alone where such writers as Dickens and Thackeray, having access to the shrine and image of Truth, have only to go into the temple'. See Clement Shorter, *Charlotte Brontë and Her Circle* (New York: Dodd, Mead & Company, 1896), p. 410. For a discussion of Victorian literary professionals, including Thackeray, see Julia Swindells, *Victorian Writing and Working Women* (Minneapolis: University of Minnesota Press, 1985).

22 *DC*, 278.

23 See Diane Sadoff, *Monsters of Affection* (Baltimore: Johns Hopkins University Press, 1982), p. 45. Many other Dickens critics make similar observations, but Sadoff's discussion is especially useful for its clarity and fullness of detail.

24 Steven Connor explains the mutual engagement of intense looks as a Lacanian mirroring relationship. See the discussion of *Great Expectations* in *Charles Dickens* (New York: Blackwell, 1985), Chapter 6.

25 Seltzer, *Bodies and Machines*, p. 63. Also see Helena Michie on decorporealisation: *The Flesh Made Word: Female Figures and Women's Bodies* (New York: Oxford University Press, 1987).

26 Mary Poovey, *Uneven Developments* (Chicago: University of Chicago Press, 1988). Poovey's chapter on *David Copperfield* and the professional writer illustrates how fidelity of the Victorian woman 'guaranteed legitimacy and neutralized the effects of the internal division essential to this paradigm of identity – whether the identity was of the individual, the family, or the nation'. Poovey also argues persuasively that 'this view of woman depends on normalizing assumptions about class'. See p. 115.

27 D. A. Miller has argued for homoerotic feelings being put in the service of social control through domestication. A father who cannot love his friends in public, say, may love his sons in private. See his essay on *The Woman in White* in *The Novel and the Police* (Berkeley: University of California Press, 1988). Miller's chapter on *David Copperfield*, which I discovered late in the writing of this essay, also treats secrets, subjectivity and interpretation. We differ in the use of this material.

28 Francis Barker, *The Tremulous Private Body: Essays on Subjection* (New York: Methuen, 1984), p. 63.

29 This phrase is adopted from a poem by Boris Vian, quoted by Michel de Certeau in *The Practice of Everyday Life* (Berkeley: University of California Press, 1988), p. 193.

8

Past and present: *Bleak House* and *A Child's History of England*

JOHN LUCAS

In January 1830, Thomas Macaulay published in the *Edinburgh Review* an essay which soon established itself as the credo for a newly confident Whig interpretation of history. Macaulay's ostensible subject was Robert Southey's recently published *Sir Thomas More: or, Colloquies on the Progress and Prospects of Society* in which, as might be expected of that radical-turned-reactionary, Southey mourns the gradual degeneration of England from 'the golden days of good Queen Bess' to the nadir of the present and the emergence of 'the manufacturing system'. There is nothing, Macaulay assures us, which Southey hates so bitterly as he does this system. 'It is, according to him, a system more tyrannical than that of the feudal ages, a system of actual servitude, a system which destroys the bodies and degrades the minds of those who are engaged in it. He expresses a hope that the competition of other nations may drive us out of the field; that our foreign trade may decline; and that we may thus enjoy a restoration of national sanity and strength.' But Southey fails to produce a single fact to support his views; and much of Macaulay's essay is given over to showing that there are facts which lead to a very different conclusion.[1]

I don't intend here to follow through Macaulay's argument. It is suffi-cient to note that his essay is a passionately eloquent account of the ben-efits of what used to be called the industrial revolution; and that he batters his opponent with remorseless details of the benefits of 'the manufactur-ing system' Southey so detests. The following passage, in which he begs to differ from Southey's belief that the labouring classes were 'better fed three hundred years ago than at present', is a fair example of Macaulay's strategy.

We believe that he is completely in error on this point. The condition of servants in noble and wealthy families, and of scholars at the Universities, must surely have been better in those times than that of wealthy day-labourers; and we are sure that it was not better than that of our work-house paupers. From the household book of the Northumberland family, we find that in one of the greatest establishments of the kingdom the servants lived very much as common sailors do now. In the reign of Edward the Sixth the state of students at Cambridge is described to us, on the very best authority, as most wretched. Many of them dined on pottage made of a farthing's worth of beef with a little salt and oatmeal, and literally nothing else. This account we have from a contemporary master at St. John's. Our parish poor now eat wheaten bread. In the sixteenth century the labourer was glad to get barley, and was often forced to content himself with poorer fare. . . . The advice and medicine which the poorest labourer can now obtain, in disease, or after an accident, is far superior to what Henry the Eighth could have commanded. . . . We do not say that the lower orders in England do not suffer severe hardship. But, in spite of Mr Southey's assertions . . . we are inclined to doubt whether the labouring classes here really suffer greater physical distress than the labouring classes of the most flourishing countries of the continent.[2]

The onward and upward march of (English) civilisation being effectively proved, Macaulay ends his essay with the confident, even knowing assertion that future progress will not be achieved by

the omniscient and omnipotent State, but by the prudence and energy of the people. . . . Our rulers will best promote the improvement of the nation by strictly confining themselves to their own legitimate duties, by leaving capital to find its own most lucrative course, commodities their fair price, industry and intelligence their natural reward, idleness and folly their natural punishment, by maintaining peace, by maintaining property, by diminishing the price of law, and by observing strict economy in every department of the state. Let the Government do this: the People will assuredly do the rest.[3]

Reading this, it is easy to understand why Lord Acton should have said that Macaulay's essays provided 'a key to half the prejudices of our age'.[4] Southey's contention for a nation in decline is dismissed by a combination of powerful rhetoric and an impressive array of facts. This is important. Macaulay means to use facts not as Mr M'Choakumchild does in *Hard Times* but in order to bring the past alive. For this he was greatly dependent on his reading of Scott. As J. W. Burrow remarks, 'in recommending, in his essay on History, a new kind of historiography, Macaulay was speaking of things which are separable though intelligibly related: of a justification for "social history" and of the availability to the historian of the novelist's discoveries in rendering reality'.[5] And Burrow goes on to suggest that Macaulay's dramatic re-enactment of the nation's past lends potency to his particular view of that past.

But Macaulay's view of the past is determined by and determines his view of the future, and in 1830 the future was looking good. Twenty years later it looked far less satisfactory. We know that Macaulay was shaken by the events of 1848 and much else besides. But perhaps the first clouding of his view came in 1836. In that year William Lovett gave and then published his *Address to the Working Men of the United Kingdom by the Working Men's Association*. Here, Lovett sets out what will become the Chartist demands: 'FREE PRESS, UNIVERSAL SUFFRAGE, the Protection of the BALLOT, ANNUAL PARLIAMENTS, EQUAL PRESENTATION, and PROPERTY QUALIFICATIONS for members'. Lovett comes to these demands by way of arguing that the poor can expect no justice from those who control power. 'Under a just system of government there would be but one party, *that of the people:* whose representatives would be actuated by one great motive, *that of making all the resources of our country tend to promote the happiness of all its inhabitants.*' Lovett then sketches in the kinds of men who make up Parliament at present, their professions and occupations, in order to show that they cannot be trusted to promote such happiness.

> Is the MANUFACTURER or CAPITALIST, whose exclusive monopoly of the combined powers of wood, iron, and steam, enables him to cause the destitution of thousands, and who has an interest in forcing labour down to the *minimum* reward, fit to represent the interests of working men?
> Is the MASTER, whose interest it is to purchase labour at the cheapest rate, a fit representative for the WORKMAN, whose interest it is to get the most he can for his labour?[6]

In most of his historical writing, including the essay on Southey, Macaulay sees England as radically altered by two key events of the seventeenth century: the execution of Charles I, whom he clearly detested, and the 'glorious revolution' of 1688. Between them, these made possible the emergence of England as a modern nation state, its constitution able to hold out the promise of freedom and happiness to all. In this important sense Macaulay is a constitutional historian. But freedom and happiness are matters that belong just as much if not more to social history, a distinction that might not have occurred to Macaulay in 1830 but which

Lovett's Address was bound to draw to his attention. And how could confident assertions about the parish poor having wheaten bread and so being better off than their Elizabethan counterparts, be they never so factually based, cope with Lovett's equally confident assertion, equally based on fact, that the manufacturer could cause the destitution of thousands? Capital's own most lucrative course might very well not flow in channels that would prove of benefit to the people.

That is certainly what the people Lovett was addressing thought. Hence the events of 1839, which most historians agree is as near as England came to revolution; hence, the repeated protests and petitions of 1842 and 1848.[7] These are the most obvious upheavals of a period during which the view of a smoothly unrolling future all but disappeared. For some – perhaps for many – these upheavals were the foreshocks of a coming cataclysm. Much writing of the period therefore engages with the question of how to prevent that from happening, or how to turn it to account; and this in its turn requires a re-thinking of English history. *Can the future be read from the past, and if so how?*

One of the crucial issues, perhaps the most crucial of all, was the monarchy. Macaulay and the Whigs took for granted that the execution of Charles I did away with arbitrary power. Others were not so sure. Neither were they at all sure that the appeal of Charles wasn't still being assiduously promoted by some who were set against the emergence of a modern democratic society. Hence Browning's play *Strafford*, which was performed in 1837, the year of Victoria's accession to the throne, and whose major argument is that it's a mistake for people to put their trust in kings. Patrick Brantlinger sees nothing particularly political in this and I will not here repeat arguments which I have used elsewhere to dispute the plausibility of his view.[8] I will, however, note that one of W. J. Fox's *Lectures: Addressed Chiefly to the Working Classes*, published in four volumes in 1845, is called 'On the "Form of Prayer, With Fasting," For the Thirtieth of January – "Martyrdom of King Charles the First"'; and that Fox's angry wit is aimed at those members of the establishment whom he sees as doing their best to re-align monarchy and Church so as to enhance the power of both.

Fox's main target is undoubtedly the Church of England and in particular a number of the Church's 'occasional services'. These are remarkable, he says, for 'the base servility of their politics'. There may be only a few such services, but 'small as is their number, the events are chosen with marvellous infelicity. One is the deliverance of James the First from the Gunpowder Plot; another for what is called the Martrydom of Charles the First; and a third for the restoration of his successor, Charles the Second.' And precisely what, Fox would like to know, 'is so peculiarly divine in this deposed royal race that around them should be clustered the religious associations of the country through all generations?' Precious little, is the answer. 'I really think that the Church places the present monarch in very bad company for the chief magistrate of a great, and what should be a free, people.' The people Fox had in mind, who *should be free*, are clearly not the same as the People whom Macaulay had referred to at the end of his essay on Southey. They *were* free. It is a crucial point.

For of course Fox is speaking to and for those who are still unenfranchised. The people he is primarily concerned with are the people Lovett had addressed. Accordingly, he very cleverly suggests that if Victoria is to be a constitutional monarch to her people she will have to shrug off habits that separate her from them. She will have in some way to become a democratic queen (although Fox well knows that this is a contradiction in terms).

> The persons who made such an outcry against Lord Melbourne for introducing Mr Robert Owen to her Majesty, should perceive the much more improper association in which Queen Victoria stands in the prayer book, with the Jameses and Charleses of the Stuart race, certainly by no means as respectable and decorous personages as the founder to the co-operative system.[9]

Fox is one of a number of middle-class radical republican intellectuals who, during the 1830s and 1840s, did a great deal to try to establish common cause with the emergent working class. Hence, his wonderful lectures which were, so a prefatory note tells us, given on Sunday evenings during 1844 at 'The National Hall of the Working Men's Association' in Holborn. And hence the wide range of topics chosen for these lectures, from the justified claims for Irish Independence ('The Irish People are a nation – why should they not have that mode [of an independent parliament] of expressing it?'), through celebrations of poets, painters and sculptors *rather than* 'warriors who have slain their thousands and tens of thousands', a commemoration of the acquittal of 'Hardy, Tooke, Thelwell, And Others, in 1794',[10] to an attack on Young England, a lecture on the storming of the Bastille, several on poets of the day (including a significant number of women poets), and key addresses on the People's Charter, in which Fox spends much time attacking the exclusion of women from the franchise and, by implication, from the Charter's proposals for 'universal' suffrage.

As such a list will suggest, Fox is part of a political-cultural continuum that reaches back through Shelley, whom he adored, to the great radical republicans of the 1790s. In the 1830s Fox had been the centre of a significant group of writers and intellectuals, and as editor of the radical journal *The Monthly Repository* (which ceased publication in 1838) he had considerable influence in promoting radical republican causes. Robert Browning was a contributor, as was R. H. Horne, who would become one of the most trusted contributors to *Household Words*. In common with the rest of Fox's circle, Horne adored Shelley. (There is a story that he met Mary Shelley when she returned to England after her husband's death, went down on bended knee before her and promised her his undying allegiance.) Horne was author of *Orion*, the famous 'farthing epic' (so called because he wanted to sell it at that price in order that it might be affordable to the poorest readers); and in 1834 he produced a 'burlesque' called *The Spirit of Peers and People*, to which he gave the subtitle 'A National Tragi-Comedy, Allegory, and Satire', and which, recalling something of Shelley's 'The Mask of Anarchy', sinks its teeth into the Church, the monarchy and Parliament. The burlesque ends with the representative of the People (Fox's rather than Macaulay's), proclaiming: 'Gold is God and Labour is the Ass / But now 'tis ridden to the precipice.' Unless change comes soon, therefore, there will follow 'the flow of fratricidal blood, / Ruin, or injury'.[11]

It might, of course, be argued that after the reverses of 1839 Horne's apocalyptic vision was bound to fade. But this would be to underestimate the continuing radical energies of the 1840s. And, after all, nobody breathing the air of 1 January 1840 could know that the events of 1839 weren't soon to be repeated, perhaps more successfully. It is that which gives urgency to so much radical writing of the new decade, that which at least partly explains the almost desperately keen desire of middle-class intellectuals to make common cause with working-class radicals, just as it makes Macaulay's cheery optimism of 1830 look decidedly vulnerable. Macaulay had there insisted that signs of discontent in fact proved that all was well in the nation. 'Does [Southey] not know that the danger of states is to be estimated, not by what breaks out of the public mind but by what stays in it?'[12] Here, then, we need to take note not only of Fox's *Lectures* but of a number of newspapers and journals of the period, including, to choose at random, *Reynolds News*, *The People's Journal* and *Howitt's Journal*.[13] Many of these were short-lived but all of them took for granted that a new political and social alliance between middle- and working-class interests was needed if national disaster were to be avoided. And typically there was common agreement on the need to extend the franchise and to unpick the powers of rank and privilege. In this context William Howitt's *The Aristocracy of England* is a key work of the period.

The Aristocracy of England first appeared in 1844 and went into a third edition two years later; and if Howitt's decision to write under a pseudonym suggests some caution, his adoption of the name 'John Hampden Jnr' clearly enough indicates the work's slant. There is an odd preface, in which Howitt pays tribute to Victoria for having 'shown herself worthy of the great throne on which she sits by her sympathies and care for her suffering people', but this should perhaps be read ironically. Before she came to the throne Victoria had been undoubtedly touted as a monarch who *would* display care for the least advantaged in the land, but that was standard practice.[14] Even George IV had been hailed by some – paid, no doubt – as saviour of his grateful people. What *is* true is that, for all Albert's efforts to make his wife acceptable to the public at large, the campaign to rescue Victoria from unpopularity was having a lean time of it. So that although Howitt introduces the idea of a republic in order to dismiss it – 'it is a government only for men in the most perfect state' – his coolness towards the idea has to do with present conditions and is thus very different from Macaulay's rejection of republics on the grounds that the only examples of successful ones belong to antiquity, when republics were city states, not nations, and anyway the ancients had no concept of the kind of liberty enjoyed by the English. 'In almost all the little commonwealths of antiquity, liberty was used as a pretext for measures directed against everything that makes liberty valuable.'[15]

I bring in Macaulay again at this point because it has been claimed by Allan Massie among others that the radical republicanism of the late 1840s which, I want to suggest, feeds into *Bleak House* is not much different from the Whig arguments most closely associated with Macaulay himself. The truth is otherwise. Cautious as Howitt undoubtedly is, his opposition to the aristocracy is part of an attempt to think through the consequences of empowering the people as Fox and others conceive them, not as Macaulay does. Or rather, Howitt seeks to align the two in a way that Macaulay would have thought dangerous, even subversive. Change must come through Parliament, Howitt says, but this must depend on Parliament itself being thoroughly changed. Yet how? Not by violence.

> The soil of England will not willingly drink the blood of its children. The remedy is alike simple and conspicuous. All – manufacturer and farmer, gentleman and ploughman, merchant and shopman – all must combine and with one dread voice, like another Cromwell, command the aristocrats to quit the people's house, and 'give place to better men.'[16]

Howitt's history of the English aristocracy argues that they were originally placemen who were little better than thieves and murderers and as such rewarded by successive monarchs for doing their dirty work for them. The record is 'crowded with such a throng of cruel, bloody, unprincipled, unnatural, murderous, covetous, lustful, traiterous and godless monsters as puts the bare fiction of pure blood to the utmost shame'.[17] After such a catalogue of crimes against humanity, Howitt's rejection of a plea for the seizing of aristocratic property – 'Property, however got, brave people, is sacred!' – sounds decidedly hollow, as it was perhaps meant to do.[18]

Or does it reveal a muddle? If so, that would not be surprising, nor would it stand alone. Middle-class radicals were bound to find themselves facing some awkward questions. Just where *did* they stand on matters of property, on extra-parliamentary means of widening the franchise, on the roles of Church and monarchy in state affairs? Yes, they wanted a republic, but then again perhaps not yet. Yes, they wanted universal suffrage, but then again the achievement of that shouldn't threaten their own class interests. This seems to peek through even Fox's rhetoric when, in 1848, he worries about the possibility of the working class turning against their radical middle-class allies. 'By yourselves were the Corn Laws first denounced,' he tells his working-class audience, 'yet, when the great body of the middle-class flocked around that same banner which you had raised, some of you stood aloof, questioned their motives, disturbed their meetings, and struggled hard to prevent their triumph and to forfeit your right share in the celebrations.'[19]

No wonder, then, that so much radical writing of the 1840s mixes anger at the all-too-apparent injustices of a system which Macaulay had so exuberantly hymned with an anxiety about what would happen if that same system were changed out of all recognition. Suppose those decorative totems – Church, monarchy, House of Lords, property, for example – turned out to be structural supports? To take them away would send the whole edifice crashing to the ground. Suppose – just suppose – Macaulay was right when he claimed that 'Our liberty is neither Greek nor Roman; but essentially English. It has a character all its own – a character which has taken on a tinge from the sentiments of the chivalrous ages, and which accords with the peculiarities of our manners and of our insular situation'.[20] Could liberty survive if all that was associated with chivalry was wiped away? The radicals had no doubt about the absurdity of the Young England movement. As Fox remarked, 'Young England is an entire misnomer. Decrepit old age, vamped up in a gay and glittering suit, is not youth, and vainly attempts to pass for such on the world.'[21] 'The glitter-ing suit' must be an allusion to the absurdities of the Eglinton Tournament; and mocking the efforts of those who urged and yearned for a return to Camelot is part of the radical spirit of the 1840s and 1850s.[22] But though *that* particular past might hold no attractions there was still a very real question as to where and whether a past model for the future could be found; and, if not, how the future was to be imagined.

There is no space here to follow up the implications of these questions. (The nineteenth-century invention of the past, or pasts, is a hugely complex matter.) But it is necessary to note that for those who wished the future to be different from the past two problems loomed: first, could the future develop from the past or would it have to break with it; and, second, if it came to a break did middle-class radicals have the stomach for it? This may seem a decidedly simplistic way of putting the matter, but we need to recognise the fears as well as the hopes of much of the radical activity of the 1840s. And we need also, or so I think, to recognise that for those living through so difficult and *entirely new* circumstance a certain sense of muddle is to be expected. Even working-class radicals were by no means united in their sense of how to achieve the different kinds of future society they envisaged, especially since the differences were as much between themselves as with the middle-class allies – were, in fact, as much along as between class-lines. I don't find that surprising either.

Nor do I find it surprising that the Great Exhibition of 1851 should have had among its objectives a desire to unite a nation which during the preceding decade had threatened to become perhaps fatally disunited, nor that Macaulay's *History of England From the Accession of James II*, from which comes the quotation on liberty with its longer perspective on an 'unbroken' Englishness than the essay of 1830 bothered with, should have begun to appear in 1849, nor that numerous other histories should have tumbled from the presses at the same time, all of them claiming to provide a true narrative of the past in order to show how and why the present had emerged in the form it had. I don't even find it surprising that Dickens was asked to join the committee overseeing the Great Exhibition – given his pre-eminence as a popular writer he was an obvious choice; and I cer-tainly don't find it surprising that he resigned after attending one meeting.

For Dickens had his own agenda, his own radical vision, and it was very different from whatever vision guided the architects – in every sense of the word – of the Great Exhibition.

When in 1847 the Howitts took over an ailing radical journal, *The People's Journal*, and re-named it *Howitt's Journal*, they put their names to an editorial announcing that 'Education, Peace, Free Trade, Temperance and Sanitary Reform are the principles which will be advocated. . . . Everything which can shorten the hours of mere physical labour and extend those of relaxation, of mental cultivation and social domestic enjoyment . . . must have our best and most unremitting exertions.' But the journal's overriding concern was to develop co-operation and harmony between the classes. The Howitts' contributors included many of the better-known radical journalists and writers of the day, and they did their best to get Dickens, who was on friendly terms with them, to offer them something – anything. Dickens declined. It has been suggested that he sensed the journal's financial problems made its prolonged existence very unlikely; and it is true that *Howitt's Journal* collapsed within two years, leaving its founders deep in debt.[23] Yet I am reasonably certain that had Dickens, the most generous of men, suspected the journal's money difficulties he would have helped the Howitts by sending them something for its pages. The reason he didn't has more probably to do with his sure knowledge that William Howitt's radicalism tended to be of the facing-all-ways variety and, more certainly, because he was brooding over the possibility of starting his own journal.

In the event, *Household Words* began weekly publication on 30 March 1850. Edgar Johnson notes that the journal's most characteristic feature is its treatment of current problems.

> It consistently opposes radical, national, religious and class prejudices. It crusades against illiteracy, and in favour of government aid for public education and free elementary and industrial schools for the poor. It crusades for proper sewage disposal, cheap and unlimited water supply, and the regulation of industries vital to health. It demands the replacement of slums by decent housing for the poor, pleads for the establishment of playgrounds for children, and advocates systematic municipal planning. . . . It insists that industrialists must not be allowed to mutilate and kill their labourers in order to save the cost of preventing accidents. It scandalously affirms that workingmen have the right to organise into unions, and calls upon the working class to turn the 'Indifferents and Incapables' out of Downing Street and Westminster and force the government to remedy the ills from which poor men suffer.[24]

Household Words is therefore concerned with specific issues affecting the England of its day. It is not only a home for campaigning journalism, but in certain respects comes very close to the work of Henry Mayhew: it remorselessly enquires into the actual state of the poor, of workhouses, of gin shops, factories, prisons, hospitals. It is therefore very different from the cloudy if good-hearted generalities that fill many of the pages of other radical journals of the time; different too, in that it doesn't adopt their habit of addressing the 'people' as an undifferentiated mass, even though these journals may differ among themselves as to the particular mass they are addressing. *Household Words* is Macaulay's new historiography brought up to date. It is the social history of the present.

But it also makes use of the past. In particular, it uses Dickens's *A Child's History of England*, and, given the nature of what Dickens has to say about English history and that he says it *during 1851*, this is clearly of great significance. *A Child's History* has been said to take up a position in no wise different from Macaulay, and to the extent that Dickens ends his narrative with the accession of William and Mary to the throne and given that his chief villains are the Stuart Charleses, there is some truth in this.[25] But it has to be added that Dickens finds precious little good in any monarch he mentions, and this must have been an intendedly defiant note to sound *in 1851*. For the Great Exhibition was in large part a celebration of a monarchical nation. There is also the matter of Dickens's praise for Wat Tyler, whom he presents as a man of the people betrayed by a crooked monarch. *A Child's History* provides a vivid summary of the Peasants' Revolt and its tragic outcome. Dickens ends his account as follows:

> So fell Wat Tyler. Fawners and flatterers made a mighty triumph of it, and set up a cry which will occasionally find an echo to this day. But Wat was a hard-working man, who had suffered much, and had been foully outraged; and it is probable that he was a man of much higher nature and a much braver spirit than any of the parasites who have exulted since, over his defeat. . . . The king's falsehood in this business makes such a pitiful figure that I think Wat Tyler appears in history as beyond comparison the truer and more respectable of the two.[26]

Dickens's Wat, the hard-working man – 'respectable' as Robert Owen is 'respectable' – is in sharp contrast to the image presented in another popular history of 1851, Charles Knight's *Half-Hours of English History*. Knight was an indefatigable compiler and publisher of works aimed at the new reading public, and for his *History* he fossicked among a variety of chroniclers and historians in order to put together extracts which between them provide a wonderful muddle of opinions and points of view. But Knights is in no sense a republican. His extract on the Peasants'

Revolt is lifted from Hume's *History of Great Britain* and includes Hume's claim that the peasants were led 'by the most audacious and criminal of their associates, who assumed the feigned names of Wat Tyler, Jack Straw, Hob Carter, and John Miller, by which they were fond of denoting their mean origin. . . . [They] committed everywhere the most outrageous violence on such of the gentry or nobility who had the misfortune to fall into their hands.' In this account, King Richard displays 'an extraordinary presence of mind' when Tyler falls. The King advances and asks the 'mutineers, "What is the meaning of this disorder, my good people? Are ye angry that ye have lost your leader? I am your king: I will be your leader."' Hume concludes that 'The populace, overawed by his presence, followed him'.[27]

It is hardly stretching a point to say that the mass movements of the 1840s could be accommodated to 'Wat Tylerism', and if we are tempted to think otherwise we should recall the widening of streets around Hyde Park during the erection of Paxton's gigantic edifice that was to house the Great Exhibition. The official explanation for this street-widening was that it would give the public easier access. The truth was that the authorities were worried about the possibilities of violent demonstrations and protests against the exhibition – as the Duke of Wellington remarked, 'Glass is damned thin stuff' – and were advised that wider streets would make it easier for the cavalry to ride three abreast if and when they were sent out to put down trouble. Dickens's identification with Wat Tyler, the man who had 'suffered much, and had been most foully outraged', is, then, at one with his prompt resignation from the committee overseeing the exhibition. Like Shelley, he knew whose side he was on.

This will help to explain the ardent manner of his writing about Cromwell, which takes up the two parts of Chapter 34 of *A Child's History*. Cromwell emerges from this chapter as the great, good man. There is no space here to detail Dickens's account of Cromwell's doings, but it is worth noting that in his Lecture on the Martyrdom of Charles I Fox had listed both the failings and successes of the Commonwealth, and although he remarks that its chief failing was precisely that it *wasn't* a commonwealth – 'it really was nothing more than the temporary triumph of party' – it nevertheless left behind 'the suggestion and first enactment of much that is most valuable in our subsequent legislation'.[28] We can link this to the coda to *A Child's History*, where Dickens compares the United States of America with modern England and suggests that the USA is rather better at protecting its 'subjects'. (An interesting slip: even Dickens can't shake off the habit of thinking that citizens are subjects.) 'Between you and me,' he tells his readers, 'England has rather lost ground in this respect since the time of Oliver Cromwell.'

The readers were, or were intended to be, children. Dickens is writing for those who have responsibility for England's future. This is what gives an especial edge to his *History* and why it is nonsense to try to argue that there's not much more than a cigarette paper between his and Macaulay's positions. For Dickens's is an essentially *republican* account of England – nobody could possibly be taken in by the per-functory way with which he concludes by saying that the present monarch is Queen Victoria and 'She is very good, and much loved. So I end, like the crier, with GOD SAVE THE QUEEN!' (In the preceding paragraph he has been praising the days of Oliver Cromwell.) It is also a *people's* history. Dickens invariably takes the side of those who opposed unjust authority, and in his account authority usually *is* unjust. And the very fact that he doesn't say much about England after 1688 must mean that he has little wish to accept the Whig argument that a constitutional monarchy has made possible the emergence of a nation newly devoted to liberty and freedom. Or rather, Dickens would no doubt wish to ask, as those radical republican intellectuals of the 1840s had been asking, liberty and freedom for whom? And against the bland assurance of the Archbishop of Canterbury who, in the prayer he composed for the grand opening of the Great Exhibition, thanked God for being so much in favour of the monarchy – 'Of Thee it cometh that violence is not heard in our land, wasting nor destruc-tion within its borders . . . it is of Thee that there is peace within our walls and plenteousness within our palaces'[29] – against this there is the testimony of *Household Words*, in whose pages *A Child's History* first appeared, that there was indeed wasting within England's borders. The journal also provides ample testimony to the fact that while there might be plenteousness within the palaces there was a marked lack of it elsewhere and that this lack might well occasion in the future, as it had in the recent past, violence and destruction. Wat Tyler might still rise up against the palaces of contemporary London, whether crystal or Buckingham or Lambeth or Westminster.[30] For what *Household Words* above all reveals is that England is not a united people but a divided nation and that the determining factor in this is class. And this is what Dickens's novel is about: class as the defining characteristic of a nation which is therefore in no sense a society of mutual, shared knowledge. England can only, and paradoxically, be known by and to those who resist the knowingness of Whig and Tory, both of whom construct images of 'the people' which manage to leave the people out of account. Much more than *Household Words* even, *Bleak House* provides the historiography of the present.

'London.' That is how *Bleak House* opens. This is no fiction, the one-word sentence says, this is the modern city. But what has the word to do with the title, and why the frontispiece of a country house, a vast gothicky pile seen past wintry trees and under a heavy sky (plate 8)? Is this the house intended by the title (plate 9), whose lettering is set out in such contradictory ways? 'Bleak' is designed in fanciful curlicues but tethered to the altogether more four-square 'House', its individual letters made up of bricks so obdurately constructed that 'House' could be a prison. Underneath the title is a London street scene with a small crossing-sweeper in the foreground propped against a bollard and leaning disconsolately on his besom. Which, then, is Bleak House: London or the country house which faces it across the page divide and yet has no apparent connection to the city?

What these illustrations do is to open up questions which haunt the novel. There *are* connections between the country house and the city, but who is to understand them, how are they to be weighed, what do they mean? And since both country house and city are English, what does this tell us of England? That it contains two antithetic ways of life or that somehow or other it can be understood as a unified whole? Macaulay intended to speak for England when he spoke to and for 'the people', yet the people he addressed were, as we have seen, very different from the people Lovett and Fox and his circle had in mind. And the Young England movement had a still very different concept of a united people: one that virtually excluded the middle class in favour of a dream of uniting noble and – well, not vassal, but labourer, perhaps. Given such different meanings, such variant readings of the people, could anyone speak with true authority of knowing England? Wasn't it far more likely that England was becoming unknowable?

Yet the voice which introduces us to *Bleak House* gives every impression of knowing. 'London', it says. At the time he was planning *Household Words* Dickens told his friend John Forster that he imagined much of it being written by a kind of super-reporter: 'a certain *shadow* which may go into any place . . . and be in all homes, and all nooks and corners, and be supposed to be cognisant of everything, and go everywhere, without the least difficulty . . . a kind of semi-omniscient, omnipresent, intangible creature'.[31] It is a perfect description of the ambitions of the realist novelist, even down to 'semi-omniscient, omnipresent'. The novelist must go everywhere even if he can't always understand what he sees. This is the

BLEAK HOUSE

CHARLES DICKENS

LONDON.

BRADBURY & EVANS, BOUVERIE STREET.

shadow-novelist whose voice introduces us to *Bleak House*. Or rather it is both voice and recording eye. It lifts up for a panoramic view: 'Fog on the Essex marshes, fog on the Kentish heights.' It zooms in for close-ups: 'fog in the stem and bowl of the afternoon pipe of the wrathful skipper, down in his close cabin; fog cruelly pinching the toes and fingers of his shivering little 'prentice boy on deck'. It sees people from unusual angles: 'chance people on the bridges looking over the parapets into a nether sky of fog, with fog all round them, as if they were up in a balloon, and hanging in the misty clouds'. The speed with which this shadow moves from view to view, place to place, and the use of the continuous present – as though these scenes are not sequential but co-terminous – makes for a sense not so much of randomness as of sure intent. For the shadow suddenly dives down among the muddy streets in order to lead us to 'the very heart of the fog' where sits 'the Lord High Chancellor in his High Court of Chancery' (49–50).

The majesty of the law. But the law, though stuffed with legal knowledge, declines to have any other knowledge. It has knowledge without understanding. Hence the policeman, who knows it his duty to move Jo on but not why, nor where to – ' "My instructions don't go to that" '(320). Hence Guppy and his friend, who see in their grubbily acquired knowledge a way to make money but have no understanding of the harm they do to other people's lives. Hence Tulkinghorn, that friendless, 'dingy London bird', who knows everyone's secrets and is absolutely without the imagination to grasp their human significance. Hence Vholes, who is content to take Rick's money but not to take responsibility for what he might otherwise know is happening to Rick. Wherever you look in the novel you find the law. England is a land of law. In *The Great Arch: English State Formation as Cultural Revolution*, Philip Corrigan and Derek Sayer point out that in the first third of the nineteenth century, 'the most comprehensive battery of legislative, practical and other regulatory devices against the emergent working class' comes into existence.[32] And they might have added that together with this battery came a swelling army of lawyers; and lawyers helped make for more laws and still more laws and still more lawyers. Inspector Bucket is the human face of the legal system, the all-seeing, wise, drily compassionate man of law. But his wisdom stops short at a crucial point. There are things he truly does not know. As we shall see, he is only semi-omniscient.

facing] 8, 9   Hablôt Browne ('Phiz')
frontispiece and title-page of the first edition (1853)

The Church of England knows precious little of the nation. By the time Dickens began his novel the first religious census, of 1851, had revealed how few working-class people went anywhere near a church; and hardly any of them bothered with the established Church. It is a point Dickens draws attention to when, after Jo has been told by the policeman to move on, he sits

> munching, and gnawing, and looking up at the great Cross on the summit of St. Paul's Cathedral, glittering above a red and violet-tinted cloud of smoke. From the boy's face one might suppose that sacred emblem to be, in his eyes, the crowning confusion of the great, confused city; – so golden, so high up, so far out of his reach. (326)

For, as the Archbishop of Canterbury had implied in his prayer of 1851, people like Jo simply don't exist in England.[33]

And although adherents of the Young England movement were prepared to acknowledge the fact of poverty, their remedy of bath-houses and cricket is overshadowed in Chapter 12 when the voice speaks of those who have set up a Dandyism in religion and who would 'make the Vulgar very picturesque and faithful, by putting back the hands upon the Clock of Time, and cancelling a few hundred years of history' (211). These dandies meet at Chesney Wold, the country house depicted in the frontispiece. They know nothing of the city experience of Jo.

As for Chadband, the oleaginous voice of dissent, he may know of Jo but he certainly doesn't know what to make of him, as Chapter 25 reveals. Jo is for Chadband a subject to be 'improved'. It has been said that in making Chadband into a caricature of ignorance and greed Dickens is less than fair to the dissenting tradition; and to the extent that the tradition was more concerned with representing working-class interests than the Church of England ever was, this is so. But, as E. P. Thompson has definitively shown, the representation of those interests put an emphasis on the acceptance of suffering rather than resistance to it.[34] And it would be absurd to deny that England was well supplied with the combination of ignorance, vanity and self-serving that Chadband represents. Here as elsewhere in *Bleak House*, Dickens may choose to dwell 'on the romantic side of familiar things', as he claimed in his Preface that he would do; but Chadbandism was a familiar phenomenon of the age (as it is of *any* age).

The Church is one of the Three Estates. The nobility is another. With ruthless courtesy, the narrator homes in on Sir Leicester Dedlock, that 'honourable, obstinate, truthful, high-spirited, intensely prejudiced, perfectly unreasonable man' (57). Such poised, all-seeing certainty withers the claim to authority of country house politics. All those Coodles and Doodles and Cuffys and Buffys: they are interchangeable because they are all of a kind: placemen to interested parties who may say they speak for England but for whom a democratic nation is a terrible threat to their own position. For 'the world would be done up without Dedlocks'. That is why the apparently broad comedy of Sir Leicester Dedlock's paranoid fear of Wat Tylerism is in fact of great significance. He may dimly understand that out there, somewhere, are people who seem dissatisfied with their lot and with the nation, but he has no idea who they are. It is the sure sign of his absolute ignorance of England.

And it is shared by Victoria herself. Hence that moment where the narrator, having made his readers watch Jo's death, turns to address the Queen. 'Dead, your Majesty. Dead my lords and gentlemen. Dead, Right Reverends and Wrong Reverends of every order. Dead, men and women, born with Heavenly compassion in your hearts. And dying thus around us every day' (705). 'Your Majesty' is as specific as 'London'. The historiographer of contemporary England can speak with authority because he possesses knowledge that England's monarch lacks.

Yet Dickens is not the only person to be in possession of such knowledge. By the end of the novel his readers know as much as he does about contemporary England. So does Esther Summerson. Esther is in many ways the least knowledgeable of people. For most of the novel she doesn't even know about her own parents. You could therefore say that she is entirely without authority. But by the end of the novel she knows as much as the narrator. She sees nearly everything that he sees. And what above all she sees is that the society in which she lives is controlled not by authority but by *class*. When she is required to accompany Mrs Pardiggle, the bringer-of-good-tracts, to visit the brickmakers' families, Esther is 'painfully sensible that between us and these people there was an iron barrier, which could not be removed by our new friend. By whom, or how, it could be removed, we did not know; but we knew that' (159). And much later she is made to realise that Jo, the boy she has saved from death, is hounded to it by the actions of Harold Skimpole and Inspector Bucket. Dickens's readers can see that Skimpole is a selfish hypocrite, even though Esther's guardian can't. Esther sees more than Jarndyce, precisely because she lacks authority, has, in other words, no (or few) preconceptions. And Bucket? He is the reassuringly considerate custodian of the law. Yet he is quite prepared to warn Jo, desperately ill though the boy is, to stay out of London and to ' "maintain a bright look-out that I didn't catch him coming back again" ' (830), as he tells Esther in a glaze of calm self-satisfaction.

For much of the novel Jo's lodging place is 'Tom-All-Alone's', which Dickens had long considered taking as the title of his novel. He made in all ten different stabs at finding the title he wanted, and down to the ninth Tom-All-Alone's is still featured, together with a number of additional phrases or subtitles, such as 'The Solitary House' or 'The Ruined House'. Then, at the tenth attempt, he jotted down 'Bleak House and the East Wind. How they both got into Chancery And Never got out.' He doubly underlined those words then put a diagonal line beneath them. And then, under the diagonal line, he wrote simply 'Bleak House'.[35] The title draws in the implications of all the others. Tom-All-Alone's is crucial because it is the place of neglect, where few of the novel's protagonists would dare to go, even though it is property owned by Jarndyce of Jarndyce and Jarndyce, is situated between Oxford Street and Piccadilly, and Jo lives there.

And this is the point. Tom-All-Alone's is at once central to the novel as it is central to London and at the same time unknown, denied, as Jo is denied, by, among others, Bucket, Skimpole, the policeman who moves him on, Mrs Snagsby, Lady Dedlock, who can't stand him near her; and even Woodcourt, the humane physician, has to struggle hard to overcome his revulsion at the boy. The only people who unselfconsciously feel for him are Nemo, the man of no name, Mr Snagsby, the least authoritative of men, and of course the illegitimate Esther. A community of feeling is dependent on an absence of authority. Only there, beyond the class-bound knowledge from which authority derives its credentials, is community at all possible. Authority, a combination of monarchy, Parliament, law and Church, cannot legitimately speak for England because it doesn't *know* England, that plethora of communities the novel's narratives reveal to its readers. Early commentators on *Bleak House* complained that for all the appearance of plot there really wasn't one because there is an 'absence of a coherent story'. But that is the point. London, Chesney Wold, 'Bleak House' *don't* cohere. Or rather, they cannot be brought into coherence under any of authority's versions of a monarchical, Anglican community. England's future history, like the Roman allegory on Mr Tulkinghorn's ceiling, points, however ambiguously, in a different direction.

Towards the north, perhaps? Certainly Mr Rouncewell, the iron master, possesses new energies, even a new vision of what society might be, that are regenerative and conceivably Macaulay-like in their breezy confidence. But the implications of this are not explored in *Bleak House*. That is a matter for Dickens's next novel, *Hard Times*. And whatever the problems Dickens runs into there it can be said that the way he confronts and tries to resolve them will hardly comfort those wishing to read England's history along the lines Macaulay had laid down in 1830 and which his adherents and followers in the 1850s still thought of as pointing to a knowable future.

Notes

1 T. Macaulay, *Essays and Lays of Ancient Rome* (London: Longmans, Authorised edition 1888), p. 104.
2 *Ibid.*, pp. 116–18.
3 *Ibid.*, p. 121.
4 Quoted by J. W. Burrow, *A Liberal Descent: Victorian Historians and the English Past* (London: Cambridge University Press, 1982), p. 38.
5 *Ibid.*, p. 36.
6 In George Levine, *The Emergence of Victorian Consciousness: The Spirit of the Age* (New York: The Free Press, 1967), pp. 304–7.
7 For all this see Dorothy Thompson, *The Chartists: Popular Politics in the Industrial Revolution* (Aldershot: Wildwood House, 1984), esp. pp. 271–329.
8 See John Lucas, *England and Englishness: Poetry and National Identity, 1688–1900* (London: Chatto & Windus, 1990), pp. 166–7.
9 W. J. Fox, *Lectures: Addressed Chiefly to the Working Class* (London: Charles Fox, 1845), 4 vols, vol. 1, p. 101.
10 Tooke, Hardy *et al.* were arrested under the 'Combination Acts' and other legal manoeuvres of the mid-1790s to stamp out republican, Jacobin pro-French arguments of the time.
11 For a full account of Horne, see Anne Blainey, *The Farthing Poet* (London: Methuen, 1968).
12 Macaulay, *Essays*, p. 113.
13 I am grateful to Audrey Roulstone for much of the information about the Howitts contained in this paragraph.
14 For much of this, see my essay on 'Love of England: Patriotism and the Making of Victorianism', in D. Margolies and M. Joannon (eds), *Heart of the Heartless World: Essays in Cultural Resistance in Memory of Margot Heinemann* (London: Pluto Press, 1995).
15 Quoted by Burrow, *A Liberal Descent*, p. 5.
16 Wm Howitt, *The Aristocracy of England: A History for the People* (London, 1846, 3rd edn), p. 332.
17 *Ibid.*, p. 22.
18 *Ibid.*, p. 335.
19 W. J. Fox, *Counsels to the Working Class* (London: Charles Fox, 1848), p. 25.
20 See Burrow, *A Liberal Descent*, p. 57.
21 Fox, *Lectures*, vol. 3, Lecture XI, p. 171.
22 For the tournament and much else besides see Mark Girouard, *Return to Camelot: Chivalry and the English Gentleman* (London: Yale University Press, 1981), pp. 82–110.
23 I am grateful to Audrey Roulstone for this information.
24 See Edgar Johnson, *Charles Dickens: His Tragedy and his Triumph* (New York: Simon & Schuster, 1952), 2 vols, vol. 2, p. 714. Johnson provides a blow-by-blow account of

the typically meticulous planning that Dickens put into *Household Words*. See vol. 2, pp. 101–4.

25 Macaulay entertained some hopes that Dickens would write for the *Edinburgh Review*, but Dickens never did contribute. For this see Johnson, *Charles Dickens*, vol. 1, p. 442. And see vol. 2, p. 955 for evidence that Dickens disliked Macaulay's *History of England*.

26 There is no standard edition of *A Child's History of England*. I therefore identify references after quotations by reference to the chapter from which each comes.

27 Charles Knight (ed. and selector), *Half Hours of English History* (London: Warne & Co., 1851), 9 vols, vol. 3, pp. 4–5. Hume is also quoted on the need to use the greatest severity in putting down such uprisings as the Peasants' Revolt.

28 W. J. Fox, *Lectures*, vol. 1, p. 114.

29 For this see Eric de Mare, *London 1851: The Year of the Great Exhibition* (London: The Folio Society, 1972), unpaginated.

30 Dickens's readers would have known that Wat Tyler was the nickname of one of the northern Chartist leaders during the disturbances of 1848. See Harvey Peter Sucksmith, 'Sir Leicester Dedlock, Wat Tyler and the Chartists, the Role of the Ironmaster in *Bleak House*', in *Dickens Studies Annual* (1975), pp. 113–31.

31 John Forster, *The Life of Charles Dickens* (London: Chapman & Hall, 1893), p. 395.

32 P. Corrigan and D. Sayer, *The Great Arch: English State Formation as Cultural Revolution* (Oxford: Basil Blackwell, 1985), p. iii.

33 Having denounced the Archbishop's prayer for its ignorance of the real condition in which many in London were living, Charles Kingsley was forbidden from preaching in London for three years.

34 See E. P. Thompson, *The Making of The English Working Class* (London: Gollancz, 1963), *passim*. The Primitive Methodists broke away from the Methodist community at the beginning of the nineteenth century precisely because they realised their Church was placating and accommodating Anglican opinion and moving away from identification with the working community.

35 See Susan Shatto, *The Companion to Bleak House* (London: Allen & Unwin, 1987), pp. 298–9.

9

'Another day done and I'm deeper in debt': *Little Dorrit* and the debt of the everyday

DIANE ELAM

> None of us clearly know to whom or to what we are indebted in this wise, until some marked stop in the whirling wheel of life brings the right perception with it.
>
> Charles Dickens, Little Dorrit[1]

'All this time' (319)

'What time is it?' is an everyday question, the type that is so frequently posed that one almost forgets asking and answering it. As a question, it would hardly seem worthy of attention in literary theory or in an essay about the novel. But it is precisely because the question of time tends to be forgotten that I want to call attention to it. On the one hand, remembering the way in which the novel as a literary form incurs a debt to time merely returns to an account that seems to have been settled long ago.[2] It is nothing new to argue that narrative, including that of the novel, is always a question of temporality. Narrative is always 'in' time, as it were. And yet on the other hand, there still remains an outstanding debt. However much literary theory has remembered the temporality of narrative, it has forgotten the novel's debt to *everyday* time, to the way in which narrative engages not only with abstract temporality but also with an everyday experience of time. The reason for this memory lapse is as simple as everyday expressions themselves: because everyday time seems so familiar, we forget to think of it as a problem. That is to say, we have forgotten the actual complexity inherent in what *seem* like simple everyday expressions of time, and likewise we have not sufficiently considered the ways in which a novelistic narrative could engage the complexity of everyday time through its very insistence on these everyday phrases. For this reason, I would like to suggest that it is only by making our everyday experience of time sound, in some sense, *less* familiar that we can begin to pay off the forgotten debt. I want to argue that the novel can allow for such a defamiliarisation and can thus cause us to remember our temporal commitment.

I have chosen to collect on an example which is a particularly overdrawn account: Charles Dickens's novel *Little Dorrit*. Although H. G. Wells's *The Time Machine* or even Dickens's own *Hard Times* (to name only two possibilities among many) might seem to offer more ready-to-hand choices, the narrative of *Little Dorrit* is itself a kind of time machine that will put our recollective energies to the test.[3] But before I turn to this particular text, it is worth saying a few general words about the debt incurred to everyday time in Dickens's novels.[4] First, from the moment of their initial serial production, the novels engage with the reading and writing of narratives as temporal activities. For instance, reading the novels as serials or instalments weaves the narrative into the fabric of everyday life, a point underlined by the advertisements for household goods included in some number parts. To possess a novel in its entirety as something to be read over a continuous and hence neutral period of time is an experience of reading that happens only as a kind of secondary reception of Dickens's work. Serial publication, that is, underlines the point that reading is an activity in the everyday world and not merely that which takes place in the homogeneous and empty 'ideal time' of contemplation (the time of the library).

That reading takes time, and takes place within temporal restrictions, leads to my second point: Dickens's novels have a quality of length (as well as sheer quantity) which also makes their reading take a lot of time. While this is obviously true of any long novel, there is something in the way in which a Dickens novel is long that differs from the way in which *Middlemarch* or *À la recherche du temps perdu* is long. What makes Dickens's novels distinctive (if not unique) is that they are *not* unifying epic projects that organise time in a trajectory. So much of the narrative time in a Dickens novel is taken up with cameos, with details, with miniature portraits encountered in the time of everyday life. It is in this context of everyday details that I wish to *set* Dickens's treatment of time. I say 'set', as one might of a clock, rather than 'explain' because the everyday does not provide an *explanatory context* for Dickens's writing. His engagement with the incongruous details of everyday life is marked by a resistance to explanatory systems that might attempt to fit those details into a coherent pattern. For this reason, it hardly seems surprising that attempts at elaborate explanation of Dickens's texts so often collapse into incoherent piles of detail: much of the allure of detail for Dickens is its status as pure detail, as ordinary rather than exemplary.

Such an attention to detail in the everyday engages questions of temporality in ways which differ significantly from those that Paul Ricoeur finds important. Arguing that 'narrative structure confirms the existential analysis' of time (a position for which I have some sympathy), Ricoeur then goes on to stress that certain quest narratives (*The Odyssey* and Augustine's *Confessions* would be two examples) 'reach a deep level of repetition' and establish 'human action at the level of authentic historicality'.[5] For Ricoeur the seemingly banal encounters with everyday time cease to take on importance for serious considerations of temporality. Ricoeur ironically seems to have lost sight of the everyday in his own reading of Heidegger's existential analysis of everyday temporality. By contrast, Dickens concentrates on the very strangeness of the details of everyday time in such a way that Heidegger's understanding of everyday temporality seems anachronistically to enter the pages of Dickens's novel.

To work out more precisely what is at stake in Dickens's engagement with everyday time, this chapter will move from a consideration of time and narrative form, through the thematisation of time and debt in *Little Dorrit*, to an argument which suggests that Dickens's concern with the everyday moves him to rephrase the work of memory as an excess of indebtedness over any narrative consciousness. Hence, the theory of narrative is not finally adequate to deal with the condition of time for Dickens, since such theory seeks to settle a debt that Dickens insists upon as unpayable. The everyday is not a field into which theory might intervene to explain memory as a temporal effect; rather the conflicting temporalities characteristic of the everyday mark the effects of memory as a *resistance* to theory, a debt that resists *epistemological* accounting.

While I will return later to these accounting problems, for the moment I want to stress that time is 'in' Dickens's novels but not in any simple way, for if time is 'in' the novels, then what time is it? What exactly would it mean to tell the time in Dickens's novels? To formulate an answer for each text would certainly take more time than I have in this chapter, so I will, as I mentioned earlier, limit my investigation to telling the time in *Little Dorrit* in order to say something about 'the times' of the everyday that the novel represents. It is crucial, however, to recognise that the phrase 'the times' does *not* refer casually to a particular historical period. Reading the time in Dickens's novel will not consist of viewing a single historical 'time' within the novel as if it were a clock-face; *Little Dorrit* does not offer us a window on the past, a transparent look at 'the times' about which Dickens writes. The historical is not transparent in that the novel will not allow us to separate the historical times (Victorian England) from a theory of historical time that would delimit or isolate such a period. Instead, the novel offers competing theories of time, which can help us to understand what makes a recovery of historical time problematic. As we shall see, historical and everyday time are not simply opposing ways of accounting for time, rather Dickens's text suggests that what makes historical time so problematic is that it can be accounted for only in everyday time. For this reason, it may even be more proper to speak of the *temporality* of the times.

To put the issue this way is not to suggest, however, that we need to develop a historical theory of time and then bring its explanatory powers to the specific context of the everyday.[6] Such an approach both underestimates the complexity of the everyday (its capacity to be theoretical) and incorrectly assumes theory to be somehow other to or outside of everyday life. Theory is already within the everyday and figured as the problem of accounting *for* everyday time while still remaining *within* everyday time.

With these temporal economics in mind, I want to propose that the *time of debt* ('present' narration) and the *debt to time* (narrated time undermined by the time of narration) form the double context in which Dickens's novel engages with the everyday. In the most general of terms, this means that narration is hopelessly in debt to time in that there is a gap between the time of narration and narrated time – *Little Dorrit*, after all, opens with the words 'Thirty years ago', which separates the time of narration from the narrated time. The time of narration is not the time that is narrated, just as the time of Dickens's writing must differ from the time of a reader's reading. Narration is hopelessly *in debt to time*, so much so that the economy of narration is always a debtor's economy. This is something we've known about in novels since *Tristram Shandy*: the attempt to pay off, to tell the story, itself gets in the way of the story. Realist narrative ceaselessly and impossibly struggles to close the gap between the time of narration and narrated time – writing goes both backwards and forwards in that the 'now' both is and was.

That the time of narration is always an impossible time (the time of the present cannot be reconciled with the time of the past) is the problem that Dickens's Mrs Ticket puts before us when she remarks that 'all times seem to be present, and a person must get out of that state and consider before they can say which is which' (584). Narrators could be said to fall under Mrs Ticket's prescription, because they must leave the present in order to tell what time it is, to find a 'present' narrative voice *in the time of debt*. However, getting out of the present is also a getting into debt, into the Marshalsea, as it were, since the narrator's aim of telling what time it *is* is always that of recapturing the present of those times, be they best or worst. At the risk of being too much of an *arche*ologist, I might even go so far as to say that the *founding* possibility of narrative is its unpayable debt to time, its inability to make present the *time of debt* in which the *debt to time* could be repaid.[7]

'But there is plenty of time, plenty of time' (124)

One kind of essay would stop right here, pointing out a congruity of thematic content (debt) and formal framework (the temporal condition of the narrative) in *Little Dorrit* that redounds to the credit of Dickens the artist. The everyday articulation of the historical would turn out to be merely a formal debt. But to make this the stopping place would actually be avoiding the crucial problem of what everyday time is. Instead, I want to keep the clock ticking on this project and propose that the problem of time and debt is related to the difficulty of thinking about everyday life and its stubbornness in the face of explanatory mechanisms – those of either the novel, the clock or the literary theorist. If theory is not something we bring to explain the everyday, neither is there simply a single theory of time that we can locate within the everyday. It is precisely the sense of multiple and competing temporalities that I want to call 'the everyday'.[8]

To see how this is indeed the case, it is worth turning to the interplay of the various temporalities or 'times' in *Little Dorrit*. Dickens's novel juxtaposes three conflicting systems of accounting for time, which for simplicity's sake I will call 'clock time', 'organic time' and 'psychic time'. As I have already suggested, none of these will serve as Dickens's own time-keeping system, none will account for the novel itself. For this reason, it is worth repeating that the unaccountable co-existence of multiple and heterogeneous temporalities characterises the time of everyday life for Dickens. Everyday time is always in difficulties when it comes to accounting for itself.

The first theory of, or method for, keeping track of time that I will address is clock time. Dickens's characters seem unable to escape the overwhelming influence of clocks, so much so that it is little wonder that Dickens refers to everyday life in *Little Dorrit* as 'the clock of busy existence' (388). Since the entire novel virtually ticks and chimes, all of the references to clocks chiming and striking the hour would be too tedious to enumerate, but suffice it to say that once John Baptist makes reference in the first chapter to the fact that 'the mid-day bells will ring – in forty minutes' (42), the bells hardly stop ringing: bells regulate life at the Marshalsea, Clennam listens to the Sunday evening church bells announce the service (67), the next day Mrs Clennam is wheeled to her tall cabinet as the city clock strikes nine in the morning (84), then 'the church clock [strikes] the breakfast hour' at the Meagleses' house (245), and so on and on.

These examples are not meant to suggest, however, that the only clocks in the narrative are public instruments for keeping time; the novel is also filled with watches and everyday household clocks. For instance, the first thing that we learn about Mr Flintwinch is that 'there was nothing about him in the way of decoration but a watch' (72). As for Mrs Clennam, her parlour sports a 'large, hard-featured clock on the sideboard' (72). Mr Dorrit joins their company with his own concern for the relationship between debt and watches: he announces his need to purchase a watch as he leaves debtor's prison, and then reversing the sequence, when he believes that he has returned to the Marshalsea, the first item he wants to pawn is his watch (475, 712). Finally, this list of examples could not fail to mention the 'very remarkable watch' inscribed with the letters 'D.N.F.', which plays such a large part in the narrative action (405).

And yet for all of these examples, the references to clocks in *Little Dorrit* are not exhausted. The most excessive account of the everyday in terms of clock time is Casby's house – in which everything from the parlour fire to the servant is said to tick:

> There was a grave clock, ticking somewhere up the staircase; and there was a songless bird in the same direction, pecking at his cage, as if he were ticking too. The parlour-fire ticked in the grate. There was only one person on the parlour-hearth, and the loud watch in his pocket ticked audibly.
>
> The servant-maid had ticked the two words 'Mr Clennam' so softly that she had not been heard; and he consequently stood, within the door she had closed, unnoticed. The figure of a man advanced in life, whose smooth grey eyebrows seemed to move to the ticking as the fire-light flickered on them, sat in an arm-chair with his list shoes on the rug, and his thumbs slowly revolving over one another. (186)

It would not be too far-fetched to say that the measurement of time as clock time has invaded everything but Mr Casby's revolving thumbs, which might just as well be moving parts in a clock.

In the face of all of these references, the question to ask here is the simple one that Heidegger has already posed: 'What does it mean to read time from a clock?'[9] What does it mean for being to be constituted by clock time? The answer to which Dickens's text leads us is also in part Heidegger's:

> The time I am trying to determine is always 'time to', time *in order to* do this or that, time that I need *for*, time that I can permit myself *in order to* accomplish this or that, time that I must take *for* carrying through this or that . . . We are always already reckoning with time, taking it into account, before we look at a clock to measure the time. If we observe that each time we use a clock, in looking at it, there is present already a reckoning with time, then this means that time is already given to us before we use the clock.[10]

Clocks stand in Dickens's novel, as they do for Heidegger, as the mark that time is already being reckoned with, that narrative action is always already taking place in time. To look at the clock, to listen to chiming bells, is merely to affirm that within-time-ness. We could, then, read the comic description of the Casby household as the ultimate illustration of being within-time-ness.

But Dickens is not simply a version of Heidegger *avant la lettre*. Dickens's reckoning of clock time produces a bottom line that would be more familiar to Marx than it would to Heidegger, for *Little Dorrit* also reveals that clock time is alienating and external to being. On the most rudimentary level, the repeated references to clock time in *Little Dorrit* suggest the reduction of the everyday to monotony – the repetitive, habitual, even mechanical rhythm of existence that takes as its extreme form the regulated Benthamite prison. Thus, the Casby household is not only a comic instance of being-within-time-ness but also the terrifying abstraction of being reduced to the ticking of time. In this sense, clock time is the very model of the universal abstraction of value that grounds commodification and alienation according to Marx. Just as the capitalist has workers punch a time clock to record the duration of their labour, so too are Dickens's characters bound to the rhythms of the clock. Or to put this in a more Dickensian fashion: we are prisoners of the clock, and time is the eternal turn-key. The emblem of this condition is John Baptist, the prisoner who is always mentally aware of exactly what time it is, so much so that Rigaud tells him that he is a clock (42). Baptist has gone as far as he can to be alienated from his own labour; he is a man who is the very mechanised product of the capitalist economy of time.[11]

To speak about this matter more generally, the example of Baptist points to the way in which Dickens identifies capitalism as primarily an economy of debt and interest (rather than of production and consumption) so that the state of the economy may be measured in terms of the relation between money and time. Given the invisibility of capital itself, its working appears only in the time of interest as a return on capital. Speculative disaster proceeds from the over-acceleration of this time, money made too quickly to be understood. There is thus a debt to time on the part of the creditor, as Pancks hurries to collect rents due before sums owed accumulate in sublime proportions.

Such is the relationship between capitalism and the novel as well: the temporality of narration can be linked to Marx's account of capitalist social relations, where the experience of time *as* debt *is* the condition of life. Wage slavery introduces an irreversible loss of time: the narrator, like the labourer, exchanges real time as clock time for congealed abstract time (wages or narrative) and loses out in the process. As Marx explains, 'the capitalist *forces* the worker where possible to exceed the normal rate of intensity, and he forces him as best he can to extend the process of labour beyond the time necessary to replace the amount laid out in wages'.[12] The worker makes a permanent loan to the capitalist, and the capitalist each day gets deeper in debt to the worker who has been 'squeezed' (to borrow Pancks's phrase) by the capitalist's ticking clock. Likewise, the realist must spend a lifetime struggling to catch up with her/himself: one can only tell one's story completely from the vantage point of, and within the luxurious deadlines imposed by, death. If death is the final entry in the debt column, it also makes its double entry in the credit side of the time sheet. Here we find first that the right regulation of debt is a matter of payment 'on time' in a society of credit, and failure to pay on time condemns one to the *timeless* sentence of debtor's prison, which once again only death can mark as complete. Thus, in an age of spiralling budgets and rapidly accelerating technology, *Little Dorrit* seems to acquire a new relevance, even if Mr Merdle has been replaced in our own day by that rather anonymous figure, Mr Savings and Loan.[13] The obscurity of Mr Merdle's actual means of coining the money with which to saturate society does not simply indicate the non-productive function of speculative capital. On either side of the balance sheet, Dickens's vision of capitalism shows humanity threatened by the unrepayable debt to time, be it the whirlwind of accumulation or the dead calm of Marshalsea. Time, one might say, is the alienating medium of the social in *Little Dorrit* in a stronger sense even than money, for time does not represent anything other than itself as it circulates.

'Time went on' (105)

And yet as exhaustive as this explanation of time might seem, there is still more time to come. Just as the characters in *Little Dorrit* find themselves surrounded by devices with which to tell the time, they are also made to exist in a world of eternal, organic time: the perpetual change in seasons, the flow of rivers, the continually staring sun. It would be tempting to say that Dickens insists upon the rhythms of the sun, of the seasons and harvest time, in order to suggest an organisation for everyday labour that would counter the alienating effects of the capitalist's clocks imposed upon a population of urban debtors. If this were so, Dickens would be another 'young Marx', bent on returning the alienated and debt-ridden proletariat to an organic freedom as producer by uniting them once more with the nature of their species-being.

However, there seems to be little that is redemptive about organic time in *Little Dorrit*, making the Marxist reading of Dickens's text insufficient. Organic time in *Little Dorrit* is as insistently circular and as monotonous as the clock time that derives from it. To use Dickens's remarks: 'Morning, noon, and night, morning, noon, and night, each recurring with its accompanying monotony, always the same reluctant return of the same sequences of machinery, like a dragging piece of clockwork' (387–8). Organic time continues on only as the eternal return of the same, to offer now an explanation that sounds more like Nietzsche than Heidegger or Marx. *Little Dorrit* marks the succession of days and seasons as purposeless return – a cycle of organic time that repeatedly returns us to the same time. For instance, the novel begins on the brink of autumn, on an August day with the burning sun's universal stare; Book Two opens during vintage time 'in the autumn of the year' (482), and the novel concludes on an 'autumn morning' with the 'sun's bright rays' shining down (895). From sun to shining sun, from autumn to autumn, the narrative takes us back to where we started. We harvest the fruit of our labours only so that we can begin to labour again. A rather vicious hermeneutic circle to say the least, in that Dickens's text strongly suggests that our debt to organic time, like clock time, can only be paid, our labours finally concluded, in the moment of death: once more the everyday can be accounted for only in time when it no longer needs to be accounted for. Organic time ironically proves to be as alienating and impoverishing as the astral abstraction that clock time can impose on the worker.

Dickens's ambivalence with regard to industrialisation can thus be understood as scepticism about the possibility of organising the events that take place in organic time as the linear temporality of historical progress – whether as technological progress via the industrial revolution or spiritual progress brought about through religious devotion. This point is made clearer in the novel's unsettling conclusion in which Dickens does deliver a conventional marriage ending between Little Dorrit and Arthur (progress Victorian-style) but does so in the context of a narrative which emphasises *descent,* not the ascent usually associated with historical progress. As Dickens tells it, Little Dorrit and Clennam:

> *Went down* into a modest life of usefulness and happiness. *Went down* to give a mother's care, in the fullness of time, to Fanny's neglected children no less than to their own, and to leave that lady going into Society for ever and a day. *Went down* to give a tender nurse and friend to Tip for some few years, who was never vexed by the great exactions he made of her in return for the riches he might have given her if he had ever had them, and who lovingly closed his eyes upon the Marshalsea and all its blighted fruits. They *went quietly down* into the roaring streets, inseparable and blessed; and as they passed along in sunshine and shade, the noisy and the eager, and the arrogant and the froward and the vain, fretted and chafed, and made their usual uproar. (895: my italics)

As the repeated references to 'went down' indicate, there is a problem with accounting for the sequence of events as representative of either simply progress or decadence. Little Dorrit's good deeds are destined to occur in a society suffering from a case of social decline, so that entry into society is itself a kind of withdrawal, another autumn as it were.

Given these mixed signals, it is difficult to know what to make of Dickens's ambivalent presentation of organic time. The Marxist reading would interpret Dickens's text as a failure to recognise the redemption awaiting us in organic time. The Heideggerian would claim that the novel goes wrong by subscribing to a false notion of external time much as did Bergson.[14] While I would not want to dismiss these objections, it is not possible to reconcile them either. *Little Dorrit* does not pose a simple accounting problem: the reckoning of clock with organic time, authentic with external time, or for that matter balancing Marxist with Heideggerian notions of time.

For that reason, I want to turn to the third, although certainly not dialectical, theory of time in the novel: the psychic account of time, to use a rather anachronistic phrase and anticipate the Freud of *The Psychopathology of Everyday Life.* Psychological time is not external to consciousness, like organic time and possibly clock time. Rather, it is the very *product* of consciousness and, as we later learn from Freud, the unconscious. Its Dickensian emblem is not from *Little Dorrit* and instead would take its most recognisable form in the character of Miss Havisham in Dickens's later novel *Great Expectations*. For Miss Havisham, clock time has virtually stopped; and, as she admits, she knows 'nothing of days of the week . . . nothing of weeks of the year' (91). She does not confirm her within-time-ness by consulting the clock.

Emblematic as Miss Havisham is of Dickens's understanding of psychic time, she also has her precursors in *Little Dorrit*. For example, Mr F.'s Aunt subscribes to a psychic time that does not run as fast as the clock or calendar. Consulting the clock does not tell her 'time for what': 'measuring time by the acuteness of her sensations and not by the clock, [she] supposed Clennam to have lately gone away; whereas at least a quarter of a year had elapsed since he had had the temerity to present himself before her' (589).

Likewise, for the character Maggie, clock time (as it relates to her own process of ageing and mental development) has ceased to run altogether. Maggie is mentally stuck in time and thinks of herself as eternally ten years old, while in fact her body is twenty-eight years old (142). Finally, Mrs Clennam feels no need to take account of either clock or organic time. Not aware of organic time, and 'unable to measure time except by the shrunken one of [her own] uniform and contracted existence', Mrs Clennam has 'stopped the clock of busy existence', as Dickens puts it (388). That Mrs Clennam asks Arthur whether it is snowing outside in September marks the extent to which her life of the mind continues as unaware of the season as it is of others' affairs (74).[15]

Psychic time, then, appears as the time of deferred action, as the traumatic crumpling of the astral time-sheet so that supposedly separate moments come into contact. In this way, *Little Dorrit* is haunted by the ghostly past of psychic time, the return of the repressed thematised as debt to one's ancestors, the paradox that makes a debt one's own, though incurred by others. Significantly, Arthur Clennam carries the marker of a debt that he initially can't read and that he subsequently cannot understand. His curiosity, which drives the plot, is the belated symptom of a pre-infantile trauma, as it were. As in Freud's account of the *Nachträglichkeit* that characterises the unconscious, the novel is caught between a symptom without a cause (Arthur's guilt) and a cause with no identifiable symptom (the message, 'D.N.F.'). The trauma is not registered at the time and appears only in another time, belatedly and inexplicably. A crime without guilt for Mrs Clennam; guilt without a crime for Arthur.

Psychic time is thus not a real alternative to the alienating monotony of organic time or the abstractions of clock time, since it is not a time in which an individual can live. Rather, the individual is torn apart by the debt to the past that psychic time imposes.

'Time for what?' (529)

In this rather lengthy survey, I've tried to show that what is striking in *Little Dorrit* is that alienation characterises all three forms of time (clock, organic and psychic), whether time is rooted in abstract rationality, natural rhythm or individual perception. However, it's hard to work out what is being alienated: whether anything other than death might offer a chance of repayment. To suggest why *Little Dorrit* is interesting on this score, I want to turn to a notion of 'everyday' time as a way to talk about the co-existence of competing temporalities. This move returns to Heidegger, for it is also Heidegger who recognises that the most banal and common everyday expressions of time actually articulate the complex relationship between being and time.[16]

Yet despite such similar projects, Dickens's text is still not offering up a before-the-fact reconciliation with Heidegger. The significant difference lies in the fact that Heidegger understands the everyday saying 'now' as 'the discursive articulation of a *making-present* which temporalises itself in a unity with a retentive awaiting'.[17] While the narrative of *Little Dorrit* can be read as rejecting the Aristotelian extreme of absolute temporality, it does not uphold the Heideggerian insistence on temporal unity and presence either. If Heidegger's project is, as Stephen Melville says, 'an attempt to think as cleanly as possible the sheer temporality of time', Dickens's project might be best characterised as an attempt to think through the sheer strangeness of everyday time.[18] The narrative of *Little Dorrit* does not propose an undivided or common present, a 'pure now' upon which alienation works.[19] The question is not one of lost 'authentic' temporality or the possible articulation of 'making-present' but rather that of unresolved strangeness and distance from the present.

For Dickens, this defamiliarising of the present is conducted through an attention to grammar, which is perhaps nowhere more evident than in his characters' relationship with language. First, with Mrs Merdle:

> In the grammar of Mrs Merdle's verbs . . . there was only one mood, the Imperative; and that Mood had only one Tense, the Present. Mrs Merdle's verbs were so pressingly presented to Mr Merdle to conjugate, that his sluggish blood and his long coat-cuffs became quite agitated. (613)

And second with Mr Pancks:

> I merely wish to remark that the task this Proprietor has set me, has been
> never to leave off conjugating the Imperative Mood Present Tense of the
> verb To keep always at it. Keep thou always at it. Let him keep always at
> it. Keep we or do we keep always at it. Keep ye or do ye or you keep always
> at it. Let them keep always at it. (871)

The present 'now' is alienation too. Capitalism demands an attention to
the present (and to the present tense) that makes it the condition of
labour's unpayable debt – one must keep always at it, must forget the
meaning or value of the labour of the past in order to make sure that capitalism is forever expanding. Pancks can never finish his work for Casby;
Mrs Merdle must make sure that the young Sparkler is gainfully employed
by the Circumlocution Office, because 'now or never was the time to
provide for Edmund Sparkler' (613). Both Pancks and Sparkler must continue to labour within the system even if what that labour might mean or
amount to may change. The problem of the now is thus the condition of
narrative debt to which I have alluded, so that if 'Now or never was the
time', 'now' is always in a sense 'never'.

It would be possible to conclude, then, that time in *Little Dorrit* is always
asynchronous, always alienating. But the question still remains: alienating
from what? The problem seems to lie with the question, since an answer
to it must be predicated on the possibility of finding a true account of
time underlying either the narrative or the material conditions of everyday life. Perhaps we should pose the problem another way in order to
understand why Dickens makes time his concern in *Little Dorrit*. Rather
than being the point where time coheres, the everyday is written across
by multiple and dividing accounts of time. Alienation is the effect of the
desire to find the point from which these accounts may be added up. That
is to say, alienation proceeds from a failed search for a universal language
of time, for a Greenwich mean standard in which the time of Being may
be spoken. Therefore, for all of these accounts *of* time, Dickens has still
failed to account *for* everyday time. We may know what time it is, according to some measuring mechanism or system, but we still do not know
what everyday time *is* as such. The distinction (which may ultimately
prove impossible to make) is one between *what time it is* and *what time is*, the
difference between 'time for what?' and 'what is time?'

In calling attention to these accounting questions, I am not bemoan-
ing a loss of Being predicated on our inability to understand time. What
I am asking – and I think that this is the point that Dickens's text makes

us confront – is what would happen if time were neither internal nor external to consciousness, belonged neither to reason, nature nor the individual? The answer in part would be that time does not so much measure Being as haunt it as the impossible condition of Being's possibility. Earlier I mentioned that time exists as the ghost, as the return of the repressed, in the everyday, and at this point I can afford to be clearer: the condition of the everyday is always haunted by the uncanniness of time, by the ghost of memory.[20] The novel's concern with time and debt figures the problem of memory as the unaccountable (ghostly) encounter with the past that activates the everyday experience of time.[21] Memory, then, is the everyday experience of time as divided from itself (the past in the present), the experience of everyday time that recognises the inseparability of the questions 'time for what?' and 'what is time?'

In speaking as I do here of memory, it is important to point out that Dickens does not equate memory with the memorialising efforts of historicism. Dickens's novel is less interested in accounting for time by historical memorialisation than it is in exploring the debt of the past within everyday life that remains the condition and function of memory.[22] This could be said to be the lesson or parable of the Circumlocution Office in *Little Dorrit*. The Circumlocution Office shares with the Chancery of *Bleak House* not simply the bureaucratic delay of progress but the realisation that time, infinitely extended, does not give rise to historical progress of any sort (a sentiment echoed in the novel's conclusion) but rather disappears into unthinkable budget deficit. Progress, that is, does not surpass its origin or historical anteriority; instead it builds up a debt to an irrecoverable origin that cannot be repaid. It is, as it were, a structural necessity of the time of narration that Mr Dorrit's debt is forgotten by the very office that processes it. The ceaseless writing of memoranda becomes, in the language of the young Barnacle, 'memorialisation', a remembering that forgets (157). The documentation of memorialisation or 'memoisation', rather than providing us with the foundation for a historical memory, creates amnesia. The absurdity of the organising principles of the Circumlocution Office, which of course give rise to the very disorder and forgetfulness its methods are designed to prevent, draws a neat parallel to historicism that seeks to pin down memory in rational, natural or individual extension – as chronology, as pattern or as life.

The larger narrative movement of *Little Dorrit*, however, does not merely repeat the actions of the Circumlocution Office. *Little Dorrit* is not a collection of historical memoranda that form a convoluted structure in which we can forget the past. For it does not lead us to understand memory as a matter of being able to have access to the way the past really was (Ranke), nor as the triumph of class consciousness (Marx), nor as the seizing hold of the past as it flashes up (Benjamin), nor finally as historically connected to anteriority and recoverable origin (Heidegger).[23] While rejecting these ways of coming to terms with the past, and while also being critical of a notion of historicism that we might later associate with Croce or Mannheim, Dickens's novel none the less treats seriously the historicality of the past.[24] *Little Dorrit* suggests that memory evokes a historical debt to the past that can neither be repaid in the insufficient currency of historicism (which gives the past value only through a genetic explanatory model) nor deferred through the possibility of its eventual recovery through an appeal to origin or presence. More properly, the novel engages memory as the encounter with a past which, like ghosts, cannot ever be fully accounted for.

And so in the very act of trying to remember our debt to everyday time, we run into an accounting problem. Instead of paying off our debt a little each day, our debt to everyday time accrues. Another day done and we're deeper in debt. And yet if our account cannot be reconciled it does not mean that we are absolved from an ethical responsibility to that account. The ghostly encounter with memory demands an ethical response to the over-arching explanatory systems of historicism, if we are to avoid forgetting the debt to the past in the very act of claiming to represent it.

'Time runs out' (846)

To state all of this as I have just done is, however, to set my own narrative clock too fast. In this final section, I want to slow the movement down and remember once again the two hands of the 'very remarkable watch' that sits on Mrs Clennam's table, for this watch most significantly marks our debt to time and calls attention to the distinction I am trying to draw between memory and memorialisation.

On the one hand, the watch is a familiar marker of our debt to astral time. It is an indicator, a signifier for the effects of memorialisation, in that it can provide the illusion of accounting for the past through clock time. There is, as I have already discussed, a certain legibility to clock time: an everyday memorialisation that makes us forget our debt to time at the very moment that we believe we are remembering it as a connectedness to past times.

Yet this particular watch's capacity to recall the past as memorial does not depend only on its ability to tell the time, for Mrs Clennam's watch also contains a timely message that is not written on the clock-face itself.

We are led to believe that the watch is the receptacle for another kind of message from the past. This is, in part, a result of Arthur's observation that his father's great concern was that the watch be sent to Mrs Clennam upon his death. 'I never knew my father to show so much anxiety on any subject', Arthur recalls (74). More significantly, though, Arthur later explains to his mother that:

> 'After my father's death I opened [the watch] myself, thinking there might be, for anything I knew, some memorandum there. However, as I need not tell you, mother, there was nothing but the old silk watch-paper worked in beads, which you found (no doubt) in its place between the cases, where I found and left it.' (75)

When Arthur sends his father's watch to his mother, he is sure that it contains some message beyond that of telling the time, but his own search for the legible memo – the memorandum that will memorialise the past – proves futile. Arthur has failed to see the important signifier written on the watch itself: the letters 'D.N.F.'.

That these letters are indeed inscribed on the watch is the contribution Blandois makes to the narrative. At first glance, he seems to have understood the hidden secret of the watch when he acknowledges its inscription: '"D.N.F. was some tender, lovely, fascinating fair-creature, I make no doubt," observed Mr Blandois, as he snapped on the case again. "I adore her memory on the assumption"' (405). While Blandois senses that the watch may have something to do with memory, none the less his reading of the inscription is as off the mark as Arthur's search for the memorandum. To assume that the watch's hidden sign is visible, like a memorandum from the Circumlocution Office, is to miss the message from the past that the watch contains. Thus, while Blandois's error is correct, in so far as he recognises that the watch must function as a reminder of the past (a forgotten love), he still fails to understand the way in which the watch also marks an unseen *obligation* to the past.

For on the other hand, the watch as marker of visible and accountable (astral) time also unaccountably marks a hidden and unaccountable past – the problem of the message 'D.N.F.'. As the narrative goes on to reveal, the letters 'D.N.F.' stand for 'Do Not Forget!' The everyday time-piece contains an everyday message. And yet the precise meaning of this phrase is far from clear: who is supposed to remember what? Something has the potential to be lost, forgotten. An outstanding obligation exists, but the terms of the responsibility are not clear. In that sense, the watch both inscribes and erases the debt of 'D.N.F.' through the very problem of trying to read the message.

This hermeneutic problem, on the most basic level, is one of choosing between conflicting readings, the possibility of which becomes apparent during Mrs Clennam's response to Rigaud:

> 'Do not forget. I do NOT forget, though I do not read it as he did. I read in it, that I was appointed to do these things. I have so read these three letters since I have had them lying on this table, and I did so read them, with equal distinctness, when they were thousands of miles away.' (846)

'D.N.F.' speaks of an unspoken gift, an unpaid debt, that is remembered but not in the way it would seem the sender of the message intended. That this tangle of responsibilities and responses remains sufficiently complex is marked by the narrative's inability (or unwillingness) to represent clearly the sequence of past events.[25] This is as much as to say that the possibility of memory does not occasion a transparent look at the past. 'D.N.F.' cannot make visible the times to which it refers; the recovery of historical time is problematic in that it will never be clear precisely what should not be forgotten.

And yet something must be remembered – the ghost of memory remains in everyday time. It is not coincidental that a series of deaths occasion the writing and reading of the letters 'D.N.F.'. The letters on the watch may be more precisely read as 'do not forget the obligations of and to the dead' in that the indebtedness to time, the responsibility of memory, is a responsibility to the dead.[26] 'D.N.F.' calls for a responsibility not only to Arthur's dead father but also to Arthur's deceased biological mother and grandfather. The inscription on the watch burdens its bearer with memory; it keeps trying to make the past, the dead, present. However, these ghosts of memory cannot in any simple way become present: an impossible presence of the dead or of the 'memory which promises the resurrection of an anterior past, a *"passé antérieur"*', as Jacques Derrida would say.[27] In these terms, Dickens's narrative – caught as it is between the debt to time and the time of debt – does not itself thematise the problem of memory so much as mark it by the empty signifier 'D.N.F.'. That is to say, 'D.N.F.' is the pure signifier of an impure and non-functional memory, of a ghost. It doesn't tell us what to remember; it reminds us not to forget our debt to the past which cannot be bought off, any more than can Little Dorrit herself, who refuses her inheritance from the codicil that might claim to settle past debts, to settle the debt of and to the past as such.

It is on this count that the novel brings together debt, inheritance, death, memory and everyday time, and ends up by insisting on the necessity of memory as unpayable debt. None of the mechanisms that account for time, nor the means by which the dead seek to pay their debts to the living (inheritance) or the living to pay their debts to the dead (memorialisation) work. Memorialisation becomes memo-rialisation; inheritance leads not to grateful memory but to oblivion (Mr Dorrit seems as clueless as Pip on the origins of his sudden wealth). What we are left with is everyday time, which is the time of a memory that cannot be settled, abstracted into epic memorial time, a time divided by a command that is heard, that obliges, but whose obligation cannot ever be satisfactorily answered or done away with. Everyday time is thus divided by a command that imparts an endless ethical debt – 'D.N.F.'.

If the experience of time in everyday life is memory, 'D.N.F.' helps us to remember that memory is not merely a matter of the abstract rationalisation or accounting for time: that everyday life is a matter of incongruous detail, of elements whose effect cannot be separated from their very resistance to meaning. In such a situation, our response to the alienation and impoverishment imposed on individuals by the capitalisation of time in the economics of 'fast food' cannot rest upon a promise of clearer historical vision or better historical accounting. Instead, memory becomes an ethical question: we must always remember in order to avoid historicist 'memorialisation', the production of ever longer tomes that merely remember to forget. However, what exactly needs to be remembered, what shape that memory must take, is the problem, and the ethos, of everyday time. Everyday life necessarily experiences temporality as an alienation: like the narrator, it is divided from its attempt to represent itself, fissured by a debt to the unpresentable. Thus, memory remains impossibly split between a past that has never been present and a future for which the meaning of the past has yet to be. In the everyday experience of time, memory does not point, like the hands on the watch, to some primordial temporality.[28] Rather, 'time shall show us' that the everyday has no time, yet must be thought, every day (221).

Notes

I would like to thank the Social Sciences and Humanities Council of Canada (SSHRC) and the Québec Fonds pour la Formation de Chercheurs et l'Aide à la Recherche (FCAR) for their financial support of this work.

1 *LD*, 787.

2 Paul Ricoeur's lengthy study of time and narrative, *Time and Narrative*, vols I–III, tr. Kathleen Blamey and David Pelleuer (Chicago: University of Chicago Press, 1984, 1986, 1988), could pose as the ultimate three-volume settlement of this account.

3 In making my argument about the way in which Dickens's novel tells the time, I am evading any direct discussion of the way in which *Little Dorrit* is also a novel about the social control of space.

4 Of course, I am hardly the first person to take up the question of time in Dickens's work. Notable studies include: Stephen Franklin, 'Dickens and Time: The Clock Without Hands', *Dickens Studies Annual*, 4 (1975); Robert L. Patten, 'Dickens Time and Again', *Dickens Studies Annual*, 2 (1973); R. Rupert Roopnaraine, 'Time and Circle in *Little Dorrit*', *Dickens Studies Annual*, 3 (1974); John Schad, 'The I and You of Time: Rhetoric and History in Dickens', *ELH*, 56 (1989).

5 Paul Ricoeur, 'Narrative Time', *On Narrative*, ed. W. J. T. Mitchell (Chicago: University of Chicago Press, 1981). While this article provides an encapsulated version of his argument, Ricoeur's full investigation of temporality and narrative is to be found in his multi-volume study *Time and Narrative*.

6 While Michel de Certeau, in *The Practice of Everyday Life*, tr. Steven Rendall (Berkeley: University of California Press, 1988), could be credited with reawakening a concern for the everyday, he has done so by making this very mistake. De Certeau strives to make 'everyday practices, "ways of operating" or doing things, no longer appear as merely the obscure background of social activity' (p. xi). No small task, especially when, as de Certeau himself admits, the success of such a project hinges on whether theory can penetrate the body of the everyday: 'This goal will be achieved . . . if a body of theoretical questions, methods, categories, and perspectives, by penetrating this obscurity, make it possible to articulate [everyday practices]' (p. xi). As de Certeau describes his project, he is a sort of a modern-day Engels, penetrating the dark, obscure recesses of the everyday, a metaphorical Manchester as it were, with his theoretical Enlightenment. The problem here is with thinking of theory as outside the everyday; or, to put this another way, the error lies in believing that theory has to be imported, like a foreign agent, in order to offer enlightenment about the significance of the everyday.

7 It is interesting to note that Heidegger makes an even stronger claim along these lines when he argues, in *Being and Time*, tr. John Macquarrie and Edward Robinson (New York: Harper & Row, 1962), that 'discourse *in itself* is temporal, since all talking about . . ., of . . ., or to . . ., is grounded in the ecstatical unity of temporality' (400).

8 In making the claim for *Little Dorrit*'s particular engagement with the everyday, I am not, of course, suggesting that there was no such thing as quotidian existence prior to the late nineteenth century. However, I do want to say that Dickens, like George Eliot, is aware of the heterogeneity of something like daily life to historical time at the same time that he thinks daily life is worth talking about.

9 Martin Heidegger, *The Basic Problems of Phenomenology*, revised edition, tr. Albert Hofstadter (Bloomington and Indianapolis: Indiana University Press, 1988), p. 257.

10 Heidegger, *The Basic Problems*, p. 258.

11 Indeed Baptist's transgression is entrepreneurial: that of excessive, contraband, trading (740).

12 Karl Marx, *Capital*, vol. 1, tr. Ben Fowkes (Harmondsworth: Penguin Books, 1979), p. 987. Marx presents perhaps his most compelling illustration of the relationship

between time and the worker when he speaks of the death of countless weavers brought about by the introduction of the power loom in India (pp. 558–9). On the question of the relationship between time and labour in nineteenth-century Britain, see also E. P. Thompson, 'Time, Work-Discipline, and Industrial Capitalism', *Past and Present*, 38 (1967).

13 Of course, the anonymity of Mr Savings and Loan only completes Dickens's picture of the nondescript Merdle, whose spouse and adopted son are, by contrast with him, veritable 'sparklers'.

14 Heidegger holds that 'the time "in which" what is present-at-hand arises and passes away, is a genuine phenomenon of time; it is not an externalisation of a "qualitative time" into space, as Bergson's Interpretation of time – which is ontologically quite indefinite and inadequate – would have us believe' (*Being and Time*, p. 382).

15 Dickens extends Mrs Clennam's condition in his characterisation of Mr Dorrit, who also attempts to turn back the clock of busy existence when, in the middle of a large dinner party, he begins to think that he is back in the Marshalsea.

16 See Heidegger, *Being and Time*, p. 422.

17 Heidegger, *Being and Time*, p. 417.

18 Stephen Melville, *Philosophy Beside Itself* (Minneapolis: University of Minnesota Press, 1986), p. 54.

19 It is perhaps important to note that I am not talking about Henri Bergson's notion of the past existing in the present, which would be one way of thinking about memory, for instance. My claim is more radical than this and would be closer, if anything, to the way in which Jacques Derrida discusses time in '*Ousia* and *Gramme*: Note on a Note from *Being and Time*', in *Margins of Philosophy*, tr. Alan Bass (Chicago: University of Chicago Press, 1982). As Derrida points out, 'The now does not belong to the essence of time; it is elsewhere. That is, outside time, foreign to time. But foreign to it as its accident' (61).

20 This remark puts me once again alongside Heidegger. But whereas Heidegger emphasises the uncanniness of Being ('we flee in the face of the uncanniness which lies in Dasein', he explains in *Being and Time*, p. 234), I want to argue for the uncanniness of *time*.

21 Dickens's concern with time fits the historical (or at least one version of the 'historical') argument proposed by critics like Jerome Buckley. According to Buckley, in *The Triumph of Time* (Cambridge, Mass.: Harvard Unversity Press, 1966), the Victorians 'were preoccupied almost obsessively with time and all the devices that measure time's flight' (2). Buckley's argument is also borne out in the words of Thomas Carlyle in *Sartor Resartus* (New York: Doubleday, 1937): 'our whole terrestrial being is based on Time, and built on Time; it is wholly a movement, a Time impulse; Time is the author of it, the material of it' (127).

22 In this context it seems significant that Dickens's next novel, *A Tale of Two Cities*, more directly engages historical time by investigating the distinction between memory and memorialisation. But even there I would argue that Dickens retains his suspicion of historicism's ability to recover the past and instead appeals to the ghost of memory.

23 See Leopold von Ranke, *The Theory and Practice of History*, ed. Georg G. Iggers and Konrad von Moltke (Indianapolis and New York: Bobbs-Merrill, 1973); Karl Marx, *Capital*, vol. 1, tr. Ben Fowkes (Harmondsworth: Penguin Books, 1979); Walter Benjamin, 'Theses on the Philosophy of History', in *Illuminations*, ed. Hannah Arendt, tr. Harry Zohn (New York: Schocken Books, 1969); and Martin Heidegger,

'What is Called Thinking?', tr. Glenn Gray (New York: Harper & Row, 1968). For a further discussion of the indispensability of anteriority and originality for Heidegger's understanding of memory, see Jacques Derrida, *Memoires for Paul de Man*, revised edition (New York: Columbia University Press, 1989), pp. 140–1.

24 See for instance: Benedetto Croce, *The Story of Liberty*, tr. Sylvia Sprigge (New York: Harcourt & Brace, 1923); Karl Mannheim, *Ideology and Utopia: An Introduction to the Sociology of the Novel*, tr. Louis Wirth and Edward Sahils (New York: Harcourt, Brace & Co., 1946).

25 Notably, the Penguin edition of the novel tries to sort out what the reader is supposed to remember by including its own explanatory appendix. But the editor of that edition has, to a certain extent, missed the novel's point: we will never be able to understand completely what it is that we are supposed to remember, just as the characters in the novel either fail to read or refuse to read the message properly. In this sense, there is no pure or proper memory as such.

26 Jacques Derrida makes a similar point in *Memoires*. Derrida's complex meditation on the role of memory reminds us from the very beginning that 'what is recalled to memory calls one to responsibility' (p. xi).

27 Derrida, *Memoires*, p. 58. My own argument is very much indebted to Derrida's articulation of the temporal condition of memory: 'Memory stays with traces, in order to "preserve" them, but traces of a past that has never been present, traces which themselves never occupy the form of presence and always remain, as it were, to come – come from the future, from the *to come*. Resurrection, which is always the formal element of 'truth', a recurrent difference between a present and its presence, does not resuscitate a past which had been present; it engages the future' (58).

28 Heidegger raises this possibility, although in a different way, towards the end of *Being and Time*: 'But while time is "immediately" intelligible and recognisable, this does not preclude the possibility that primordial temporality as such may remain unknown and unconceived, and that this is also the case with the source of the time which has been expressed – a source which temporalises itself in that temporality' (460).

10

Babel unbuilding: the anti-archi-rhetoric of *Martin Chuzzlewit*

STEVEN CONNOR

Why architecture? *Martin Chuzzlewit* rears and swarms with the embodied precipitates of the architectural impulse, and is crammed with many different kinds of building and built environment, literal and metaphorical. As ever, Dickens's imagination is possessed and propelled by made spaces and places; and a number of the central characters in the book are in varying degrees architects themselves. F. S. Schwarzbach rightly points to the centrality of the architectural metaphor, and especially the focus on different forms of housing accommodation, in Dickens's evocation of the contemporary condition of England.[1] Despite all this, there seems to be a curious indifference on Dickens's part to the actual process of designing and constructing buildings. If there are plenty of buildings in *Martin Chuzzlewit*, there is precious little building; such that Mark Tapley's sneer about the supposed spontaneous construction of buildings in Eden has a wry application to the novel itself. Although Dickens's own attitudes and preferences with regard to architecture as they emerge in letters and elsewhere are not at all easy to square with the architectural values in his novels, and especially in *Martin Chuzzlewit*, he does seem to have maintained inside and outside his novel-writing a mistrust of the (still-emerging) profession of architecture. In 1852, he wrote to Angela Burdett-Coutts, the dedicatee of *Martin Chuzzlewit*, advising her to seek second opinions (among them that of his own brother-in-law Henry Austin, who was a civil engineer) to supplement the expertise of Philip Hardwick, whom she had chosen as the architect for her project of building homes in the slum areas of the East End:

> I would not like to say this to Mr. Hardwick (knowing what tender corns architects usually have) but I have no doubt that your noble design would

benefit by such a course. They know little (but most important) things beforehand, which an architect would only find out, probably, by your experiencing the worst of them when the building was done. (*Letters*, 6.626–7)

Later in his life, Dickens dabbled in a little architectural design himself, in bringing about various alterations to his newly acquired Gad's Hill property. He wrote in 1858 that he had 'added to and stuck bits' upon it, 'so that it is as pleasantly irregular, and as violently opposed to all architectural ideas, as the most hopeful man could possibly desire' (Dexter, 3.30).

I think that earlier discussions of the representation and significance of architecture in *Martin Chuzzlewit* considerably misconstrue the architectural ethics which are developed through the book. Alan R. Burke provides an exhaustive account of the book's metaphorical allusions and metaphors in his essay on the topic of 1973; but his assumption that there is a single, labyrinthine 'architectural city' of commercial corruption, which winds through and connects the various Chuzzlewittian environments of London and elsewhere, seems to me to collapse together too many important architectural and spatial differences.[2] In another essay of a few years later, Joseph H. Gardner mounts an interesting argument for the influence of Pugin on Dickens's conception of Pecksniff, perhaps mediated through Hablôt Browne.[3] Despite the difference in style of these two essays, they share an assumption about the architectural aesthetic of the novel which I think it is hard to sustain, namely that it privileges the organicist virtues of wholeness and integrity and marks as corrupt the fragmenting distortions of manner instanced not just in Pecksniffian excrescence (he advertises himself as an architect of details rather than of total design) but in the extravagant spatial disorder of London. Such a view seems to determine Alan R. Burke's judgement that the view from Todgers's is intended to show us how 'urban space is . . . violated and exploited by selfish economic interests to the point of the almost total loss of meaningful human order and relationships'.[4]

Certainly, there are hints among the, somewhat thin, archive of comments that Dickens made about architecture, particularly during his tour of Italy during the year following the completion of *Martin Chuzzlewit*, which might bear out the negative view of architectural irregularity assumed here. *Pictures from Italy* has the following complaint about St Peter's in Rome: 'It is an immense edifice, with no one point for the mind to rest upon; and tires itself out with wandering round and round.

The very purpose of the place, is not expressed in anything you see there'
(*AN*, 367–8). Elsewhere, Dickens is to be found preferring the 'gravity and
repose' of Canova's statues to the baroque extravagance and disproportion of Bernini's saints and other such 'breezy maniacs',

> whose every fold of drapery is blown inside-out; whose smallest vein, or
> artery, is as big as an ordinary forefinger; whose hair is like a nest of lively
> snakes; and whose attitudes put all other extravagances to shame.
> Insomuch that I do honestly believe, there can be no place in the world,
> where such intolerable abortions, begotten of the sculptor's chisel are to
> be found in such profusion, as in Rome. (*AN*, 394)

But Dickens's novels seem to act out a more radical and unsettled aesthetic than his more formal statements announce. I will be saying in the
pages that follow that Dickens's disinclination or incapacity to imagine
the art and act of architecture are part of a larger accusation against it.
But it is the repertoire of meanings and metaphors associated with building and buildings and the relations between humans and their spatial
environments that Dickens uses to mount his assault on architecture, an
assault which associates it at various times with egotism, folly, abstraction, alienation, dissimulation, irresponsibility, exploitation, criminality,
vanity, vacuity, cupidity and death. The accusation mounted with, and
against, architecture is folded into a complex self-accusation against the
rhetorical architecture of narrative itself. Dickens's novel attempts to
affiliate itself with the crowded, incoherent, acoustic space which is
embodied for the ear, rather than the rational, apparent space which is
presented to the eye. *Martin Chuzzlewit* not only exacts revenge on the art
of architecture, it also posits for itself an organising aesthetic of unbuilding.

The attitude to Pecksniff's architecture is established in Chapters 5
and 6, when Pecksniff welcomes the young Martin Chuzzlewit to his
house. The chapter establishes a pattern of alternation between
soaring verticality and bathetic declension which is to recur throughout the book. (It is hinted at by the mathematical diagrams that
Pecksniff is shown tracing, which look like 'designs for fireworks' (*MC*,
134).) Martin is led by the vainglorious Pecksniff to the top of his large
house, the large 'two pair front' which is the hotbed of his architectural
genius, and is shown the evidence of it in the 'plans, elevations, sections,
every kind of thing' (137) that are there displayed. Martin is then led
back down to the parlour where he has entered, to begin the process of
subsiding aspiration that is undergone by all Mr Pecksniff's exploited

pupils. Tom Pinch is surprised by the relative grandeur of the repast that is there laid out:

> The magnitude of these preparations quite took away Tom Pinch's breath: for though the new pupils were usually let down softly, as one may say, particularly in the wine department, which had so many stages of declension, that sometimes a young gentleman was a whole fortnight in getting to the pump; still this was a banquet. (137)

The pump here is the bottom of the scale, and is associated with a metaphorical reversal of the miracle at Cana, in that it turns wine by slow degrees to water. The figure of the pump has an interesting little career in the novel. In its association with water, the movement downwards from the soaring spire of Salisbury Cathedral to the humble pump anticipates the deliquescence of Martin's dreams of architectural eminence in the oozing marsh of Eden. The pump is also Mr Pecksniff's characteristic emblem, as Joseph H. Gardner and Michael Steig have noticed.[5]

There is an extensive and proliferated pattern of thematic and metaphorical exchanges of height into lowness and vice versa. Throughout the novel, the act of fabricating deceptions, conspiracies or illusions is imaged as a perverse kind of building. It is there for example in young Martin's determination to build Tom Pinch's fortune: ' "If I should turn out a great architect, Tom . . . I'll tell you what should be one of the things I'd build . . . your fortune . . . I'd build it up, Tom . . . on such a strong foundation, that it should last your life" ' (252). Martin's habit of deluding himself in this fashion recurs in his belief that he is 'very materially elevating' Mark Tapley's prospects by having him sink his savings in the Eden debacle, prompting the lament: 'Poor Martin! For ever building castles in the air' (416). This corresponds to the 'vast quantity of Castles, Houses of Parliament, and other Public Buildings' which Pecksniff's pupils construct 'in the air' (64–5), as well as, of course, to the 'flourishing' but wholly imaginary 'architectural city' of Eden as it is advertised to Mark and Martin (419). The prostration of Martin's hopes in Eden is similarly registered in terms of architectural metaphor: 'many a man who would have stood within a home dismantled, strong in his passion and design of vengeance, has had the firmness of his nature conquered by the razing of an air-built castle' (444). Here, Dickens's careful substitution of the phrase 'design of vengeance' for the original 'thirst for vengeance' in the manuscript may make a little architectural point. Even old Martin Chuzzlewit comes to disclose

181

something like an architectural motivation for expelling his grandson from his favour, since, in choosing for himself the bride that old Martin had intended for him, he had interfered with 'the grace of his design' (888).

The pattern of movement between factitious ascent and ignominious fall, or the architectural alternatives of raising and razing, is to be found throughout the novel in the imagery of towers, monuments and edifices as they are variously erected, undermined or overthrown. Towers and toppling are insisted on in the final pages of the book, with Charity Pecksniff's humiliation at the news of Augustus Moddle's absconding, and 'the bitterness of knowing that the strong-minded woman and the red-nosed daughters towered triumphant in the hour of their anticipated overthrow' (915), intensified as it is by repetition in the (somewhat shocking) picture of the ruination of the once-lofty Pecksniff, still protesting that 'he built [Tom's] fortunes better than his own', though he himself has been 'brought down very, very low' (916). Bert Hornback and others have pointed to the dominance of the myth of Eden in *Martin Chuzzlewit* with its pattern of expulsions from and returns to felicity;[6] the examples I have congregated might suggest that this myth co-operates with the more specifically architectural myth of human overreach and fall of the tower of Babel. I can find only one explicit reference to Babel in the novel, however, in General Scadder's sneer at an old country ' "that has piled up golden calves as high as Babel, and worshipped 'em for ages" ' (413).

This Babelian exchange of high and low is found most emphatically, perhaps, in the contrast between two very different kinds of architectural perspective in Chapter 9, 'Town and Todgers's'. First of all, there is the description of what Dorothy Van Ghent famously calls 'the view from Todgers's'.[7] The view from Todgers's is an elevated view, one that offers panoramic inclusiveness: 'there were steeples, towers, belfries, shining vanes, and masts of ships: a very forest. Gables, house-tops, garret-windows, wilderness upon wilderness' (188). The perspective afforded by this view expresses and in some measure responds to that desire for panoptic percipience and command which grew up during the nineteenth century in London, a desire that led to a feverish activity of charting, mapping and epistemologically regulating the chaotic and, of course, architecturally transforming city during the 1840s. It will be expressed a couple of years later in the famous passage in Chapter 47 of *Dombey and Son* which calls for 'a good spirit who would take the house-tops off', rendering causes and relations in the city 'palpable to the sight' (738). The perspective offered here is contrasted with that acquired by Mr Pecksniff later in the same chapter as he retreats from the house of the brass and copper founder's in Camberwell after having delivered his message to Pinch's sister, attempting the while to ingratiate himself with the owner by means of 'a familiar exposition of the whole science of architecture as applied to dwelling-houses':

> 'If you look,' said Mr. Pecksniff, backing from the steps, with his head on one side and his eyes half-shut that he might the better take in the proportions of the exterior: 'If you look, my dears, at the cornice which supports the roof, and observe the airiness of its construction, especially where it sweeps the southern angle of the building, you will feel with me – How do you do, sir? I hope you're well!' (197)

Pecksniff's attempts to elevate himself in the proprietor's estimation are unavailing, for the latter has appeared at the upstairs window only to demand that Pecksniff get off his lawn and leave the premises. Dickens plainly intended to structure this chapter around the perspectival contrast between the coign of vantage afforded the imaginary observer on the roof of Todgers's and the worm's-eye view given to Pecksniff, for in the rudimentary notes for Chapter 9 which are attached to the manuscript of the novel in the Victoria and Albert Museum he writes: 'Birds Eye View from housetop/Miss Pinch - Come off the Grass'.[8] But, as often in Dickens, thickening the contrast also throws it into spasm. In both the view from Todgers's and the view of Camberwell there is in fact a competition between aerial and terrestrial lines of sight. Pecksniff's attempt to gain a vantage-point on the house comes up against the proprietorial and perspectival advantage of the owner; Pecksniff looks up only to see himself being looked down upon. There is a similarly comic collision between perspectives as, looking out over the rooftops from Todgers's, the imaginary observer is drawn with unaccountable intensity to look downwards: you begin, we are told, by knocking your head against the door as you come out and being choked 'from having looked, perforce, straight down the kitchen chimney' (188). The bewildering crowd of detail which looms up from the prospect quickly impels the imagined observer to seek the retreat of the ground floor, and to testify afterwards that 'if he hadn't done so, he would certainly have come into the street by the shortest cut: that is to say, head-foremost' (189).

This passage also contains one of the most striking examples of the inversion/alternation of the vertical and the horizontal, in the detail of the shadow of the Monument. The Monument, designed by Christopher Wren, probably with the assistance of Robert Hooke, is a Roman Doric column in Fish Street which commemorates the Great Fire of London of 1666. Its height of 202 feet is said to be exactly the distance to the west that the fire started in Pudding Lane. The shadow of the Monument, as well as symbolically opposing ruin and architectural erection, suggests a direct rotation of the vertical axis into the horizontal, as well as the unstable reversibility of distance and proximity, as the observer's eye follows the shadow of the Monument 'stretching far away, a long dark path', but then recoils from its distant top to 'the tall original [that] was close beside you' (188). Thus, while the two contrasting passages of architectural observation in Chapter 9 may have begun as a simple contrast between height and lowness, they effect a chiasmic interchange of the conventional associations between height, distance, and wholeness of view on the one hand, and the conventional associations between lowness, proximity and intimate partiality of view on the other.

The principle of elevation seems also to be under threat in *Martin Chuzzlewit* from the more violent levellings wrought by conflagration or explosion. As Alan R. Burke has noticed, the Great Fire of London is called to mind repeatedly in the references to the Monument, as well as in more sinisterly specific details like the presence of 'strange solitary pumps . . . hiding themselves for the most part in blind alleys, and keeping company with fire-ladders' (186).[9] The explosive hint that Guy Fawkes may have been a Chuzzlewit (52) is amplified by the suggestion that the mysteriously disconnected cellarage of Todgers's may be filled with 'casks of gunpowder' (188) and by the fact that among the items in Mr Pecksniff's inventory of architectural designs is a 'powder-magazine' (137). The explosive metaphor becomes quite explicit in the evocation of the undermining power of change at the beginning of Chapter 18:

> Change begets change. Nothing propagates so fast. If a man habituated to a narrow circle of cares and pleasures, out of which he seldom travels, steps beyond it, though for never so brief a space, his departure from the monotonous scene on which he has been an actor of importance, would seem to be the signal for instant confusion. As if, in the gap he had left, the wedge of change were driven to the head, rending what was a solid mass to fragments; things cemented and held together by the usages of years, burst asunder in as many weeks. The mine which Time has slowly dug beneath familiar objects, is sprung in an instant; and what was rock before, becomes but sand and dust. (361)

This passage seems oddly to compound two different kinds of mine, the excavation of the earth and the kind of explosive that, from medieval times onwards, was placed in such excavated spaces (the close association in practice between excavation and explosion is presumably the reason for the migration of the word's meaning). But in collapsing this association into metaphorical identity, this passage identifies in a strange way the different though often associated risks of subsidence and explosive discharge. This is not without significance in a novel in which the subterranean space of the city has such importance. Such space is hauntingly indeterminate in *Martin Chuzzlewit*, whether in the 'grand mystery' of Todgers's cellarage, which 'within the memory of man had no connexion with the house, but had always been the freehold property of somebody else' (187), or in the ghostly sound of clinking halters which can be heard from 'deep among the very foundations of these buildings [where] the ground was undermined and burrowed out into stables' (187). The last example is an important reminder of the ambivalence of underground city space. For if it is true that the underground is the dark converse of architectural elevation, it is also manifestly the case that the underground spaces of the city are themselves *built* spaces. The allure and menace of the underground come from a certain vulnerability of architecture *to itself*, since the mining that is the underground equivalent of building is never far away from being an undermining.

This is connected throughout the novel with imagery which suggests the loss of foundation in the abrupt opening of gulfs, pits, chasms and cavities. These fears are concentrated in the apprehension of Jonas Chuzzlewit as he plans the murder of Montague Tigg that 'the fatality was of his own working; the pit was of his own digging' (791). It recurs in the extraordinary melodramatic question that is asked as Jonas leaves London, which suggests that his homicidal itinerary is literally underground: 'Did . . . no burrowing rat, scenting the work he had in hand, essay to gnaw a passage after him, that it might hold a greedy revel at the feast of his providing?' (797). The opening of gulfs is important in the dream of the apocalyptic city which Jonas has in the coach down to the West Country: his guilty excitement turns the horizontal disposition of space in the city into the sickening depths and drops of a complex verticality: 'these streets were very precipitous, insomuch that to get from one to another, it was necessary to descend great heights by ladders that were too short, and ropes that moved deep bells, and swung and swayed as they were clung to' (798). Jonas's preoccupation with depth is appropriately consummated in the dell into which he must go 'down, down, down' to commit the murder (801).

There is a broader significance in the architecture of the underground which is also purposeful in terms of the total design of *Martin Chuzzlewit*. The developments in engineering techniques and technology which made it feasible for the space-hungry nineteenth century to go below the surface, to build the underground travel, communication and sanitation systems that are still in use today in cities like London and Calcutta, made the underground just as representative as an architectural location of the modern as the towering pinnacle of the multi-storey building.[10] But the excavation of the ground also of course brings the city into contact with the remains of its past. To build downwards is thus simultaneously to advance and to retreat in time, architecture becoming archaeology. This is, in turn, not without application to the presentation in *Martin Chuzzlewit* of the United States, which is similarly pledged to the future and founded on the active forgetting of the past, but whose architectural aspirations slither back into the form-annulling mire of disavowed beginnings.[11]

However, there is an important distinction between the subterranean in nature and the underground spaces of the city. The movement towards and into the ground, whether in the collapse into swampy indeterminacy in Eden, or the slow subsiding of Tigg's corpse, 'sopping and soaking in among the leaves that formed its pillow; oozing down into the boggy ground' (802), is a collapse of spatial differentiation itself. The underground space of the city, by contrast, though it may threaten such subsidence, is constructed, architectonic space, which accounts for its extreme ambivalence. Only in the city, it appears, can the underground be simultaneously inside and outside the constructed habitat of the human. Hence the curious co-operation between the horror of spatial vacancy conveyed in the imagery of undermining and the delight in underground or quasi-underground enclosure which is to be found at various points in *Martin Chuzzlewit*, for example, in the semi-submerged tavern room, 'a little below the pavement' (621) in the sea-port (unnamed, but, I suppose, Liverpool), where Martin and Mark take their ease on their return from America:

> It was one of those unaccountable little rooms which are never seen anywhere but in a tavern, and are supposed to have got into taverns by reason of the facilities afforded to the architect for getting drunk while engaged in their construction. (621)

The remark that the room has 'got into' the tavern rather than being constructed at the same time as the rest of it suggests a hollowing adaptation of some previously entire space. This quality of architecture from the inside out seems to be a feature of other snug burrows in the novel, such as Tom's and Ruth's triangular apartment in Islington (650) or the snug chambers in Furnival's Inn where John Westlock resides (766). In the end, the novel attempts to transform the fissuring of horizontal space in Jonas's Dostoyevskian nightmare of the city into a more benign disposition of different dimensions in the city in which John Westlock and Ruth Pinch conduct their courtship. The restoration of the ordered linear perspective that has become so disturbed through this book is accompanied by the suggestion that the eruption of subterranean energies may be controlled by the coy dallying of Ruth's foot with the broken ground at her feet:

> The day was exquisite; and stopping at all, it was quite natural – nothing could be more so – that they should glance down Garden Court; because Garden Court ends in the Garden, and the Garden ends in the River, and that glimpse is very bright and fresh and shining on a summer's day. Then oh little Ruth, why not look boldly at it! Why fit that tiny, precious, blessed little foot into the cracked corner of an insensible old flagstone in the pavement; and be so very anxious to adjust it to a nicety! (896)

Architectural metaphor is used in *Martin Chuzzlewit* not merely to embody the dynamic dispositions of high and low, construction and demolition, but also to mark out a more fundamental contrast between what might be called coherent or 'architectural' space and, on the other hand, incoherent, or 'social', space. Some of the qualities of this architectural space are signalled in the work that Pecksniff displays to Martin on his first arrival:

> 'You see,' said Mr. Pecksniff, passing the candle rapidly from roll to roll of paper, 'some traces of our doings here. Salisbury Cathedral from the north. From the south. From the east. From the west. From the south-east. From the nor'-west. A bridge. An alms-house. A jail. A church. A powder-magazine. A wine-cellar. A portico. A summer-house. An ice-house. Plans, elevations, sections, every kind of thing.' (136–7)

The architectural perspective is here distanced, abstract and formalised. It divides Salisbury Cathedral into a series of views, or perspectival slices. It separates observer and observed, in order better to serve the purposes of ocular appropriation and regulation. It promises visual wholeness in the rounding of all the perspectives into three-dimensional solidity, but in fact delivers only a flattened, purely formal totality. The reduction of space to geometry – 'plans, elevations, sections' – makes it at once mathematical and miscellaneous: the 'every kind of thing' displayed so casually in Pecksniff's various architectural projects.

There is in *Martin Chuzzlewit* a powerful antidote to this rationalised and architectural perspective, and once again it can be seen dramatised in the view from Todgers's. When trying to assess the larger significance or meaning of this view, it is easy to come to rest prematurely at the end of the first paragraph, with its climactic summary of the whole picture, as 'a very forest . . . wilderness upon wilderness. Smoke enough for all the world at once' (188). But what we are offered in the following paragraph substantially undermines the panoptic command that is implied in the availability of this view and judgement. The anti-architectural perversity of this perspective refuses the graduated, geometrical disposition of near and far and the evaluative orderings it implies. Distance suddenly lurches into proximity, ground is wrenched into figure and vice versa:

> After the first glance, there were slight features in the midst of this crowd of objects, which sprung out from the mass without any reason, as it were, and took hold of the attention whether the spectator would or no . . . The man who was mending a pen at an upper window over the way, became of paramount importance in the scene, and made a blank in it, ridiculously disproportionate in its extent, when he retired. (188)

The disturbed relations of background and foreground recur in the novel in the description of the storm during Jonas's and Montague's journey down to see Pecksniff in Chapter 42. The photographic intermittence produced by the 'crooked and dazzling' lightning, such that 'the eye, partaking of the quickness of the flashing light, saw in its every gleam a multitude of objects which it could not see at steady noon in fifty times that period' (720), replicates the volatility of the view from Todgers's. This loss of perspective in the general or traditional sense is one of the features stressed in Dorothy Van Ghent's essay on the view from Todgers's, but it is anticipated in the surprisingly precise complaint from a reviewer, probably Thomas Cleghorn, in the *North British Review* of May 1845: 'There is no judicious perspective, and withdrawing from view of disagreeable particulars. We stand as close to the most offensive object, and see its details as nakedly, as if it were the most agreeable.'[12] In the view from Todgers's, objects in the field of view refuse to remain merely objects. Looking back on the looker-on, they suggest the presence within the spreading scene of alternative and incommensurate lines of sight: 'the revolving chimney-pots on one great stack of buildings, seemed to be turning gravely to each other every now and then, and whispering the result of their separate observation of what was going on below' (188).

Most importantly, the view from Todgers's is a scene without coherent intervals. Where architectural vision offers the continuity of a divisible space, which supplies and requires gaps *between* objects, the view from Todgers's, in which 'the host of objects seemed to thicken and expand a hundredfold' (188), and the more general social spatiality for which it stands in *Martin Chuzzlewit*, is a crammed and mobile plenitude of impingements. Seen in this light, the most important spatial contrast in the novel may be that between space itself, in the ordinary sense, and congestion. In her book *Dickens the Designer*, Juliet McMaster has an interesting discussion of the relations between egotism and space in *Martin Chuzzlewit*, in which she suggests convincingly that selfish characters in the novel are all spatially covetous. She reads Pecksniff's profession as an architect as a desire for the appropriation of others' space, and points to the many examples in the book of cramping or congestion as the effect of a similar kind of spatial greed, instancing in particular a number of accounts of crowded conditions in coaches, which arise at different times from the selfishness of young Martin, Jonas and Anthony Chuzzlewit and Sarah Gamp.[13] It seems to me, however, that the architectural impulse against which Dickens inveighs in *Martin Chuzzlewit* is expressed not just in the desire to take up space but more generally in the desire to take it over. Such a desire is expressed not so much in the occupation of space as in the abstract or ocular command over it displayed for example in the jeer the narrative allows itself at the fact that Pecksniff styles himself not only as an architect but also as a land surveyor: 'In one sense, and only one, he may be said to have been a Land Surveyor on a pretty large scale, as an extensive prospect lay stretched out before the windows of his house' (64). Pecksniff appropriates space not by physically expanding into it but by a kind of remote control exercised through and at distance. (Hence the seemingly incongruous spatial generosity shown by Pecksniff when leaving Martin to go to London: ' "We leave you in charge of everything. There is no mystery; all is free and open . . . you are forbidden to enter no corner of this house; but are requested to make yourself perfectly at home in every part of it" ' (142).)

The novel sets the homeliness of crowded, constricted or burrowed-out space against this airy but commandeering expansiveness; one of the signs of the obvious narrative approval of Tom Pinch is his capacity to effect architectural improvements under confined conditions – for example in the home he makes for old Martin in the Temple, or in the cramped conditions of the coach he shares with Martin and his box:

> It was not precisely of that convenient size which would admit of its being squeezed into any odd corner . . . It was all on Mr. Pinch's side, and Mr.

> Chuzzlewit said he was very much afraid it would encumber him; to which
> Tom said, 'Not at all;' . . . the cold air came from Mr. Pinch's side of the
> carriage, and by interposing a perfect wall of box and man between it and
> the new pupil, he shielded that young gentleman effectually. (130)

Dickens's suspicion of the remote control of space that he attributes to
architectural aspiration also seems to result in appreciative depictions of
various kinds of obstructed or myopic interior perspective, for example
in the narcotic bedroom at the Blue Dragon, with its absence of colours
or details to stimulate the eye, and its heavy draperies that 'act as non-
conductors to the day and getting up' (80), or the back parlour at
Todgers's, which 'commanded, at a perspective of two feet, a brown wall
with a black cistern on the top' (184). Dickens also enjoys the discomfited
space of the vulgar mansion in Camberwell, whose pretensions to
grandeur of scale are comically undermined. Here the sociable principle
of proximity thwarts the desire for the stretching of space into a symbolic
diagram of class and status; as with the view from Todgers's, architectural
intervals are here suppressed, leading to an uncomfortable jamming
together of the house's front gate, lodge and hall door.

> There was a great front gate; with a great bell, whose handle was in itself
> a note of admiration; and a great lodge; which being close to the house,
> rather spoilt the look-out certainly, but made the look-in, tremendous. At
> this entry, a great porter kept constant watch and ward; and when he gave
> the visitor high leave to pass, he rang a second great bell, responsive to
> whose note a great footman appeared in due time at the great hall-door,
> with such great tags upon his liveried shoulder that he was perpetually
> entangling and hooking himself among the chairs and tables, and led a
> life of torment which could scarcely have been surpassed, if he had been
> a blue-bottle in a world of cobwebs. (192)

The last detail looks forward to the inconvenient epaulettes of General
Fladdock, which similarly frustrate the desire to maintain the formal distinctions between objects: raised to his feet after tripping over his sword at
the house of the Norrises, General Fladdock is forced to move 'edgewise
that he might go in a narrower compass and be in less danger of fraying
the gold lace on his epaulettes by brushing them against anything' (352).

Most effectively as an instance of positively incoherent space in the
novel, there is the 'unaccountable' room in the Liverpool tavern that I
have already referred to. If in one sense it displays an extravagant excess
of detail over form, then looked at another way the room's tipsy eccentricity is also a peculiar instance of form expressing and arising from

function. The tavern room provides a benign version of that collapsed internal space of the house at Camberwell, with its elaborate provision of 'a bell that rang in the room itself, about two feet from the handle, and had no connexion whatever with any other part of the establishment' (621). In its semi-sunken condition, and in its sociable proximity to the pavement, the tavern room gives us the same packed, spasmodic space, with the same sudden reversals of distance and proximity, as are given in the view from Todgers's: 'fearful boys suddenly coming between a thoughtful guest and the light, derided him, or put out their tongues as if he were a physician; or made white knobs on the ends of their noses by flattening the same against the glass, and vanished awfully, like spectres' (621). Typically for Dickens, this shrinking of distance is registered in the way in which sight gives way to sound; the window of the tavern is so close to the street that 'the passengers grated against the window-panes with their buttons, and scraped it with their baskets'.

However, there is no simple distribution in this novel of architectural or regulated space as opposed to social or contiguous space. Many have observed the disconcerting similarities between the largely benign stuffiness and tightness of fit of Todgers's and the oppressiveness of the room, opening on to a blind alley, in which Jonas immures himself to establish his alibi (796), and between the confusing interior walls and partitions of Todgers's, especially in its drawing-room (202), and the glass doors and skylights of Anthony Chuzzlewit's, later his son's house (237, 796). We might say that the impulse to squeeze spatial separation into contiguity is so strong that it affects even the metaspatial disposition of relatively open and closed spaces, closing up, or 'telescoping' (in that other meaning which is never far away from its primary one in Dickens) the very space which allows one metaphorically to distinguish the relations between open and closed space. There is no abstract field of view in which to dispose the different spatial regions or qualities relative to each other, since the metaphorical distinctions between spaces are subject in this novel to the same distortions and convulsions as affect the individual spaces themselves.

In evoking these topological relations and disturbances, Dickens suffers from the apparent disadvantage of working in a verbal medium; for the language of narration can evoke and describe spatial relations but cannot itself mime or embody them. One of the ways in which Dickens seeks to remedy this, here and in other novels, is through his narrative's co-operation with its illustrations. Indeed, at times, it is almost as though the language of the novel were straining to abolish itself in the condition of fixed and palpable visibility that is achievable in the illustrations.

Dickens's narrative process builds towards moments of climax that are simultaneously revelatory, in that they show the sudden, stark emergence of a truth which has hitherto been kept implicit, and static, in their pet-rifaction of such revelation in posture, position or expression: in this novel, for instance, the arrival of Nadgett to condemn Jonas, or Martin's striking down of Pecksniff. But if Dickens in this sense attempts to spa-tialise his own narrative, he also architecturalises some of the language of characters in the novel. Pecksniff in particular piles up language as a sub-stitute for the raising of actual buildings, as is indicated ironically by his sanctimoniously anti-rhetorical rhetoric at the laying of the stone of the grammar school stolen from Martin's designs: ' "My duty is to build, not speak; to act, not talk; to deal with marble, stone, and brick: not lan-guage" ' (626). The reading of the grandiloquent Latin inscription to the building, with its relish for every 'good long substantive, in the third declension, ablative case, with an adjective to match' (625), appears to contradict this verbal parsimony. This archi-rhetorical association between building and language is perhaps given its rationale by the myth of Babel, which evokes the liability to collapse of both architectural and linguistic aspirations.

The most important way in which Dickens attempts to mediate between the immaterial word and the material form of architecture is through the idea of music. It is of more than passing significance, as John Schad has noticed, that Tom Pinch is a musician rather than (or perhaps as well as) an architect.[14] There are two important instances in the novel of the replacement or supplementation of architectural space by the acoustic architecture of music. The first is the description of Tom Pinch playing the organ in Salisbury Cathedral in Chapter 5; the second is the evocation of Tom Pinch at the organ which concludes the book and pro-vides the form for Hablôt Browne's summarising design for the fron-tispiece of the novel. In both, the particular quality of music to which Dickens directs attention is its capacity to pervade and connect shapes and locations. As Tom Pinch plays in Chapter 5, his music resembles and blends with 'the yellow light that streamed in through the ancient windows in the choir . . . mingled with a murky red' (126). In contrast to the insecure alternations between upper and lower dimensions that affect architectural designs of all kinds in the novel, the 'grand tones' of Tom's music are confirmed rather than confounded by the 'echo in the depth of every ancient tomb' which they awaken. The communication of differ-ent spatial dimensions itself is accompanied by a metaphorical blending of different times, since 'the feeling that the sounds awakened, in the moment of their existence, seemed to include his whole life and being'

(126). Where architectural design establishes form through the geometrical division of space, as imaged in Pecksniff's compendium of views, of 'Salisbury Cathedral from the north. From the south. From the east. From the west. From the south-east. From the nor'-west' (137), this acoustic architecture has an imaginary power to establish form through the permeation of space.

Doubtless it is this power that suggests to Dickens the plan of concluding his novel with an evocation of the enlarged blending of the narrative's past, present and future in Tom's organ-playing (916). The imagined capacity of this music to mould the disjoined planes and particles of plot into an organic volume is made clear in the answering contrast between the frontispiece it suggested and the design employed on the monthly wrappers. Both designs offer a total vision of the novel, but in markedly different ways. The initial wrapper design (plate 10) flattens the theme of the novel into formulaic, fabular contrasts, rich and poor, success and failure, pleasure and suffering, which it separates off to the left and the right of the image. Interestingly the structure of the whole, with its contrasting compartments, seems to be secured by a kind of scaffolding; in the lower right this modulates by a visual pun into a judicial scaffold. There is room for interesting speculation about the relation between the architectural raising of fortunes and 'the drop' of the scaffold in the fate of Jonas, for this association recurs in at least two other illustrations; in Sarah Gamp's hanged facsimiles in the illustration to Chapter 49, and in the tripod-shaped scaffold which secures the foundation stone of 'Pecksniff's' grammar school in the illustration to Chapter 35, which is transformed into the Bosch-like apparatus from which Pecksniff dangles in the frontispiece illustration (the detail is below and to the right of the central figure of Tom Pinch). The frontispiece does not allow for the visual distance and separation, the morally distributed space of the wrapper design. In place of its left-hand/right-hand, snakes-and-ladders dichotomies, the frontispiece coils together the crowded, perverse, pervaded space that I have been calling social space.

Music is a more sociable art than architecture, suggests Juliet McMaster, because it is temporal as well as spatial, and thus implies the co-presence of separated spaces.[15] Music itself has its own metaphorical architectonics, of course, in its capacity to mould empty duration into rhythm, pulse and pattern; but the aspect of music that impresses Dickens most in this novel is its power to pervade and transform space, to dissolve distinctions and – to adopt the architectural metaphor that is so potently employed in the novel itself – to cross thresholds. The unmasking of Jonas brings about one of those public explosions of disclosure which will recur in later novels (most remarkably, perhaps, the literal bursting out into the street of the case of Jarndyce in *Bleak House*). The appearance of Nadgett on the threshold of Jonas's room unleashes a torrent of sound, whose jostling energy both saturates and dissolves space:

> Hark! It came on, roaring like a sea! Hawkers burst into the street, crying it up and down; windows were thrown open that the inhabitants might hear it; people stopped to listen in the road and on the pavement; the bells, the same bells began to ring: tumbling over one another in a dance of boisterous joy at the discovery . . . and making their airy playground rock. (783)

Sound both loosens the congestion of the city in *Martin Chuzzlewit* and expresses the principle of interpenetration that accompanies it. This is suggested by the description of the labyrinthine streets near Todgers's, which are so stopped up by obstruction that 'when a stray hackney-coach or lumbering waggon came that way, they were the cause of such an uproar as enlivened the whole neighbourhood, and made the very bells in the next church-tower vibrate again' (866). Usually, in *Martin Chuzzlewit*, the sound of bells transmits itself through and across the spatial distinctions and obstructions of the city, in an irresistible acoustic contagion; here, in a neat inversion, the bells are themselves sounded by the ringing clamour of the city. The bells which resound through the novel, in premonition, vengeance and celebration, suggestively enact the passage from the divisive architecture of crime to the associative architecture of music. Bells belong to and express the principle of architectural elevation, but resist the abstraction of spaces and places that is otherwise associated with elevation in the novel. They are ubiquitous in the novel both in the sense that they are heard everywhere and in the sense that they draw together every different location.

Dickens's fascination with the dissolving powers of sound seems at times to outweigh his interest in the resolving powers of music. This may be suggested by the havoc he wreaks upon the claims of music in his comic account of the serenade performed by the gentlemen at Todgers's. This music aspires to the architectural ordering of place and distance, with its final evocation of Pecksniff, the 'architect, artist, and man', as the performers 'gradually withdrew to bed to give the music the effect of distance' (247). But Dickens comically yet forcefully subdues the performance of this piece to his own narrative performance of it. His narrative of the episode both holds its music together and pulls it apart, his focus on the expressionist performance of the flautist Augustus Moddle rendering it as an image of the baroque unpredictability of place typical of

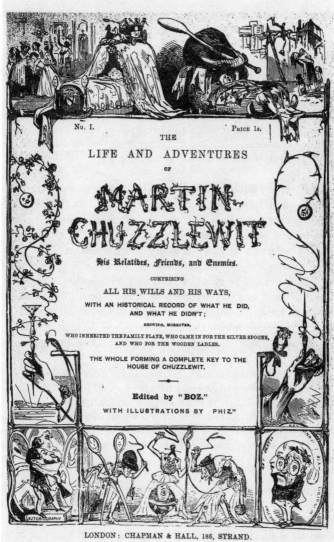

10   Hablôt Browne ('Phiz')
cover design for the serial (1843)

Todgers's and undermining its pretensions to classical, quasi-architectural composure:

> The flute of the youngest gentleman was wild and fitful. It came and went, in gusts, like the wind. For a long time together, he seemed to have left off, and when it was quite settled by Mrs. Todgers and the young ladies, that, overcome by his feelings, he had retired in tears, he unexpectedly turned up again at the very top of the tune, gasping for breath. He was a tremendous performer. There was no knowing where to have him; and exactly when you thought he was doing nothing at all, then he was doing the very thing that ought to astonish you most. (246)

The wildness and fitfulness of Moddle's flute-playing associates it with the decidedly an-architectural, though not wholly anarchic, wind that gusts through *Martin Chuzzlewit*. Like the fog of *Bleak House*, the wind that springs up in Chapter 2 of the novel serves both to disrupt and to reconfigure the orderings of space. It anticipates the movement of the novel itself in rushing through Pecksniff's house on the way to sport itself out in the open ocean. The effect of wind and sea is both to collapse all distinctions of form and to assert a more dynamic principle of unity in the principle of force transmitted over what Dickens evocatively calls 'angry space', in a passage which gives us accelerated versions of the various kinds of spatial enfoldings and collapses which occur through the novel:

> On, on, on, over the countless miles of angry space roll the long heaving billows. Mountains and caves are here, and yet are not; for what is now the one, is now the other; then all is but a boiling heap of rushing water. Pursuit, and flight, and mad return of wave on wave, and savage struggle, ending in a spouting-up of foam that whitens the black night; incessant change of place, and form, and hue; constancy in nothing, but eternal strife. (308)

The wind contributes to the anti-architectural design of the book because, like sound itself, it is a disturbance of the air which moves through and across spatial distinctions. The association between the wind and the art of music established in the description of Augustus Moddle's playing is thus very apt. The question of the power of music to move across distinctions is central to the architectural aesthetics and ethics of the book as a whole, which, as I said at the beginning of this chapter, have a more radical form than that suggested by Dickens's own views and preferences about architecture as they are expressed outside the novel.

Hablôt Browne's frontispiece illustration (plate 11) is a marvellous

11   Hablôt Browne ('Phiz')
frontispiece of the first edition (1844)

transposition of the musical into visual form; but, inasmuch as it is a spa-tialisation of the non- or trans-spatial, it is also, inevitably, a kind of failure. There is the sting of rivalry here, within the convivial association of word and image; for it is important for Dickens's purpose that the image should be set against itself, should be forced, to the very degree that it succeeds in conjuring up the temporal totality of the novel, to testify against the tendency of images to freeze and formalise emergence and duration, a tendency which has also been associated accusingly through-out the novel with architecture. The image is so successful an evocation of the text it supplements that one cannot merely *see* this image; one is forced to *read* it, as attentively as any portion of the text. Indeed, there is significant reading matter in it. At the top of the text, there is a (literally) overarching and unifying architectural motif, meant to stand, no doubt, for Salisbury Cathedral, which shades on the left into the Blue Dragon and on the right into Pecksniff's architectural area (which includes his architectural signature, the pump). Written across the spines of the enor-mous books there are some phrases which remind us of the famous epitaph to Sir Christopher Wren's tomb in St Paul's: 'Si monumentum requiris, circumspice' – 'If you look for his monument, look about you'. The epitaph tells us that words are inadequate, and that what can be seen is richer and more substantial testimony to the glory of Wren's achieve-ment. The imaging of these words, with their ironic application (is the monument to Pecksniff his pump?), delivers us to the visual music of asso-ciations which unrolls around Tom Pinch, but in so doing also takes us back to the text to which they are subsidiary.

On its own, Dickens's textual evocation of the memories that rise up with Tom's organ-playing is feeble enough, for it thins out and formalises the density and crowded complexity of the novel that it concludes. In pro-viding us with a mere 'elevation' or 'section' of the novel, the conclusion might even be seen as an involuntary lapse into the architectural mode that Dickens disdains and comically molests throughout its length. By going beyond the narrative to which it restores our attention, but also falling short of its capacity to evoke a crowded world of emergence, the frontispiece closes the uncomfortable interval between the novel and its own formalised conclusion. The illustration is thus a relay to transmit the novel to itself. In the end, it is the powers of his own narrative to dispose, disclose and connect that Dickens wishes to set against the mythifying, monumental powers of the architect. Narrative delivers, and delivers itself to the interruptions, impingements and comminglings that are dis-avowed in the will-to-architecture. *Martin Chuzzlewit* organises itself with peculiar and paradoxical purposefulness around the narrative principle of unbuilding. The fascination of *Martin Chuzzlewit*, as a transitional novel between the earlier, more fluidly extemporised works and the later, more comprehensively architectonic novels, is the curious, collapsing integrity it derives from its ruination of the architectural.

Notes

1 See the chapter '*Martin Chuzzlewit*: Architecture and Accommodation', in F. S. Schwarzbach, *Dickens and the City* (London: Athlone Press, 1979), pp. 80–100.
2 Alan R. Burke, 'The House of Chuzzlewit and the Architectural City', *Dickens Studies Annual*, 3 (1973), 14–40. Despite my disagreements with this essay, it will be plain what a considerable resource it has been to me in my thinking about this topic.
3 Joseph H. Gardner, 'Pecksniff's Profession: Boz, Phiz, and Pugin', *The Dickensian*, 72 (1976), 75–86.
4 Burke, 'The House of Chuzzlewit and the Architectural City', p. 25.
5 Joseph H. Gardner, 'Pecksniff's Profession', pp. 79–80, Michael Steig, *Dickens and Phiz* (Bloomington and London: Indiana University Press, 1978), pp. 64–5.
6 Bert G. Hornback, *Noah's Arkitechture: A Study of Dickens's Mythology* (Athens: Ohio University Press, 1972), pp. 41–52.
7 Dorothy Van Ghent, 'The Dickens World: The View From Todgers's', *Sewanee Review*, 58 (1950), 419–38.
8 *Martin Chuzzlewit*, ed. Margaret Cardwell (Oxford: Clarendon Press, 1982), p. 835.
9 Burke, 'The House of Chuzzlewit and the Architectural City', pp. 15, 22.
10 For a history of the development of underground engineering in London, see Richard Trench and Ellis Hillman, *London Under London: A Subterranean Guide* (London: John Murray, 1984).
11 Rosalind Williams, in her *Notes on the Underground: An Essay on Technology, Society, and the Imagination* (Cambridge, Mass. and London: MIT Press, 1990), traces the relations between the imagination of the urban underground and the fascination with the excavation of origins in nineteenth-century geological science.
12 'Writings of Charles Dickens', *North British Review*, iii (May 1845), repr. in *Charles Dickens: The Critical Heritage*, ed. Philip Collins (London: Routledge & Kegan Paul, 1971), p. 190.
13 Juliet McMaster, *Dickens the Designer* (Totowa, NJ: Barnes & Noble, 1987), pp. 63–8.
14 John Schad, *The Reader in the Dickensian Mirrors* (Basingstoke: Macmillan, 1992), p. 107.
15 McMaster, *Dickens the Designer*, p. 65.

11

Dickens's idle men

DAVID TROTTER

The opening chapter of *American Notes* (1842) describes the two stages of Dickens's embarkation on the steam-packet *Britannia*, 'twelve hundred tons burden per register, bound for Halifax and Boston, and carrying Her Majesty's mails' (53). The first stage begins in sharp disillusionment, as a preliminary inspection exposes the inadequacy of the ship's facilities, and concludes, after a survey of a stewardess's 'merry eyes' and some convincing nautical bustle, with spirits partially recovered, and a return to solid ground for the night. The second stage begins with the final journey out to the packet, and a revival of Dickens's writerly interest in his fellow-passengers. The ship attracts murmurs of admiration.

> Even the lazy gentleman with his hat on one side and his hands in his pockets, who has dispensed so much consolation by inquiring with a yawn of another gentleman whether he is 'going across' – as if it were a ferry – even he condescends to look that way, and nods his head, as who should say, 'No mistake about *that*'. (58–9)

The lazy gentleman has made the passage thirteen times before, and soon acquires the status of a veteran, an expert, an oracle. He remains utterly unperturbed by the 'bewildering tumult' of departure.

> In the midst of all this, the lazy gentleman, who seems to have no luggage of any kind – not so much as a friend, even – lounges up and down the hurricane-deck, coolly puffing a cigar; and, as this unconcerned demeanour again exalts him in the opinion of those who have leisure to observe his proceedings, every time he looks up at the masts, or down at the decks, they look there too, as wondering whether he sees anything wrong anywhere, and hoping that, in case he should, he will have the goodness to mention it. (59–60)

One person who clearly has the leisure to observe these proceedings, and to admire the unconcerned demeanour they reveal, is the author himself. The lazy gentleman establishes, through sheer laziness, a position which the observer, encumbered not only by luggage and friends but by the duties of observation, would dearly like to occupy. I shall suggest that Dickens occasionally found the leisure in his fiction to reflect upon displays of unconcern; and that these moments are worth commenting on because they are, like the one in the opening chapter of *American Notes*, wonderfully poised and inventive.

There can be no doubt about the lazy gentleman's dedication to laziness. Dickens encounters him once more on the voyage out when, miserably sea-sick, he stumbles up on deck in the middle of a storm.

> Even in that incapable state, however, I recognised the lazy gentleman standing before me: nautically clad in a suit of shaggy blue, with an oilskin hat. But I was too imbecile, although I knew it to be he, to separate him from his dress; and tried to call him, I remember, *Pilot*. After another interval of total unconsciousness, I found he had gone. (65)

One might hallucinate a function for this layabout by addressing him as 'pilot'. But he is not to be defined in that way. He has no function, either in life, as far as one can tell, or in the narrative. His departure from the tale, during the 'interval of total unconsciousness', is as abrupt as his entrance into it. He never reappears. Dickens accords him an epithet, but not a name, not a part to play.

This chapter is about the imaginative appeal of unconcern, of vacancy, of lack of purpose. I will try to demonstrate, first, that there is a connection between the idler's neglect of purposeful activity and his narrative inconsequence; and, second, that it is the narrative inconsequence which frees Dickens to write with a particular and extraordinary command. When he contemplates his lazy gentlemen, he becomes momentarily as lazy as they are, as unencumbered. I do not claim any great significance for them. Indeed, I shall suggest that it was precisely their marginality which made them so attractive to him.

Descriptions

In Dickens's fiction, the lazy gentlemen constitute a technique for the description of city life. In this respect, they perhaps have something in common with the *flâneurs*, those dandyish observers of the urban crowd who supposedly made the nineteenth-century arcades their own, and whose self-display and inquisitive detachment have been seen as symptomatic of the formation of recognisably modern attitudes to the city.[1] Indeed, John Rignall has argued convincingly that in nineteenth-century realist fiction the *flâneur*'s remote yet curious gaze 'duplicates that of the novelist himself, who confidently assigns meaning to details of physical appearance, dress and milieu, and reads the visible exterior as a clue to the truth or life behind it'. However, the novelist's self-mirroring is not necessarily uncritical: the *flâneur*'s frequent inability to make sense of what he sees, the perplexity in which his observations appear so often to involve him, might be taken to mark the limits of realist technique.[2] Rignall's thesis illuminates the part played by strolling spectators in *Bleak House* and other novels. But the lazy gentlemen I wish to draw attention to differ from these spectators in two respects: first, their gaze does not so much duplicate that of the novelist as offer an enticing alternative to it; second, they make no effort to make sense of what they see, and therefore cannot be said either to succeed or to fail as interpreters.

In Chapter 32 of *Nicholas Nickleby* (1832–33), Nicholas and Smike arrive in London by stagecoach. The spectacle which greets them exemplifies the baffling heterogeneity of city life.

> Streams of people apparently without end poured on and on, jostling each other in the crowd and hurrying forward, scarcely seeming to notice the riches that surrounded them on every side; while vehicles of all shapes and makes, mingled up together in one moving mass like running water, lent their ceaseless roar to swell the noise and tumult. (*NN*, 488)

The noise and tumult happen *to* Nicholas and Smike, on the stage-coach roof, but not *for* them. They do not respond to it, and it does not reveal or provoke anything in them. Who, then, *is* it for? Dickens uses an impersonal construction ('it was curious to observe') to define the point of view from which the tumult is observed. The spectacle activates a generalised curiosity which might be thought to include Nicholas and Smike, but which does not belong to them. Half a page later, Dickens delivers a moralising exegesis of it which is pretty clearly outside their current preoccupations. 'Life and death went hand in hand; wealth and poverty stood side by side; repletion and starvation laid them down together' (*NN*, 489).

Dickens knew that he could not rely on his characters to convey what he himself knew about London. In *Oliver Twist*, Oliver and Sikes, *en route* from Bethnal Green to Chertsey, pass through Smithfield Market, 'from which latter place arose a tumult of discordant sounds that filled Oliver

Twist with amazement' (*OT,* 203): there follows a description of tumult so resourceful that it evidently cannot be attributed to the dumbfounded child-hero. Which would be fine, except that Dickens usually did feel obliged, I think, to attribute such descriptions to someone. The pseudo-biblical cadence of the passage I have quoted from *Nicholas Nickleby* ('repletion and starvation laid them down together') shows him invoking the wisdom of ages as a perspective on modern urban experience – and thus perhaps missing its specificity. What he needed was a point of view confined neither to the particular nor to the general.

Chapter 37 of *Nicholas Nickleby* introduces both the hero and the reader to the counting-house of the brothers Cheeryble, situated in a pleasant backwater in the City.

> It is a quiet, little-frequented, retired spot, favourable to melancholy and contemplation, and appointments of long-waiting; and up and down its every side the Appointed saunters idly the hour together, wakening the echoes with the monotonous sound of his footsteps on the smooth worn stones, and counting first the windows and then the very bricks of the tall silent houses that hem him round about. (553)

There is a new feeling here, about London: one of melancholy, perhaps, but a melancholy which does not incapacitate. The Appointed is kept waiting, and the wait subjects him to some monotonous pacing and calculating. But a man who 'saunters idly' is not a man whom the delay of business has reduced to anxiety or anger. He has that much in common with the lazy gentleman of *American Notes.* Idle sauntering is perhaps what he does best; and doing that best is an activity which reveals aspects of city life barely perceptible to those whose appointments are strenuously kept. It is an activity, we might note, which steadfastly refuses to become a point of view (a position from which meaning can be grasped or ascribed). Whereas the *flâneur* reads the city like a book, ceaselessly decoding manner and behaviour, Dickens's lazy gentlemen count bricks or stare into space.

This absolute failure to produce meaning dissociates the lazy gentlemen both from the wisdom of ages and from the novel's characters, whose narrative destinies require of them some measure of intentionality. The Appointed has no name. He plays no part in events. His disappearance, like his appearance, is abrupt and unmotivated. He constitutes a degree zero of narrative as well as of hermeneutic momentum. And yet he does make something happen. He makes possible a rhetorical event, in the ensuing description of the square. 'It is so quiet that you can almost hear the ticking of your own watch when you stop to cool in its refreshing atmosphere' (553). Dickens steps outside the novel, for a moment, outside the current preoccupations of his characters, in order to reveal an aspect of urban experience; and yet he does not feel the need to invoke a panoramic perspective. The silence in which you listen for the sound of your own watch reproduces the hermeneutic degree zero of the silence in which the Appointed counts bricks; and it creates a further narrative degree zero, a bubble of inconsequence. For a moment, Dickens occupies the position marked out by an unnamed idler. The idler may or may not be refreshed by the square's atmosphere; the author certainly is, by this temporary suspension of narratorial responsibilities.

There is some reason to think that those responsibilities might have been weighing heavily on the author's shoulders. When Nicholas returns to London, in Chapter 32, it is in response to an urgent message from Newman Noggs. Not finding Newman at home, he wanders the streets, as he often does when anxious, and eventually turns into an expensive hotel for a pint of wine and a biscuit. There he overhears two dissolute men-about-town, Sir Mulberry Hawk and Lord Verisopht, discussing his sister Kate in far from complimentary terms. *Nicholas Nickleby* is a novel about class, about the proper definition of gentility; and this stage-managed coincidence serves the purpose of introducing Nicholas at first hand to a gentility defined by status and appearance rather than by conduct. When he returns to London in Chapter 32, he returns to an allegorised city where rakes transparently abuse class privilege in the pursuit of virtuous maidens. He will shortly encounter a gentility defined by conduct in the shape of the self-made and unsparingly charitable Cheeryble brothers. Chapter 37, which begins with the Appointed counting bricks, ends with a transparent display of Cheeryble-ness, as the brothers throw a party for their faithful old retainer, Tim Linkinwater. I would suggest that the former's inconsequence offered Dickens blissful if momentary relief from the gathering momentum of his own allegory. Unlike the *flâneurs*, Dickens's lazy gentlemen do not appear to be dandies; their function is to see, not to be seen. And yet they are men of leisure, or at least men unperturbed by the delay of business. It may be that their idleness, like that of the *flâneurs*, only in a more radical fashion, constitutes an implicit reproach to narratives which endorse strenuous self-making.

The tendency of criticism has been to tuck these loose ends back into the allegorical weave. A famous essay by Dorothy Van Ghent proposes that the view from the roof of Todgers's boarding-house, in *Martin*

Chuzzlewit (1843–44), a view attributed to an unnamed and not notably purposeful observer, should be understood as characteristic of 'the Dickens world'. 'The prospect from Todgers's', Van Ghent argues,

> is one in which categorical determinations of the significance of objects – as of the chimney pots, the blank upper window, or the dyer's cloth – have broken down, and the observer on Todgers's roof is seized with suicidal nausea at the momentary vision of a world in which significance has been replaced by naked and aggressive existence.[3]

While there is undoubtedly some truth in this account, it may insist too much on the scene's centrality, and on the extreme nature of the break-down it portrays.

Todgers's features prominently enough in the action of the novel. The Pecksniffs board there, and are visited there by Jonas Chuzzlewit, among others. Yet none of the main characters ever makes it as far as the roof. Whatever it is that happens there happens incidentally, by way of distraction from the gathering pace of events: events in which the unnamed observer plays no part at all. Indeed, the scene which unfolds would seem to be removed from action of any kind, or indeed repre-sentativeness of any kind, by its interest in the mechanics of perception. 'After the first glance, there were slight features in the midst of this crowd of objects, which sprung out from the mass without any reason, as it were, and took hold of the attention whether the spectator would or no' (*MC*, 188). The interlude on the roof allows Dickens to explore, as Edmund Husserl and Maurice Merleau-Ponty were later to do, the phe-nomenology of perception: to grasp the way in which the world appears to us by bracketing off conscious acts of mind (willing, judging, expect-ing and so on).[4]

'The man who was mending a pen at an upper window over the way, became of paramount importance in the scene, and made a blank in it, ridiculously disproportionate in its extent, when he retired' (*MC*, 188). The disproportion of the effect indicates that perception is never unmediated: that the mind makes sense of the world by processing sensory data in the context provided by data stored in the memory. The gap left by the pen-mender's retirement from the window is a gap left not so much *in* what is perceived as *between* what is seen and what is remem-bered: a gap created, one might say, in the mind's grasp of experience, in the illusion of stability it seeks to create. The rupture of that illusion might well be thought to provoke unease. But it is scarcely a moral or social unease. Dickens's phenomenology of perception scrupulously avoids, as yet, any gesture at 'naked and aggressive existence'. By exceeding the preoccupations of the novel's characters without recourse to a panoramic perspective, by delineating a roof which is neither place of rendezvous nor panopticon, it makes for him a moment of blissful unconcern.

From this point on, however, the scene becomes increasingly self-conscious, and it is this self-consciousness, I would argue, which has been mistaken for a protest against naked and aggressive existence.

> The gambols of a piece of cloth upon the dyer's pole had far more interest for the moment than all the changing motion of the crowd. Yet even while the looker-on felt angry with himself for this, and wondered how it was, the tumult swelled into a roar; the hosts of objects seemed to thicken and expand a hundredfold; and after gazing round him quite scared, he turned into Todgers's again, much more rapidly than he came out; and ten to one he told M. Todgers afterwards that if he hadn't done so, he would certainly have come into the street by the shortest cut: that is to say, head-foremost. (*MC*, 188–9)

This looker-on, unlike those I have discussed so far, is not entirely immune to narrative. He even extrudes a micro-narrative of his own, a story of panic and hasty descent, of 'suicidal nausea'. But we should note that the panic is to some extent self-induced. The looker-on feels guilty for allowing himself to find greater interest in the gambols of a piece of cloth (or in the appearance and disappearance of a man mending a pen) than in the changing motion of the crowd. He feels guilty because he has taken a holiday from the exegetic responsibilities of the strolling spectator. It is only *after* his guilt has become manifest that his failure to make sense of what he sees begins to unsettle him, and he feels sick. At this point, he enters a story, a story about the modern city, about naked and aggressive existence. While I would concede that the story he then recounts to M. Todgers is a disturbing one, I think that its significance lies less in the vision it conveys than in the speed with which it is hashed up. To my mind, the looker-on's belated guilt is also the novelist's. Dickens recoils from the pleasures of unmotivated observation into a micro-narrative whose hysteria betrays its origin. Another moment on the roof and he might have *become* Merleau-Ponty.

Inspectors

In Chapter 4 of *Nicholas Nickleby*, we encounter a variant of the 'lazy gentleman' trope. Nicholas and his uncle seek out Mr Wackford Squeers at the Saracen's Head, Snow Hill. Dickens identifies the yard of the Saracen's Head as a site at once inside and outside the novel.

> When you walk up this yard, you will see the booking-office on your left, and the tower of Saint Sepulchre's church darting abruptly up into the sky on your right, and a gallery of bedrooms on both sides. Just before you, you will observe a long window with the words 'coffee-room' legibly painted above it; and looking out of that window, you would have seen in addition, if you had gone at the right time, Mr Wackford Squeers with his hands in his pocket. (90)

On this occasion, the phantom observer is neither named nor designated by epithet. But he or she is like the lazy gentleman and the Appointed in conspicuously having no business, at a moment when the main characters are preoccupied with business; and in having no further part to play in the tale.

Chapter 4 opens in more abstract fashion, identifying the Saracen's Head not by the appearance it might present to an observer but by its proximity to nearby landmarks: Newgate, Smithfield Market and the 'squalid tottering houses' of Snow Hill (*NN*, 89). These landmarks are defined institutionally, so to speak, through the position they occupy within a social and economic system: 'at the very core of London, in the heart of its business and animation'. We can sense, as Dickens lengthens his rhetorical stride in the paragraphs which describe them, something of the threat they posed, in his mind, to the very possibility of business and animation. What emerges here is an institutional apprehension of the city which the later novels were to extend and refine considerably. The stroller in the yard thus obtrudes his or her laziness not only against Nicholas's embryonic career but also against an institutional apprehension of the city, and indeed against the very idea that novels might have a strenuous diagnostic function.

Social commentary had always been an important feature of Dickens's novels. In the early 1840s, however, the emphasis altered from attacks on relatively isolated abuses like Poor Law reform or the Yorkshire schools to a general mapping of social and economic malaise. Dickens began to believe that the way to ensure the wealth of the nation was to ensure its health. One of his closest friends was his brother-in-law, Henry Austin, an engineer who had become involved in the politics of public health while working on the construction of the Blackwall Railway in East London. In 1842, Edwin Chadwick asked Austin to present a copy of his *Report on the Sanitary Condition of the Labouring Population of Great Britain* to Dickens. Dickens was at first suspicious of Chadwick, holding him responsible for the tyrannies of the 1834 Poor Law Amendment Act. But he soon relented. Throughout the 1840s he worked closely with Austin to promote sanitary reform, collaborating on articles and speeches. In 1848, Austin became Secretary to the General Board of Health. K. J. Fielding and A. W. Brice, who have examined this collaboration in detail, conclude that Dickens 'not only had access to the most important central authority on public health, on the sanitary problems brought by the great cities, and on measures to be taken against the dreaded visitation of cholera, but . . . was also enlisted as an ally and received help with his own writing in return'.[5] In the preface to the 1849 edition of *Martin Chuzzlewit*, he claimed that he had taken 'every possible opportunity' to expose in his novels the 'want of sanitary improvements' in the dwellings of the poor (*MC*, 40).

The sanitary reformers argued that bad housing and bad drainage cause disease. Organic matter accumulated in cesspools and blocked drains putrefies and gives off a foul miasma, a 'disease-mist' or noxious gas; anyone inhaling the miasma sickens. Chadwick's solution was to pump water through a comprehensive system of glazed sewers, and so sweep away any deposits of solid matter before they could putrefy. He believed that 'continuous circulation' should be the fundamental principle of sanitary reform. In cities as in bodies, malfunction was caused by blockage. Clear the blockage and you restore the organism to health.

Sanitary reform was conceived as part of an ambitious programme of economic, social and moral discipline. In *The Health of Nations*, a posthumous epitome and review of Chadwick's work published in 1887, the essays on wealth and population are supplemented by others on every imaginable aspect of social and moral policing. Few things were beneath his notice. The last essay he wrote urges the issue of tricycles to the Metropolitan Police, for reasons of fitness as well as efficiency. Another draws attention to the disciplinary effects of Dickens's novels on an apprentice who, since he preferred reading to working, was invited to read aloud. 'The idle apprentice read from *Pickwick*, and soon the laughter became epidemic, with such an improvement in the rapidity of the work that the master appointed idle Tom to be reader in general, with the best success.' Chadwick reported the experiment to Dickens, assigning to Tom 'the function, economically, of a fifer or drummer to animate, regulate, and quicken the march of production'.[6]

The credence Dickens gave to the metaphor of circulation produced in his later novels an almost obsessive recurrence to examples of blockage such as Newgate prison, Smithfield Market and the Snow Hill slum.

The sticky, foul-smelling deposits lodged in attic-rooms and burial- grounds find analogies in financial irregularity and administrative incompetence, in repressed feeling and the 'perpetual stoppage' (*BH,* 211) of fashionable society. Dickens's rhetoric clots and exfoliates as he regards the effects of obstruction.[7] In a world mapped by metaphor there is, one might think, as little room for an idle observer as there is for an idle apprentice. His early novels create a place for a different kind of observer, a strenuous observer, a man with a keen and perhaps officially sanctioned appetite for meaning.

Consider, for example, the description of the Three Cripples, in *Oliver Twist* (1837–39), an inn notable for the moral 'repulsiveness' of its customers.

Cunning, ferocity, and drunkenness in all its stages, were there, in their strongest aspects; and women: some with the last lingering tinge of their early freshness almost fading as you looked: others with every mark and stamp of their sex utterly beaten out, and presenting but one loathsome blank of profligacy and crime; some mere girls, others but young women, and none past the prime of life; formed the darkest and saddest portion of this dreary picture. (237)

The distended syntax of this sentence reveals a desire at once to draw a general 'picture', from the moralist's position of relative detachment, and to savour novelistically its most pungent detail: to narrow the focus first to the women present, and then to those women who most vividly display, for the benefit of an observer whose position is distinctly if faintly marked, the very process of corruption ('almost fading as you looked'). The excitement of observation, of simply being there, in such spectacularly low company, has to be reframed ('this dreary picture') while the sentence advances so as to include a justifying alertness to social symbolism.

This alertness comes into play again as the novel reaches its climax, in Chapter 50, with the pursuit of Sikes to Jacob's Island, in Southwark, a neighbourhood which must rank as 'the filthiest, the strangest, the most extraordinary of the many localities that are hidden in London, wholly unknown, even by name, to the great mass of its inhabitants'. A neighbourhood so strange, so wholly unknown, is not susceptible to casual description. It requires a map, a plan of action. 'To reach this place, the visitor has to penetrate through a maze of close, narrow, and muddy streets.' It is through the eyes of the intrepid visitor that we see Jacob's Island.

> Jostling with unemployed labourers of the lowest class, ballast-heavers, coal-whippers, brazen women, ragged children, and the raff and refuse of the river, he makes his way with difficulty along, assailed by offensive sights and smells from the narrow alleys which branch off on the right and left, and deafened by the clash of ponderous waggons that bear great piles of merchandise from the stacks of warehouses that rise from every corner. (*OT*, 442)

The emphasis on class differences ('unemployed labourers of the lowest class', 'raff and refuse of the river') serves to separate out and identify the visitor, even before we have registered the difficulties and dangers he faces on his journey. This is no idle observer. The only possible explanation for his presence among such offensive sights and smells is official business. He belongs, or might well belong, to the growing band of Chadwickian reformers. The next two paragraphs record the evidence such a man might want to examine: 'every repulsive lineament of poverty, every loathsome indication of filth, rot, and garbage' (*OT*, 443). In these lineaments and indications is the meaning the reformer seeks.

Passages such as this develop a position for the figure prepared institutionally and rhetorically by the social reform movement. Reports such as James Kay's *The Moral and Physical Condition of the Working Class* (1832) had already imagined the cholera doctor as an urban explorer.

> He whose duty it is to follow the steps of this messenger of death, must descend to the abodes of poverty, must frequent the close alleys, the crowded courts, the overpeopled habitations of wretchedness, where pauperism and disease congregate round the source of social discontent and political disorder in the centre of our large towns, and behold with alarm, in the hot-bed of pestilence, ills that fester in secret, at the very heart of society.[8]

Dickens was not blind to the authority and the dramatic potential of the narrative position marked out by the reports of reformers like Kay. Where an implicitly purposeful 'visitor' or 'stranger' ventures in the early novels, an explicitly purposeful doctor or engineer will venture in the later novels. *Dombey and Son* (1849) contrasts the magistrate's abstract denunciation of the poor with the reformer's empirical knowledge: 'follow the good clergyman or doctor, who, with his life imperilled at every breath he draws, goes down into their dens, lying within the echoes of our carriage wheels and daily tread upon the pavement stones' (737). In *Bleak House*, we follow Allan Woodcourt into such dens. It was through the eyes of such men that Dickens increasingly chose to view urban experience.

Enigma and its antidotes

One kind of blockage which worried and excited Dickens was any obstruction of the flow of information upon which the business of the world depended. The metaphor of circulation which had given both shape and savour to his imagining of social process turned excessive or malevolent secrecy into an object of compelling horror. Think, for example, of the lawyer Tulkinghorn, in *Bleak House* (1853), a 'silent repository' of 'family confidences' (58) who hoards information as others hoard money. Tulkinghorn's calling is, as Lady Dedlock points out, 'the acquisition of secrets, and the holding possession of such powers as they give him, with no sharer or opponent in it' (567). The criminality of his conduct needs (and receives) no explanation, because miserliness represented to Dickens the worst kind of 'perpetual stoppage'. In the later novels, the secretive secrete. Like a tumour, they extract matter from the bloodstream of society; and the matter they have extracted stagnates and festers in its hiding-places. *Bleak House* abounds in characters dedicated to the acquisition of secrets which they hope to exploit for personal gain.

Such blockages could be cleared only by a new type of specialist: Nadgett, in *Martin Chuzzlewit*; Inspector Bucket, in *Bleak House*; and Pancks, in *Little Dorrit*. These men do not merely resolve the particular mysteries which at once bind together and isolate the main protagonists. They enact the resolution of mystery itself. They cleanse and disinfect a landscape fouled by secretiveness. In this respect, they might be said to constitute a counter-type to the lazy gentlemen of the early novels. They are neither lazy nor gentlemen. Strenuously purposeful, tenacious to a fault, they do not merely scan a scene, as a stroller would, but devour it instantly, extract its essence and then move on.

Dickens slyly compares type and counter-type by allowing his detectives to masquerade, on occasion, as idlers. Mr Nadgett, who makes enquiries on behalf of the Anglo-Bengalee Disinterested Loan and Life Assurance Company, is always keeping appointments in the City, 'and the other man never seemed to come'. He sits for hours in business coffee-houses, occasionally drying a damp handkerchief before the fire, and 'still looking for the man who never appeared' (*MC*, 517). Even when in hot pursuit of a suspect, Inspector Bucket still manages to seem at a loose end. He 'pervades' houses and 'strolls about an infinity of streets: to outward appearance rather languishing for want of an object' (*BH*, 768). No wonder lazy gentlemen are something of a rarity in the later novels: their very *modus operandi* has been requisitioned for official purposes.

It is those official purposes which now expose and render the city.

Inspector Bucket, in search of Jo the crossing-sweeper, dives into a street 'reeking' with such smells that his companion Snagsby, who has lived in London all his life, can scarcely believe his senses (364). His pursuit of Lady Dedlock takes Esther Summerson and himself down the 'narrowest and worst streets' in the capital (858). The very extremity of the pollution requires an informed and committed presence: a detective, a sanitary inspector. But Dickens could not quite bring himself to relinquish altogether the pleasures of vacancy. He occasionally revived them, in the later novels, by temporarily de-commissioning, as it were, a minor character: by releasing him or her, for a spell, from any obligations to the narrative.

The solicitor's clerk William Guppy, in *Bleak House*, belongs to a group of virulently malign petit-bourgeois blackmailers which also includes the Smallweeds, the Chadbands and Mrs Snagsby. The resentment and acquisitive fury of this group brings down the Dedlocks. Chadband expresses their philosophy when he flaunts their hoarded knowledge in front of Sir Leicester. ' "Air we in possession of a sinful secret, and doe we require corn, and wine, and oil – or, what is much the same thing, money, for the keeping thereof? Probably so, my friends" ' (789). Guppy's inquisitiveness about Esther Summerson is a milder, although potentially harmful, version of this malevolence. But in Chapter 20 he is released for a blissful moment from his demented social climbing.

Much of the novel's action takes place during a hot summer when the law courts are in recess and the clerks at Kenge and Carboy have little to do but swelter and chafe. 'Mr Guppy has been lolling out of window all morning, after trying all the stools in succession and finding none of them easy, and after several times putting his head into the iron safe with a notion of cooling it' (327). While lolling out of the window, 'surveying', as the Appointed had done in *Nicholas Nickleby*, 'the intolerable bricks and mortar' (*BH*, 328), he spots his friend Tony Jobling. The moment of vacancy generates a virtuoso comic interlude, as Guppy and Jobling repair, with Guppy's colleague Bart Smallweed, to a chop-house known as the Slap-Bang.

During this interlude, Bart Smallweed, otherwise barely perceptible, comes stupendously alive. In the office, he is Guppy's pale and obsequious shadow. But the Slap-Bang enables him to deploy to brilliant effect his profound knowledge of life in general and waitresses in particular. He supervises the ordering of an epic meal. Towards the end of the meal, Guppy resumes his narrative function, thus distinguishing himself from his deputy, who has none. He proposes that Jobling should rent a room above Krook's rag and bottle shop, with a view to acquiring some of the old man's secrets. Smallweed, who later turns out to be Krook's nephew, shows no interest in the project. While Guppy and Jobling hurry off to see Krook, he stays behind in slap-bang heaven, reading the papers, the very antithesis of purposeful activity. The *Times* is so large in proportion to himself that when he holds it up to run his eye over the columns he 'seems to have retired for the night, and to have disappeared under the bedclothes' (*BH*, 337). Bart Smallweed is to some extent dissociated from the utterly repellent Smallweed clan (342–7), and he escapes the punishment meted out to them. He is not present when the older Smallweeds and the Chadbands invade Chesney Wold, to blackmail Sir Leicester, and are defeated by the guileful Inspector Bucket (785–91). Nor is he present when Guppy, accompanied by Jobling, renews his suit to Esther Summerson, and is suavely dismissed by Jarndyce (915–20). Bart Smallweed is a connoisseur of vacancy, and as such exempted from the possessive hermeneutic fury which sours Guppy and Jobling, corrodes the rest of the Smallweed clan and kills Tulkinghorn.

Harmlessness

I want by way of conclusion to examine briefly two issues connected with Dickens's lazy gentlemen: the company they keep, and the ground they occupy. For although they are marginal figures, their influence is, to a limited extent, contagious. They disseminate laziness. And this laziness, though scarcely commendable in the moral and political terms proposed by the novels, does no harm.

In *Nicholas Nickleby*, the Appointed is not the only person hanging around in the City square where the Cheeryble brothers have their head-quarters. 'The ticket-porter leans idly against the post at the corner, comfortably warm, but not hot, although the day is broiling. His white apron flaps languidly in the air, his head gradually droops upon his breast' (553). London ticket-porters were licensed to carry messages and run errands, but in Dickens's novels they seem strangely untroubled by anything in the nature of business. 'A crop of grass would grow in the chinks of the stone pavement outside Lincoln's Inn Hall', we learn in *Bleak House*, 'but that the ticket-porters, who have nothing to do beyond sitting in the shade there, with their white aprons over their heads to keep the flies off, grub it up and eat it thoughtfully' (313). These benign ruminants are a reproach to the obsessiveness of law-court and counting-house.

Dickens rarely missed an opportunity to introduce small groups of loafers. Each group constitutes a miniature utopia of unconcern: utopias created, in some cases, in the teeth of a prevailing concern which motivates not only the main participants in the scene but the novel itself. For example, the members of the crowd gathered outside the magistrate's house where Pickwick and his entourage have been taken, in Chapter 25 of *The Pickwick Papers* (1836–37), are so desperate to know what is going on, and so incensed by the lack of information, that they express their feelings by 'kicking at the gate and ringing the bell, for an hour or two afterwards' (421). They might almost be the novel's impatient readers. But the pursuit of meaning does not drive everyone in the crowd to the same frenzied activity. Three or four 'fortunate individuals', having found a grating in the gate which 'commanded a view of nothing', stare through it with 'indefatigable perseverance' (422). Their perseverance is, I think, a reproach to curiosity: they know that nothing will come of a view of nothing.

In *Great Expectations*, Pip spends the night before his first visit to Miss Havisham in Pumblechook's house in the nearby market town. It is the only time he does so, and his stay serves little purpose except to afford us a glimpse of Pumblechook's shop and of the high street.

> The same opportunity served me for noticing that Mr Pumblechook appeared to conduct his business by looking across the street at the saddler, who appeared to transact *his* business by keeping his eye on the coach-maker, who appeared to get on in life by putting his hands in his pockets and contemplating the baker, who in his turn folded his arms and stared at the grocer, who stood at his door and yawned at the chemist. (84)

The chamber of commerce appears to have reconstituted itself as a chamber of idleness: these ruminants are the middle-class version of the herbivorous ticket-porters. But the scene also contains another group of loafers. The only tradesman in the high street who does any work at all is the watch-maker, 'always poring over a little desk with a magnifying glass at his eye, and always inspected by a group of smock-frocks poring over him through the glass of his shop-window' (84). The smock-frocks point back down virtually the whole length of Dickens's career to the scene outside the magistrate's house in *The Pickwick Papers*. They have a view of something, to be sure, but it might just as well be nothing, for all they are likely to make of it: a vacancy captured immaculately by the ironic repetition of 'poring' and 'glass'. Again, I think, the novel glimpses utopia as it hesitates for a moment in the approach to Satis House and the relentless pursuit of meaning which will be inaugurated there.

To return to *Pickwick*, the three or four fortunate individuals who gaze at nothing do so with the perseverance of people who 'flatten their noses against the front windows of a chemist's shop, when a drunken man, who has been run over by a dog-cart in the street, is undergoing a surgical inspection inside' (422). There, as in *Great Expectations*, the microscopic inspection which repairs the damaged fabric of man or mechanism seems to require as its complement a macroscopic inspection which, applied through the lens of grating or window, produces absolutely nothing at all. Dickens wanted both of these benevolences. The former he was able to embody in a figure like Allan Woodcourt, in *Bleak House*; his acknowledgement of the latter proved irregular, but rather more vivid.

There is also a connection, although admittedly a more distant one, between the lazy gentlemen and the spaces they inhabit. Dickens warmed to the portrayal of one kind of space in particular: a reality which, had he been alive today, he might have defined as virtual reality. I am thinking, for example, of Dick Swiveller's apartments, in *The Old Curiosity Shop* (1841), a 'single chamber' which 'was always mentioned in the plural number'.

> In its disengaged times, the tobacconist had announced it in his window as 'apartments' for a single gentleman, and Mr Swiveller, following up the hint, never failed to speak of it as his rooms, his lodgings, or his chambers, conveying to his hearers a notion of indefinite space, and leaving their imaginations to wander through long suites of lofty halls, at pleasure. (101)

The fiction is sustained by an ingenious piece of furniture which doubles as bookcase and bedstead: its bedstead function being firmly suppressed during the day, its bookcase function at night. Another obvious example of virtual reality is Wemmick's 'Castle' in Walworth, in *Great Expectations*. In this case, the fiction is sustained by a painted gun-emplacement and a moat. 'It was worth any money to see Wemmick waving a salute to me from the other side of the moat', Pip remarks, 'when we might have shaken hands across it with the greatest ease' (312). The garden contains a bower which is about twelve yards from the back door but approached 'by such ingenious twists of path that it took quite a long time to get at' (229–30). The important aspect of these illusory spaces, for my purpose, is the essential innocence of the illusions they foster. Dick Swiveller's bookcase–bedstead is an indication that, however callow and self-absorbed he may seem, he will turn out all right in the end; while Wemmick's 'castle' harbours his integrity and kindliness. Similarly, the sinister but essentially benevolent Nadgett, in *Martin Chuzzlewit*, constitutes a one-man virtual reality. He spends much of his time sending letters which never arrive anywhere, 'for he would put them into a secret place in his coat, and deliver them to himself weeks afterwards, very much to his own surprise, quite yellow' (517).

Some of this innocence rubs off on the lazy gentlemen. In the opening chapter of *American Notes*, Dickens's spirits are restored by a stewardess who, producing sheets and table-cloths from the entrails of sofas, demonstrates that his cabin is not quite as small as he had at first thought. Each nook and corner, each article of furniture, is something other than what it pretends to be: 'a mere trap and deception and place of secret stowage'. The traps and deceptions revealed by the stewardess's preparations are as well-meaning as her 'piously fraudulent' account of safe January voyages. The cabin is rendered harmless by its exposure as virtual reality: 'by this time it had expanded into something quite bulky, and almost boasted a bay-window to view the sea from' (*AN*, 56–7). Thus fortified, Dickens is able to relish, on his return to the ship, the lazy gentleman's equally benevolent laziness.

My faith in the harmlessness of the view from Todgers's roof, in *Martin Chuzzlewit*, is strengthened by the establishment's position at the centre of a kind of benevolent maze. 'Nobody had ever found Todgers's on a verbal direction, though given within a minute's walk of it.' Here is another array of harmless traps and deceptions.

> A kind of resigned distraction came over the stranger as he trod these devious mazes, and, giving himself up for lost, went in and out and round about and quietly turned back again when he came to a dead wall or was stopped by an iron railing, and felt that the means of escape might possibly present themselves in their own good time, but that to anticipate them was hopeless. (185)

This observer, like the Appointed, seems to have business in the area; but he, too, does not seem terribly concerned about his failure to carry it out. Similarly, people who have been invited to dine at Todgers's, and fail to find it even though they have for some considerable time its chimney-pots in view, return home 'with a gentle melancholy on their spirits, tranquil and uncomplaining' (185). The harmlessness of the maze underwrites the harmlessness (the bliss) of not getting where you're going to, of not fulfilling your commitments. The looker-on on Todgers's roof seems at least to have found the place; but I can't believe that he, any more than the fortunate individuals who gaze perseveringly through gratings and shop-windows, or chew grass in city squares, will come to any harm – or do any harm.

Notes

1 See Keith Tester (ed.), *The Flâneur* (London: Routledge, 1994).
2 John Rignall, *Realist Fiction and the Strolling Spectator* (London: Routledge, 1992), p. 2.
3 Dorothy Van Ghent, 'The Dickens World: The View from Todgers's', *Sewanee Review*, 58 (1950), 419–38. The passage quoted is on p. 426.
4 Edmund Husserl, *Cartesian Meditations*, tr. Dorion Cairns (The Hague: Martinus Nijhoff, 1977); Maurice Merleau-Ponty, *The Phenomenology of Perception*, tr. Colin Smith (London: Routledge & Kegan Paul, 1962).
5 K. J. Fielding and A. W. Brice, '*Bleak House* and the Graveyard', in *Dickens the Craftsman*, ed. Robert B. Partlow (Carbondale: University of Illinois Press, 1970); 'Dickens and the Tooting Disaster', *Victorian Studies*, 12 (1968), 227–44.
6 Edwin Chadwick, *The Health of Nations*, ed. Benjamin Ward Richardson, 2 vols (London: Longmans, 1887), vol. 1, pp. 354–5.
7 See David Trotter, *Circulation: Defoe, Dickens and the Economies of the Novel* (London: Macmillan, 1988).
8 James Kay, *The Moral and Physical Condition of the Working Classes Employed in the Cotton Manufacture in Manchester* (London: James Ridgway, 1832).

12

The topography of jealousy in *Our Mutual Friend*

J. HILLIS MILLER

Victorian novels were written for readers who for the most part knew London or even lived there. This meant that the mention of specific streets or regions had an immediate resonance. Such place names served as a shorthand code for the social and economic status of the inhabitants. For an American reader, a good Victorian map of London, or at least a modern *A to Z Atlas of London and Suburbs*, is an essential ancillary tool in reading. Even such a map, however, does not give the social meaning of the various localities.[1]

Dickens's *Our Mutual Friend* is a cardinal example of the creation out of words of a singular mental topography. It differs slightly but in significant ways from Dickens's earlier great London novels, for example *Bleak House*. In *Our Mutual Friend*, as in *Bleak House*, the self-enclosed idiosyncrasy of the characters is signalled by their enclosure in domestic interiors that mirror their individuality and oddness. Krook's rag and bottle shop and the basement room of Grandfather and Grandmother Smallweed, in *Bleak House*, correspond, as examples of this, to Boffin's Bower, Venus's shop, the Veneering mansion, or the pub called The Six Jolly Fellowship Porters in *Our Mutual Friend*. The difference between the two novels is a difference of nuance, but it is an important nuance. *Bleak House* emphasises much more overtly the way all these apparently dispersed and unlike people, each hermetically sealed in his or her uniqueness, are nevertheless connected to one another, responsible for one another. This is elaborately worked out on the level of plot. In *Bleak House* everybody turns out to be involved in one way or another with Esther Summerson's story or with the Jarndyce case in Chancery. As Inspector Bucket says, 'the whole bileing of people was mixed up in the same business, and no other' (863). This interconnection is also worked out on the topographical level in the

12

The topography of jealousy in *Our Mutual Friend*

J. HILLIS MILLER

Victorian novels were written for readers who for the most part knew London or even lived there. This meant that the mention of specific streets or regions had an immediate resonance. Such place names served as a shorthand code for the social and economic status of the inhabitants. For an American reader, a good Victorian map of London, or at least a modern *A to Z Atlas of London and Suburbs*, is an essential ancillary tool in reading. Even such a map, however, does not give the social meaning of the various localities.[1]

Dickens's *Our Mutual Friend* is a cardinal example of the creation out of words of a singular mental topography. It differs slightly but in significant ways from Dickens's earlier great London novels, for example *Bleak House*. In *Our Mutual Friend*, as in *Bleak House*, the self-enclosed idiosyncrasy of the characters is signalled by their enclosure in domestic interiors that mirror their individuality and oddness. Krook's rag and bottle shop and the basement room of Grandfather and Grandmother Smallweed, in *Bleak House*, correspond, as examples of this, to Boffin's Bower, Venus's shop, the Veneering mansion, or the pub called The Six Jolly Fellowship Porters in *Our Mutual Friend*. The difference between the two novels is a difference of nuance, but it is an important nuance. *Bleak House* emphasises much more overtly the way all these apparently dispersed and unlike people, each hermetically sealed in his or her uniqueness, are nevertheless connected to one another, responsible for one another. This is elaborately worked out on the level of plot. In *Bleak House* everybody turns out to be involved in one way or another with Esther Summerson's story or with the Jarndyce case in Chancery. As Inspector Bucket says, 'the whole bileing of people was mixed up in the same business, and no other' (863). This interconnection is also worked out on the topographical level in the

against the front windows of a chemist's shop, when a drunken man, who has been run over by a dog-cart in the street, is undergoing a surgical inspection inside' (422). There, as in *Great Expectations*, the microscopic inspection which repairs the damaged fabric of man or mechanism seems to require as its complement a macroscopic inspection which, applied through the lens of grating or window, produces absolutely nothing at all. Dickens wanted both of these benevolences. The former he was able to embody in a figure like Allan Woodcourt, in *Bleak House*; his acknowledgement of the latter proved irregular, but rather more vivid.

There is also a connection, although admittedly a more distant one, between the lazy gentlemen and the spaces they inhabit. Dickens warmed to the portrayal of one kind of space in particular: a reality which, had he been alive today, he might have defined as virtual reality. I am thinking, for example, of Dick Swiveller's apartments, in *The Old Curiosity Shop* (1841), a 'single chamber' which 'was always mentioned in the plural number'.

> In its disengaged times, the tobacconist had announced it in his window as 'apartments' for a single gentleman, and Mr Swiveller, following up the hint, never failed to speak of it as his rooms, his lodgings, or his chambers, conveying to his hearers a notion of indefinite space, and leaving their imaginations to wander through long suites of lofty halls, at pleasure. (101)

The fiction is sustained by an ingenious piece of furniture which doubles as bookcase and bedstead: its bedstead function being firmly suppressed during the day, its bookcase function at night. Another obvious example of virtual reality is Wemmick's 'Castle' in Walworth, in *Great Expectations*. In this case, the fiction is sustained by a painted gun-emplacement and a moat. 'It was worth any money to see Wemmick waving a salute to me from the other side of the moat', Pip remarks, 'when we might have shaken hands across it with the greatest ease' (312). The garden contains a bower which is about twelve yards from the back door but approached 'by such ingenious twists of path that it took quite a long time to get at' (229–30). The important aspect of these illusory spaces, for my purpose, is the essential innocence of the illusions they foster. Dick Swiveller's bookcase–bedstead is an indication that, however callow and self-absorbed he may seem, he will turn out all right in the end; while Wemmick's 'castle' harbours his integrity and kindliness. Similarly, the sinister but essentially benevolent Nadgett, in *Martin Chuzzlewit*, constitutes a one-man virtual reality. He spends much of his time sending letters which never arrive anywhere, 'for he would put them into a secret place in his coat, and deliver them to himself weeks afterwards, very much to his own surprise, quite yellow' (517).

Some of this innocence rubs off on the lazy gentlemen. In the opening chapter of *American Notes*, Dickens's spirits are restored by a stewardess who, producing sheets and table-cloths from the entrails of sofas, demonstrates that his cabin is not quite as small as he had at first thought. Each nook and corner, each article of furniture, is something other than what it pretends to be: 'a mere trap and deception and place of secret stowage'. The traps and deceptions revealed by the stewardess's preparations are as well-meaning as her 'piously fraudulent' account of safe January voyages. The cabin is rendered harmless by its exposure as virtual reality: 'by this time it had expanded into something quite bulky, and almost boasted a bay-window to view the sea from' (*AN*, 56–7). Thus fortified, Dickens is able to relish, on his return to the ship, the lazy gentleman's equally benevolent laziness.

My faith in the harmlessness of the view from Todgers's roof, in *Martin Chuzzlewit*, is strengthened by the establishment's position at the centre of a kind of benevolent maze. 'Nobody had ever found Todgers's on a verbal direction, though given within a minute's walk of it.' Here is another array of harmless traps and deceptions.

> A kind of resigned distraction came over the stranger as he trod these devious mazes, and, giving himself up for lost, went in and out and round about and quietly turned back again when he came to a dead wall or was stopped by an iron railing, and felt that the means of escape might possibly present themselves in their own good time, but that to anticipate them was hopeless. (185)

This observer, like the Appointed, seems to have business in the area; but he, too, does not seem terribly concerned about his failure to carry it out. Similarly, people who have been invited to dine at Todgers's, and fail to find it even though they have for some considerable time its chimney-pots in view, return home 'with a gentle melancholy on their spirits, tranquil and uncomplaining' (185). The harmlessness of the maze underwrites the harmlessness (the bliss) of not getting where you're going to, of not fulfilling your commitments. The looker-on on Todgers's roof seems at least to have found the place; but I can't believe that he, any more than the fortunate individuals who gaze perseveringly through gratings and shop-windows, or chew grass in city squares, will come to any harm – or do any harm.

Notes

1 See Keith Tester (ed.), *The Flâneur* (London: Routledge, 1994).
2 John Rignall, *Realist Fiction and the Strolling Spectator* (London: Routledge, 1992),
3 Dorothy Van Ghent, 'The Dickens World: The View from Todgers's', *Se Review*, 58 (1950), 419–38. The passage quoted is on p. 426.
4 Edmund Husserl, *Cartesian Meditations*, tr. Dorion Cairns (The Hague: Marti Nijhoff, 1977); Maurice Merleau-Ponty, *The Phenomenology of Perception*, tr. C Smith (London: Routledge & Kegan Paul, 1962).
5 K. J. Fielding and A. W. Brice, '*Bleak House* and the Graveyard', in *Dickens Craftsman*, ed. Robert B. Partlow (Carbondale: University of Illinois Press, 197 'Dickens and the Tooting Disaster', *Victorian Studies*, 12 (1968), 227–44.
6 Edwin Chadwick, *The Health of Nations*, ed. Benjamin Ward Richardson, 2 vol (London: Longmans, 1887), vol. 1, pp. 354–5.
7 See David Trotter, *Circulation: Defoe, Dickens and the Economies of the Novel* (London: Macmillan, 1988).
8 James Kay, *The Moral and Physical Condition of the Working Classes Employed in the Cotton Manufacture in Manchester* (London: James Ridgway, 1832).

stress on the way you can get from one of these strange interiors to any of the others. The itineraries are often carefully given. The omniscient narrator of *Bleak House* expresses this interconnectedness in the form of questions the novel answers by way of the revelation of the central mystery of Esther's parentage:

> What connexion can there be, between the place in Lincolnshire, the house in town, the Mercury in powder, and the whereabout of Jo the outlaw with the broom, who had the distant ray of light upon him when he swept the churchyard-step? What connexion can there have been between many people in the innumerable histories of this world, who, from opposite sides of great gulfs, have, nevertheless, been very curiously brought together! (272)

As I say, it is a matter of nuance, but the result, at least in my own mental mapping, is that I have a much clearer image of the relation of places to one another, as of the relation of the characters and plots, for *Bleak House* than for *Our Mutual Friend*. This might be exemplified by a juxtaposition of the famous opening of *Bleak House* with an episode set in a London fog in the middle of *Our Mutual Friend*. In the opening of *Bleak House* there is 'fog everywhere' (49). Dickens gives a long list of the places where it is foggy: up the river, down the river, everywhere in London, finally zooming in, as one might say, on the Court of Chancery, where the fog is densest. The fog in *Bleak House*, however, more joins people together than it separates them, just as the case of Jarndyce and Jarndyce makes everyone in the novel interconnected.

The fog in *Our Mutual Friend*, at the opening of Book Three, on the contrary, more separates people than joins them, or it joins them in the common fate of death as the ultimate separation. The fog in *Our Mutual Friend* is a great sea that drowns everything and everybody. This could be seen, the narrator tells the reader, from a perspective outside London on high ground. The ubiquitous motif of drowning in *Our Mutual Friend* is in this passage universalised as the condition of all those who live in London. Londoners are already figuratively drowned even before some of them are literally drowned. The fog separates each person from his or her neighbour. It puts each in a condition likened to death by drowning. The fog at the same time joins them in that all are drowning in the fog and all are coughing and choking with the same gigantic head cold. Though all Londoners are cut off from one another, the fog and the catarrh are the mutual friends, so to speak, of each. They are joined by what separates them:

From any point of the high ridge of land northward, it might have been discerned that the loftiest buildings made an occasional struggle to get their heads above the foggy sea, and especially that the great dome of Saint Paul's seemed to die hard; but this was not perceivable in the streets at their feet, where the whole metropolis was a heap of vapour charged with muffled sound of wheels, and enfolding a gigantic catarrh. (479)

In the next paragraph after the passage just cited, Riah makes his way from Pubsey and Co. in Saint Mary Axe to Fascination Fledgeby's chambers in the Albany by an itinerary that is exactly named. Like so many of the itineraries in *Our Mutual Friend* it could be followed today on a street map or on foot in the real London, 'by Cornhill, Cheapside, Fleet Street, and the Strand, to Piccadilly and the Albany' (480). Nevertheless, what Dickens here emphasises is the way each of these locations is separated from the others by the dense fog: 'Almost in the act of coming out at the door, Riah went into the fog, and was lost to the eyes of Saint Mary Axe' (480). Though Fledgeby is himself 'Pubsey and Co.', the difference between Riah's shabby office in Saint Mary Axe and Fledgeby's luxurious flat in the Albany works to hide the connection. Riah, with his long staff and skirt, seems to those who see him to appear out of the fog and then disappear into it, as if he must be an apparition – strange, ghostly or uncanny. The fog makes Riah a species of Baudelairean revenant, like those seven identical old men who appear on a foggy day in Paris, in Baudelaire's 'Les Sept Vieillards': 'Fourmillante cité, cité plein de rêves, / Où le spectre en plein jour raccroche le passant!' (Swarming city, city full of dreams, / Where the ghost in broad daylight accosts the bypasser!).[2] Londoners, however, have more a habit of rationalising or suppressing uncanny urban apparitions than does the Baudelairean persona: 'Thither he went at his grave and measured pace, staff in hand, skirt at heel; and more than one head, turning back to look at his venerable figure already lost in the mist, supposed it to be some ordinary figure indistinctly seen, which fancy and the fog had worked into that passing likeness' (480).

In *Our Mutual Friend*, moreover, in spite of many passages that give an exact description of the movement by one of the characters from one interior to another, street by street, and in spite of the fact that, as in *Bleak House*, all of the grotesque 'minor' characters are involved in one way or another in the larger plots, there are nevertheless some hints of the extreme difficulty of mapping a way to get from any one of these places to at least some of the others. Dickens, in spite of the sovereign command of London's geography he himself had (and ascribes to his narrator), is in *Our Mutual Friend* sometimes a little unusually vague, for him, about how to get there from here. Dickens emphasises repeatedly, for example, the difficulty of finding the Six Jolly Fellowship Porters and its waterside milieu. When in the third chapter Mortimer Lightwood and Eugene Wrayburn are taken by Charlie Hexam from the Veneering mansion first to Charlie's father's house and then to the nearby police station where they view the dead body that is presumed to be John Harmon's, the narrator specifies the route taken by the carriage but not so exactly that the reader might find these locations on a map (63).

Much later on in the novel, Riah and Jenny Wren, the dolls' dressmaker, have considerable difficulty finding the tavern near Hexam's house:

> When they had plodded on for some time nigh the river, Riah asked the way to a certain tavern called the Six Jolly Fellowship Porters. Following the directions he received, they arrived, after two or three puzzled stoppages for consideration and some uncertain looking about them, at the door of Miss Abbey Potterson's dominions. (496)

The most elaborate and extended account of this relative failure in mapping, however, is John Harmon's unsuccessful attempt to reconstruct just what happened to him, and where, when he was drugged and then thrown into the river to drown: 'Perhaps I might recall, if it were any good to try, the way by which I went to it [Limehouse Church] alone from the river; but how we two went from it to Riderhood's shop, I don't know – any more than I know what turns we took and doubles we made, after we left it. The way was purposely confused, no doubt' (424); 'As to this hour I cannot understand that side of the river where I recovered the shore, being the opposite side to that on which I was ensnared, I shall never understand it now' (427). Harmon's plunge into the Thames to emerge first as Julius Handford and then, when he changes his name again, as John Rokesmith, echoes the many drownings or near-drownings that precede and follow it in the novel: those of his double George Radfoot (who is drowned in his place), of Gaffer Hexam, Rogue Riderhood (twice drowned, once to be recovered, once to drown for good), Eugene Wrayburn and Bradley Headstone, not to speak of metaphorical drownings like Wegg's being pitched head foremost into a scavenger's cart, 'with a prodigious splash' (862), or Fascination Fledgeby, after he has been thrashed by Alfred Lammle and has had pepper put on the plasters Jenny Wren applies, 'plunging and gambolling all over his bed, like a porpoise or dolphin in its native element' (793).

All those drownings, near-drownings or metaphorical drownings in a manner of speaking confound the rationalities of cognitive mapping. Scattered everywhere, all over the map, though especially anywhere on the river that winds its sinuous way from up-country through the city and down to the sea, are places that may allow a momentary or permanent entry into a region of otherness and anonymity, a region where one ceases to be oneself and may (or may not) emerge transformed. Even though the entry spots into this realm of otherness may often be located, they all lead to the same place, a ubiquitous underwater locus of meta-morphosis. These entryways are different places and yet they lead to the same place. As is suggested by John Harmon's inability to reconstruct just what ways he went to enter and escape from the Thames, the transition from the mappable spot where a drowning took place to and from the unplaceable place where one may die or be changed cannot be rationally traced.

Another form of the missing transition is the way Dickens in *Our Mutual Friend* leaps from one enclosed location to another even more abruptly and with less explanation than in *Bleak House*. The sign of these transitions is most often the blank between the end of one chapter and the beginning of the next. Even though the all-knowing and all-seeing narrator might have been able to provide detailed itineraries showing how to get from one of these places to the other, he often chooses not to do so. He juxtaposes without any intervening mark but the blank space on the page two incommensurate locales. The result is to suggest that London exists as an unimaginably large conglomeration of self-enclosed and idiosyncratic milieux, each to some degree cut off from all the others and heterogeneous to them, even though a knowing topographer might be able to find a way from one to another. The river in Chapter 1, for example, is replaced without transition or explanation by the Veneerings' mansion in Chapter 2. These unbridged discontinuities of milieu between one chapter and another are even more pronounced in *Our Mutual Friend* than in *Bleak House*. The reader is left more on his or her own to try in retrospect, after finishing the novel, to put all these dispersed locales together in a unified topography. *Our Mutual Friend* lacks the con-tinuities provided in *Bleak House* by Esther Summerson's narrative and, in a different way, by Inspector Bucket's detective unifications or by the omniscient narrator's ruminations about how all persons and places are connected.

The different threads of the stories, moreover, are less neatly unravelled in the denouement of *Our Mutual Friend* than in *Bleak House*. Wegg's serio-comic punishment, that of Fledgeby, the death of Bradley Headstone, the resurrection and transformation of Eugene Wrayburn, the smash-up of the Lammles, the revelation that Noddy Boffin is not a miser after all, the happy marriage of John Harmon and Bella Wilfer – these are a little dispersed. The novel ends by shifting from one climax to another, not by tying them all together. The different plots are bound together by analogy, by all having, as one might say, as mutual friend the central motif of drowning or near-drowning and resurrection, but they are not, as in *Bleak House*, quite so systematically intertwined at the level of plot.

The mediated similarity of characters and plots, in *Our Mutual Friend*, is not, I am claiming, quite the same thing as the demonstration, in *Bleak House*, that everything and everybody is interconnected and interdependent. One further way to talk about this nuance of difference between *Bleak House* and *Our Mutual Friend* is by identifying the significance of the latter's title. If in *Bleak House* 'the whole bileing of people was mixed up in the same business, and no other', in *Our Mutual Friend* this sharing of stories is considerably more mediated and indirect. The title names that mediation. Strictly speaking, the phrase 'our mutual friend', as any dictionary will tell you, is a solecism, an incorrect usage, but it is one so common that many usage experts now allow it to pass. 'Mutual' means 'shared', 'held in common', as in 'mutual affection' used to name the love two people have for one another. 'Mutual' can be used to name a friend we share only by a kind of illicit but significant extension of its literal meaning. A certain person is my friend. He or she is also your friend. Though we may not know one another at all and therefore have no mutual feelings of friendship or antipathy, we share a feeling of friendship for the same person. Our friendship for the third who links us is 'mutual'. We are related to one another, have mutual feelings after all, by way of a third person. The words 'our mutual friend' are used in the novel by the uneducated Mr Boffin, which may excuse Dickens for the mistake. Boffin uses the phrase to name John Rokesmith, alias John Harmon. Rokesmith is Mr Boffin's secretary and also the Wilfers' lodger, so Mr Boffin says to Mrs Wilfer: 'I may call him Our Mutual Friend' (157).

The use of the phrase as the title for the whole novel, however, suggests a wider reference. This reference extends even beyond the centrality of John Harmon to the novel's melodramatic intrigue, the way John Harmon is mutual friend of all the characters. The novel is full of situations in which one person is related to another not directly but by way of a third person whom both know. This motif of mutual friendship, as it might be called, is closely associated with the motif of doubling, with its overtones of homosexual desire or at any rate of homosociality. This motif is ubiquitous in the novel, most often as chains of doublings in which one character doubles another and is doubled in his[3] turn by yet another. The melodramatic plot depends on the similarity in appearance of George Radfoot and John Harmon, but Harmon later on doubles and redoubles himself by becoming first Julius Handford and then John Rokesmith. Rogue Riderhood is a kind of double, in appearance and profession, of Gaffer Hexam, but Bradley Headstone later dresses as the double of Rogue Riderhood, in order to put the blame for his planned murder of Eugene Wrayburn on Riderhood. Headstone and Riderhood drown locked in one another's arms. Wrayburn and Headstone are doubles in their rival loves for Lizzie Hexam. Mortimer Lightwood so models himself on his idol, Eugene Wrayburn, that they are in a manner of speaking doubles. Boffin becomes his own antithetical double when he pretends to become miserly.

The brotherly doubling of Wegg and Venus in their 'friendly move' to cheat Mr Boffin is a hilarious comic version of the motif of doubling. The scenes presenting this are at the highest level of Dickens's admirable pantomimic notations and wild verbal imagination. In the scene in which Wegg and Venus wrestle on the floor in an ecstasy of quasi-sexual greed, the homosexual component in such doubling is almost scandalously explicit. As Wegg reads to Mr Boffin stories of misers who have buried fortunes up chimneys or in dungheaps ('One of Mr Dancer's richest escretoires was found to be a dungheap in the cowhouse', . . . etc. (544)), Wegg's wooden leg rises spontaneously in the air and he falls against Venus who is sitting beside him on the settle: 'Nor did either of the two, for some few seconds, make any effort to recover himself; both remaining in a kind of pecuniary swoon' (545).

Later the same evening, after they have spied on Boffin taking a Dutch bottle from its hiding place in the mounds, Venus has forcibly to restrain Wegg from chasing after Boffin. At a slightly earlier stage, when Boffin has just left, 'Wegg clutched Venus with both hands'. Venus responds by 'clutching him with both hands, so that they stood interlocked like a couple of preposterous gladiators' (548). After Boffin leaves with the Dutch bottle, their embrace rises to a sort of climax: 'As in his wildness he [Wegg] was making a strong struggle for it [to free himself so he can chase after Boffin], Mr Venus deemed it expedient to lift him, throw him, and fall with him; well knowing that, once down, he would not be up again easily with his wooden leg. So they both rolled on the floor, and, as they did so, Mr Boffin shut the gate' (553). The doubling relation between Wegg and Venus is mediated by their mutual greed for the treasures supposedly buried in Harmon's dust-mounds. The dust-mounds are analogous to the depths of the Thames both in the way that what they hide may be anywhere under their surface and in the way they serve as a link between persons not otherwise related. Wegg and Venus desire one another by way of their greed and curiosity as to what the mounds may hide.

The most extreme form of a doubling mutual friendship is the relation of Bradley Headstone and Eugene Wrayburn. They are joined in that both love Lizzie Hexam. 'Our mutual friend' – it is almost a recipe for jealousy. A is a friend of B. C is a friend of B. A and C are related by way of their mutual friend, B. But if I am A, how do I know if B is the same for me as he or she is for C? Does B love C better? There is no direct connection between me and C, only by way of B. It is not the case that the friend of my friend is my friend. Quite the contrary. Almost certainly I am jealous if my friend has another friend, perhaps ragingly jealous if I suspect that my friend is sexually betraying me with his or her other friend, or even, as in the case of what Bradley Headstone suspects of Lizzie, no more than secretly prefers the other friend to me. I have used abstract letters rather than names both to indicate the universality of this pattern and to suggest that anyone who is trapped within its irresistible force loses his or her independent selfhood. Such a person becomes a mere node in a pattern of irresistible and potentially lethal affective forces.

Jealousy is a way of being tormentedly related to the wholly other by way of curiosity about the other's other. Let me try to explain this somewhat gnomic formulation by way of Bradley Headstone's jealousy of Eugene Wrayburn. Or does one say his jealousy of Lizzie? We are jealous both of the beloved and of the beloved's supposed beloved, the other's other. The English word jealousy comes from the Greek word *zēlos*, meaning emulation, zeal, jealousy. All the meanings given in the *OED* stress the way jealousy is first and foremost a strong affect. Jealousy, according to the *OED*, means '1. Zeal or vehemence of feeling against some person or thing; anger, wrath, indignation. *Obs.*'; '2. Zeal or vehemence of feeling in favour of a person or thing; devotion, eagerness, anxiety to serve. *Obs.*' Jealousy may be either wrath or devotion, either against or for, but in either case it is primarily a vehemence of feeling. It is by way of both these now obsolete meanings that the King James Bible translates Exodus 20.5, the commandment against idolatrous worship of graven images: 'Thou shalt not bow down thyself to them, nor serve them: for I the Lord thy God am a jealous God'. The fourth meaning in the *OED* defines amorous jealousy. It is only one form of jealousy among others: '4. The state of mind arising from the suspicion, apprehension, or knowledge of rivalry: a. in love, etc.: Fear of being supplanted in the affection, or distrust of the fidelity, of a beloved person, esp. a wife, husband, or lover'. Amorous jealousy is a 'state of mind', an exceedingly unpleasant one. It is not necessary to know that the beloved is unfaithful in order to be jealous.

If Marcel Proust is right, it is impossible ever to know. The furor of jealousy comes from a desire to know what in principle can never be known. 'Suspicion', 'apprehension', 'fear', 'distrust' – these are enough to make the lover violently and perhaps even murderously jealous, as in the cases of Othello and Bradley Headstone. The result of jealous suspicion is that every least thing seen may be a sign of the beloved's infidelity. Therefore everything must be remembered as a possible clue. As Alain Robbe-Grillet puts this: 'La jalousie est une passion pour qui rien jamais ne s'efface: chaque vision, même la plus innocent, y demeure inscrite une fois pour toutes' (Jealousy is a passion for which nothing ever effaces itself: everything seen, even the most innocent, remains inscribed there [in the jealous passion] once and for all).[4] Proust's admirable extended treatment in *À la recherche du temps perdu* of Marcel's jealousy of Albertine, a jealousy that even lasts beyond her death, shows how this desire to know whether or not the beloved is betraying me cannot ever be satisfied, even though it generates an obsessive inspection and scrutinising of everything she or he says and does. The least gesture or slip of the tongue may be a clue.

Jealous curiosity cannot be satisfied because the vehemence of jealousy puts the lover in a performative rather than cognitive situation. Everything the beloved says is turned by jealousy into a potential sign by a speech act on the part of the lover that posits significances that may or may not be there. This means that it becomes impossible ever to find out for sure whether the beloved is lying or not. Contrary to what most people assume, a lie is a speech act, not a false cognitive statement, or, to be more precise, it has a strong performative component that keeps it from being verified as true or false. A lie is a speech act because it can, if it is believed, bring about the condition it names. An example is the way Marcel's lying assertion that he does not love Albertine and wants her to leave brings about her departure. A lie belongs to the regime of witnessing, not to the regime of true or false statements. The written (as opposed to writing) Marcel's inability to understand this sad truth or to accept it when he has glimpses of it causes him intense suffering. It also generates the ironic comedy of a large part of the *Recherche*, since so much of the novel has to do with Marcel's relation to Albertine.

For Bradley Headstone too everything he sees becomes a potential sign inscribed permanently on his jealous passion. He follows Eugene Wrayburn everywhere, spying on him night after night, on the false assumption that he may thereby get confirmation of his jealous suspicion that Lizzie has refused him because she loves Eugene. But whatever he sees remains just that, a sign inscribed on his jealousy. It does not contain in itself the rules for its interpretation or for the verification of an interpretation. The meaning he gives such a sign is performatively posited by him, not intrinsic to the sign itself. As a result, the reading of each such sign, however he reads it, only exacerbates his jealousy. The reading of each such sign is something for which the jealous Bradley Headstone is responsible, or rather the autonomously working mechanism of his jealousy that works against his will to destroy him is responsible. His reading is itself a performative speech act, a blind unverifiable positing, not a verifiable epistemological interpretation, just as in the case of Marcel's conflicting hypotheses about Albertine's supposed lies. Bradley's error, like Othello's or Marcel's, is to assume that he can get solid irrefutable evidence that will justify action – Bradley's attempted murder of Eugene Wrayburn, Othello's murder of Desdemona, Marcel's decision to break with Albertine (at the very moment she takes matters into her own hands and leaves him). But nothing external can justify such actions. They are unjust, an unauthorised taking of the law into one's own hands.

Dickens in his presentation of Bradley Headstone stresses, however, another feature of jealousy. This is the way the inevitably frustrated rage to know the other person wholly and to know also the other's relation to the other's others, the beloved's supposed secret lovers, leads also to an encounter with the other within the self. The jealous suspicion that the beloved is betraying me springs from an impossible desire to know and possess the other wholly. This desire is wonderfully mimed in those scenes in Proust in which Marcel watches the sleeping Albertine. He thinks she cannot betray him while she is no more than innocent, unconscious, sleeping flesh, though she is at that moment farthest from him and most inaccessible. What is permanently unknowable in the other is the other's participation in something wholly other, that other to which Jacques Derrida refers when he says in *Aporias*: 'Tout autre est tout autre' (Every other is completely other).[5] This anonymous and ubiquitous otherness is expressed, in *Our Mutual Friend*, in the figure of the river's dark depths. Anyone who enters those depths at whatever point on the topographical surface goes into the same place. My own selfhood, however clear and distinct it may seem to me in my self-consciousness, floats on the same dark depths that are the forever hidden regions of the beloved person and reaches down to them. John Harmon, in the passage in which he attempts to reconstruct what happened to him when he was drugged and thrown into the Thames, stresses the loss of his 'I' or ego in that experience: 'This is still correct? Still correct, with the exception that I cannot possibly express it to myself without using the word I. But it was not I. There was no such thing as I, within my knowledge' (426). The rage of jealousy, which may be defined as wrath born of the impossibility of knowing the other's other, may stir up dark depths of otherness within my own self-hood and bring me to destroy myself.

The scene in which Bradley Headstone proposes to Lizzie Hexam is one of the high points of Dickensian melodrama. Bradley says all the wrong things, the things least likely to persuade her to love him. As he says, his love for her is so violent that it leads him to say things he does not mean to say. He ceases to be himself and becomes a spokesperson for his ungovernable passion:

> 'No man knows till the time comes, what depths are within him. To some men it never comes; let them rest and be thankful! To me, you brought it; on me, you forced it; and the bottom of this raging sea,' striking himself upon the breast, 'has been heaved up ever since.' (454)

As this scene makes clear, the words about the depths of the raging sea are not a metaphorical transfer from the literal naming of the River Thames, in all the scenes of drowning or near-drowning, including Headstone's drowning proleptically foreshadowed in this passage. It is the other way around. The anonymous and unnameable energy within each person is figuratively expressed by the river's black depths. This scene ends with Headstone, after Lizzie's refusal, repeating obsessively the name 'Mr Eugene Wrayburn', after 'bringing his clenched hand down upon the stone with a force that laid the knuckles raw and bleeding' and exclaiming, 'then I hope that I may never kill him!' (456). The bare name is a prosopopoetic catachresis for what he has a rage to know but can never know, the otherness of the other, the other's other. This is personified for him as Lizzie's secret feelings about Wrayburn and so is embodied in the name 'Mr Eugene Wrayburn'.

Eugene Wrayburn himself is drawn to Lizzie just as Headstone is. He too, when Headstone savagely beats him and leaves him for dead in the river, enters watery depths that stand for internal depths that are the same for each person. In Eugene's case, however, his near-death is the occasion of a transformation that brings him back a changed man, worthy now to break class barriers, marry Lizzie and live happily ever after, just as John Harmon is changed by his near-drowning, while Headstone plunges into the water at Plashwater Weir Mill Lock to carry his double, the undrownable[6] Rogue Riderhood, to a joint death, locked in an embrace that expresses their unity and similarity.

The word 'energy', used by the narrator of Headstone ('The wild energy of the man . . . was absolutely terrible' (454)), names an impersonal power in which all the novel's characters participate. This energy is the inner depth of each. It is a power both for good and for evil, both for death and for life. This energy is Dickens's version of the wholly other. It serves as what one might call a mutual friend for all the characters, male and female alike. It links them across class and gender barriers as well as across barriers of good and evil.[7] Jealousy is one way, though by no means the only way, to break through to a confrontation with an impersonal power alien to the ordinary world of everyday life. This power underlies each person and, for Dickens, is present everywhere in nature too. This ubiquitous force resists rational mapping. It interferes with the reader's efforts always to locate every person and every milieu in *Our Mutual Friend* in some place that might be identified according to familiar spatial coordinates.

As Northrop Frye says, this hidden energy is both destructive and creative, both Thanatos and Eros. It provides the drive for behaviour on the surface, but that behaviour rapidly becomes mechanical and sterile unless there is a periodic reimmersion in anarchic depths. The wild comic surface and mad linguistic verve of Venus, Wegg, Podsnap and Mrs Wilfer are the indirect manifestation of an energy that appears more directly in Headstone's insane jealousy. Dickens's comedy and his melodrama arise from the same sources and are fuelled by the same fire. As Frye saw, surface behaviour is likely gradually to become more and more cut off from the energy that gives it force. This detachment makes people from both high and low in society behave and speak by rote, like unconscious automatons.

Frye's word 'humours' makes it sound a little as if these forms of behaviour and speech are primarily psychological quirks. It can easily be shown, however, that they are ideologically motivated. The characters of *Our Mutual Friend* are trapped within Victorian assumptions about class and gender. Victorian ideology and the damage it does to those of both sexes in all levels of society are Dickens's main target in *Our Mutual Friend*. Bella, who has been forced into a gender mould and left to John Harmon in old Harmon's will, 'like a dozen of spoons' (81), is as much a victim of this ideology as is Eugene Wrayburn. Wrayburn's father's wealth has given him an inability to turn seriously to his profession and an unwillingness to consider marrying Lizzie, since she is the daughter of a man who makes his living by finding dead bodies in the Thames. Wegg's mind too is a crazy jumble of received ideas, in this case lower-class ones governed by the clichés of popular culture. This victimisation by Victorian ideology is as much the origin of the crazy imitation of genteel speech in Mrs Wilfer as of the inane nationalist stupidities of Mr Podsnap or the calculated upper-class pretences of the Veneerings and Lammles. Bella's conviction that she cares only for 'money, money, money, and what money can make of life' (520) has the same source. It is equally out of touch with the energy that lies behind her charming self-deceptions. Her reformation can come only when her response to Boffin's pretence that he has become a selfish miser puts her more directly in touch with the depths of feeling within her.

Another example of this unconscious detachment from underlying 'reality' is the admirable comedy of the zany conversations between Wegg and Venus. Note, in particular, the scene in which Wegg comes to try to buy his own leg and foot bones back from Venus. Venus has bought them from the hospital to add to his collection of human bones to be articulated. 'I can't work you into a miscellaneous one [skeleton], no how', says Mr Venus. 'Do what I will, you can't be got to fit. Anybody with a passable knowledge would pick you out at a look, and say, – "No go! Don't match!" ... No, I don't know how it is, but so it is. You have got a twist in that bone, to the best of my belief. I never saw the likes of you' (124). Wegg's response is to ask Venus, 'What will you take for me?' As he explains, 'I have a prospect of getting on in life and elevating myself by my own independent exertions, ... and I shouldn't like – I tell you openly I should *not* like – under such circumstances, to be what I may call dispersed, a part of me here, and a part of me there, but should wish to collect myself like a genteel person' (126–7).

Wegg's habit of working verses from popular songs and ballads in altered form into his conversation is a brilliant dramatisation of Dickens's insight into the way the formulas of popular culture insinuate themselves into our unconscious presuppositions and have political force there. One example among many is Wegg's adaptation of 'Home, Sweet Home' to describe Venus 'floating his powerful mind in tea' in his bone-articulating and taxidermy shop:

'A exile from home splendour dazzles in vain,
O give you your lowly Preparations again,

The birds stuffed so sweetly that can't be expected to come at your call,
Give you with these the peace of mind dearer than all.
Home. Home, Home, sweet Home!'

– Be it ever,' added Mr Wegg in prose as he glanced about the shop, 'ever
so ghastly, all things considered there's no place like it.' (562)

Now it might be thought that the superficiality, inanity and lack of self-
awareness in the comic characters as well as the destructive violence of
melodramatic characters like Headstone might be set against some form
of direct, sincere speech in the good characters or in the narrator. This is
not the case. The narrator expresses his deepest insights not in commentary but by playing the roles of the comic and melodramatic characters,
in that extraordinary theatrical performance each great Dickens novel is.
Moreover, there are repeated examples of the way the good characters
can express their feelings for one another only through a self-conscious
artifice that is another form of role-playing. The most conspicuous examples of this are the way both Jenny Wren and Bella Wilfer express their
love for their fathers by treating them as their children. Jenny also expresses her relation to Riah by calling him her fairy godmother with
herself as Little Red Ridinghood. The narrator uses such self-conscious
figurative language too, as in his account of the marriage of John
Harmon and Bella Wilfer by way of the imagined perspective of a
Greenwich pensioner he names 'Gruff and Glum' (731–2), or in his
extended use of a metaphor calling the Veneerings' retainer the
'Analytical Chemist', 'always seeming to say, after "Chablis, sir?" – "You
wouldn't if you knew what it's made of"' (52).

A formal rhetorical way of putting this is to say that no direct, sincere,
literal expression of the impersonal underlying otherness exists. It cannot
be named directly. Each expression of it is another inadequate catachresis. The difference is that some of these catachreses, for example Bella's
loving play-acting with her father, are directly motivated by the anonymous energy and may work for good, while others have long since been
cut off from it and go on insanely repeating themselves automatically, as
for example in Mrs Wilfer's stately nonsense. Dickens's extreme relish in
inventing and inventing again speeches for Mrs Wilfer, as for inventing
the crazy dialogues between Venus and Wegg, will be felt by any reader.
This inimitable and inexhaustible linguistic exuberance is the chief greatness of *Our Mutual Friend*, as of Dickens's other work. Since it is chiefly,
though not exclusively, a comic exuberance, and since comedy is
extremely difficult to talk about intelligently (one's solemn comments

seem always somehow off the mark), criticism of Dickens often seems to be talking about peripheral rather than about essential qualities. Critics often discuss, for example, overall form, but that may be less important than the constantly renewed dazzling hyperbolic theatrical inventiveness that makes up most of the substance of Dickens's novels. This exuberance exceeds its incorporation in large-scale plot or in the repetitions that make for thematic coherences. Dickens at the beginning of his career found a way to express this inexhaustibly renewed comic inventiveness. In the Announcement at the conclusion of Part X of *Pickwick Papers* Dickens says there will be ten more monthly numbers of the novel, 'if the Author be permitted to retain his health and spirits'. Citing what 'the late eminent Mr John Richardson, of Horsemonger Lane Southwark, and the Yellow Caravan with the Brass Knocker, always said on behalf of himself and company, at the close of every performance', he promises 'that we shall keep perpetually going on beginning again, regularly, until the end of the fair' (902–3).

If Dickens's comic hyperbole depends on showing characters irrevocably trapped within ideological matrices of which they cannot be aware, and if they are in any case granted precious litle self-consciousness of any sort, how can Dickens plausibly round off his novel with a happy ending, or rather with several adjacent happy endings – the marriages of Bella and John, of Eugene and Lizzie, the foreshadowed marriage of Jenny Wren and Sloppy, and the justice done to all the villains? What makes these happy endings plausible? One answer has already been suggested. Those characters, like Jenny Wren and Bella, who can self-consciously transform their situations by living them according to extended play-acting metaphors can make a virtual escape from those situations. This also gives them a perspective on their lives that unconscious comedians like Wegg or Mrs Wilfer can never attain. This difference corresponds to the distinction Baudelaire makes in 'De l'essence du rire' between the inadvertently comic, as when a man slips, falls, and we laugh at him, and the absolute comic in which the same person is both the object of laughter and the spectator who laughs. 'The man who trips', says Baudelaire, 'would be the last to laugh at his own fall, unless he happened to be a philosopher, one who had acquired by habit a power of rapid self-division [la force de se dédoubler rapidement] and thus of assisting as a disinterested spectator at the phenomena of his own ego [de son *moi*].' Such comedians, Baudelaire says at the conclusion of his essay, 'indicate the existence of a permanent dualism in the human being – that is, the power of being oneself and someone else at one and the same time [la puissance d'être à la fois soi et un autre]'.[8]

Such a power of self-doubling play-acting as Bella Wilfer and Jenny Wren have transforms their situations without really providing an escape from them. *Our Mutual Friend* shows the possibility of the latter in all those characters who descend into the depths of an anonymous otherness and return transformed. Some can go down and return as a new person, as Eugene does and as John Harmon does. Some return without being changed, like Rogue Riderhood when he nearly drowns but is resuscitated. Some descend without returning, like George Radfoot, like Rogue Riderhood the second time, and like Bradley Headstone. The only chance for even a local change in the bad condition of society is some extreme event that breaks up petrified class institutions and begins again after immersion in that impersonal energy, in a rhythm of interruption that the novel repeatedly mimes or enacts. This interruption is extremely dangerous. Some do not come back. John Harmon and Eugene Wrayburn were in mortal danger when they were thrown into the Thames.

Moreover, this break-up of mechanised behaviour must be repeated ceaselessly. Society must be renewed again and again at different locations on its topographical surface or it becomes universally ossified, frozen in unjust class and gender configurations. No single descent and return will work as a symbolic transformation of the whole society, as happens in more traditional works like Greek or Renaissance tragedy, where, for example, Oedipus's punishment or Hamlet's death purges a whole society. For Dickens the change works only for the person in question. Bella must be tested and transformed by Boffin's pretence of becoming miserly and treating John Rokesmith cruelly. She has to make her own version of the descent and return. No one else can make that change for her. In no other novel by Dickens are so many different characters reformed, but the novel ends with a final return to a Veneering dinner party that shows the 'voice of society' still obstinately stuck in its class prejudices and still united in condemning Eugene's marriage to Lizzie. The solitary exception is poor little Twemlow. Twemlow for once speaks up to express his sense that being a lady or a gentleman transcends class distinctions:

'I say,' resumes Twemlow, 'if such feelings on the part of this gentleman, induced this gentleman to marry this lady, I think he is the greater gentleman for the action, and makes her the greater lady. I beg to say, that when I use the word, gentleman, I use it in the sense in which the degree may be attained by any man. The feelings of a gentleman I hold sacred, and I confess I am not comfortable when they are made the subject of sport or general discussion.' (891–2)

Thus Twemlow, but the Veneerings, the Podsnaps, Lady Tippins, Buffer, Boots, Brewer and the rest disagree. They are by no means changed by the changes that have made Bella, John and Eugene into new persons. Dickens definitely does not see the transformation of a single person as a synecdoche for the possible transformation of a whole society. As he puts this at the end of *Little Dorrit*, though Little Dorrit and Arthur Clennam are saved for a happy marriage, the world as a whole goes on much as it always has: 'They went quietly down into the roaring streets, inseparable and blessed; and as they passed along in sunshine and in shade, the noisy and the eager, and the arrogant and the froward and the vain, fretted, and chafed, and made their usual uproar' (895).

Of course the person who plays all of the roles, those of the good and bad alike, in one gigantic internal theatre, is Dickens himself. Baudelaire's formulas about the philosopher who can be comic and the spectator of his own comedy and about the existence of a permanent dualism in the human being are meant to apply primarily to the great comic artists, those persons, as Baudelaire puts it, 'who have made a business of developing in themselves their feeling for the comic, and of dispensing it for the amusement of their fellows'.[9] Dickens mimes within himself for our benefit many different ways of being related to prevailing Victorian ideological assumptions and many different ways of being related to the underlying impersonal otherness that gives energy to these ways of being. The novel as a whole enacts one large complex rhythm of descent and return, like a great wave made of many smaller waves that collaborate to a single end.

Here I must disagree with Frye's formulations. He says, 'The hidden world is thus, once again in literature, the world of an invincible Eros, the power strong enough to force a happy ending on the story in defiance of all probability.' Later he asserts that 'Dickens's nature is a human nature which is the same kind of thing as the power that creates art, a designing and shaping power'.[10] This grants, in my view, too happy a providential design to that anarchic underlying energy. I should rather hold that the designing and shaping power forcing a happy ending in defiance of all probability is Dickens's own histrionic invention in response to the demand made on him by the realm of otherness that, within the fiction, drives all his characters and, in the 'real world', drives him to create them. What Dickens does is authorised by that demand but not determined by it in the shape it takes. For what he does, the writing of *Our Mutual Friend*, he is responsible and he must accept that responsibility. He cannot blame it, as Bradley Headstone tries to blame what he does, on the impersonal force that works through him.

Dickens has put two examples of his own benign, life-giving theatrical creativity in the novel: Bella's transformation of her relation to her father and Jenny Wren's similar ability to live her life as though it were a fairy story. In her profession of dolls' dressmaker, Jenny may be taken as an allegorical expression of Dickens's own profession of making imaginary puppets, Wegg, Venus and the rest. These come alive for the reader through the power of his creating word, just as Jenny's dolls do for the children who come to own them. *Our Mutual Friend* as a whole is a single gigantic transformation of the Victorian world in which Dickens lived into a masterpiece of comedy in the Baudelairean sense.

This Dickens theatre will not, however, come alive without the reader's collaboration. The reader's activity is analogous to that of Bella, Jenny Wren or Dickens himself. The reader's bringing to life of the dead words on the page must be renewed again and again in what are always unique and singular acts of reading. No one can let another read for him or her. Each must read for himself or herself. If Dickens must take responsibility for what he makes of Victorian London, so must each reader take responsibility for what he or she makes of *Our Mutual Friend* as it is re-enacted on the scene of that person's own imaginary topography.

Notes

1 I have explored some of these imaginary mappings in detail in *Topographies* (Stanford: Stanford University Press, 1995). See especially the chapter on Hardy's *The Return of the Native.*

2 Charles Baudelaire, *Oeuvres complètes*, ed. Y.-G. le Dantec, Bibliothèque de la Pléiade (Paris: Gallimard, 1956), p. 159, my translation.

3 The doubles are all men.

4 Alain Robbe-Grillet, *La Jalousie* (Prospect Heights, Illinois: Waveland Press, 1990), p. 3. I owe this citation to Erin Ferris.

5 Jacques Derrida, *Aporias*, tr. Thomas Dutoit (Stanford: Stanford University Press, 1993), p. 22.

6 Riderhood has been resuscitated once from nearly drowning in the Thames at London, and he accepts the folk belief that a man who has escaped from drowning can never be drowned.

7 Northrop Frye, in one of the most brilliant essays ever written about Dickens, was for the most part right on the mark in his formulation of the way this energy works in Dickens. See Northrop Frye, 'Dickens and the Comedy of Humours', in *Experience in the Novel*, ed. Roy Harvey Pearce, Selected Papers from the English Institute (New York: Columbia University Press, 1968), pp. 49–81, esp. 75–80.

8 Charles Baudelaire, 'De l'essence du rire', *op. cit.*, pp. 717, 728; 'On the Essence of Laughter', *The Mirror of Art*, tr. Jonathan Mayne (Garden City, New York: Doubleday Anchor, 1956), pp. 140, 152.

9 *Ibid.*, p. 152.

10 Frye, pp. 79, 80.

Index

Index

Index